Jacobite Stories

Jacobite Stories

DANE LOVE

Neil Wilson Publishing Ltd.
www.nwp.co.uk

Neil Wilson Publishing Ltd
www.nwp.co.uk

© Dane Love, 2017
Reprinted July 2017
First published in October 2007.
The author has asserted his moral right
under the Design, Patents and Copyright Act,
1988, to be identified as the Author of this Work.

A catalogue record for this book is available
from the British Library.

ISBN: 978-1-903238-86-8
Ebook ISBN: 978-1-906476-43-4

Typeset in 10/14pt Bembo
Designed by Mark Blackadder

Printed and bound in the EU

Contents

Introduction

The Jacobite period in Scottish history is one of the most romanticised and misunderstood of times. The tales of Prince Charles hiding among the heather and having romantic dalliances with women of all sorts are simply not borne out by the records. Indeed, he probably presented himself on most occasions as a rather scruffy and worn-out individual, gradually getting worse as the months after Culloden passed by. Hollywood's portrayal of a dashing, handsome prince is fiction.

But what exactly was the Jacobite era? In 1688 the Glorious Revolution saw the arrival of William of Orange at Torbay in Devon to claim the throne of Great Britain for the protestant cause. The previous king, James VII of Scotland (and II of England) was William's father-in-law and had converted to Roman Catholicism. It was feared that he was planning to restore that faith as the established religion in England and Scotland. James had to flee to France where he found it more difficult to organise the restoration of the House of Stuart. A convention met on 4 April 1689 and declared that by his actions, James had forfeited the throne. His followers became known as Jacobites. The exiled 'king over the water' died in 1701.

James's son, James Francis Edward Stuart (1688-1766), was his heir and tried to reclaim the crown soon after his father's death. Known as the 'Old Pretender', his first serious attempt to restore the House of Stuart took place in 1708 when he sailed on board a French ship for Scotland. He came close to the shore off Burntisland in Fife, but the fleet failed to land and the arrival of English ships put fear into the captain and they returned to the continent. James returned in December 1715 as part of Mar's rising, but on 4 February 1716 had to flee from Montrose, heading eventually for Rome, never to return again.

His son took the reins of the cause and so commenced the last and most serious Jacobite challenge in 1745. 'Bonnie' Prince Charles Edward Stuart landed in the Western Isles and commenced a campaign that almost saw the return of the Stuarts to the throne of Great Britain. It has often been speculated that had the Jacobites not given up their march on London at Derby, they might well have won the crown, for the German House of Hanover that had succeeded William and his wife Mary was ready to escape to the continent. History records, however, that the Jacobites seem to have suffered numerous lost opportunities and this was one of the greatest. The Highlanders returned north and were eventually defeated at Culloden.

Back in France after his flight, Prince Charles virtually gave up the fight to restore the Stuarts to the throne. European politics, which had helped and hindered the Stuart cause on and off over the years, had left them behind and the German House of Hanover was becoming more accepted in Britain. Support for the cause waned and the final attempt at restoring the Stuarts failed in 1750 with the Elibank plot, an attempt to assassinate all of the Hanoverian royal household at one time, leaving the Stuarts to pick up the remains. Even in modern times, descendants of Prince Charles through a variety of lines have claimed that they would have been the king of Great Britain had things been different and a number of books detail their claims and ancestry.

Charles had thousands of supporters throughout his campaign, but one individual amongst these is the most important to me. My six-times great-grandfather, Robert Love, or Robin as he seems to have been better known, came out in support. Robin Love was born in 1716, son to John Love and Janet Smith and was baptised at Muiravonside in the county of Stirling on 28 October that year.

During the rebellion he became friendly with Bryce MacCririck, who fought in the Earl of Kilmarnock's regiment of horse. They were active in the Battle of Prestonpans and took part in the march to and retreat from, Derby. After losing at Culloden, the pair went into hiding for a number of months before Robin Love decided to head south and settle at Sanquhar in Nithsdale, near to MacCririck's home parish of Kirkconnel, both in Dumfriesshire.

John Crichton, Provost of Sanquhar, discovered that MacCririck had returned home and was determined to have him arrested for rising against the king. The provost decided it would be best to seize MacCririck whilst he was visiting his sweetheart, Agnes Corson, who lived at that time at Dumbringan, a remote cottage in the valley of the Euchan Water. When the provost and the officers arrived there, MacCririck managed to effect an escape by jumping the river at a spot known since as the 'Lover's Loup'. When Crichton tried to jump the stream he fell into the water and would have been drowned in the raging flow had MacCririck not jumped in after him and saved him. From that time onward he was allowed to live freely in the district.

Robin Love settled in Sanquhar parish, working for a time on the Eliock estate before finding employment in the local coal mines. He lived in a house in the De'il's Elbow, a row of cottages at Crawick Mill, a small clachan outside the burgh of Sanquhar. A dispute in the coal works erupted in which Robin had a main part and the men came out in strike. A warrant for his arrest was issued and the coal work's manager and the two Burgh Officers of Sanquhar arrived at his home to apprehend him. Robin asked for and was granted, permission to return to his cottage to kiss his wife, Janet Morton, goodbye. However, on his return from the cottage he was brandishing the claymore that he had used at Culloden and chased the three men away.

A similar tale to that of MacCririck then occurred. The manager, or overseer, tripped over some ropes and fell headlong into the millrace, which was in full flow at the time. He was washed down into the Crawick Water and would have drowned had Robin not rescued him. As a result the action against Robin was surprisingly quashed.

It was the interest generated by trying to find out more about my own ancestor and why he would wish to support Charles that led me to research the wider Jacobite movement. Individuals and their part in the cause have always interested me and here, in this book, I have tried to tell more about the ordinary men and women who were involved and their part in the greater Jacobite story.

DANE LOVE

Auchinleck, 2007

CHAPTER ONE

Bonnie Dundee's Highland Campaign

John Graham, who had the titles 1st Viscount Dundee and Lord Graham of Claverhouse, rode with approximately 50 cavalry to the top of Dundee Law, a prominent hill that rises 372 feet above the town of Dundee. He was dressed in a bright red coat and on the summit he stood his men in a line to witness the scene. On the small hilltop he unfurled the standard of the exiled King, James VII, in defiance of the ruling House of Orange and the Convention of Estates, as the Scottish government was known. The staff was chapped into the ground and the standard blew freely in the Spring breeze whilst the king's health was toasted and the men's allegiance sworn. It was the 16th day of April 1689 and this was the first public demonstration of support for the exiled monarch.

'Bonnie Dundee', as Graham became known in later years, was a staunch supporter of the Stewart dynasty. He was born around July 1648 and studied at St Andrews University then served in the army as a professional soldier, fighting for the French and Dutch. In 1674, at the Battle of Seneffe, it is said that he was responsible for saving the life of Prince William of Orange, but this is probably untrue. In 1677 Graham returned to Scotland and a year later was appointed captain of a troop of horse then being raised. He was appointed Sheriff-Depute of most of Dumfriesshire and Galloway where he spent the next few years hunting down Covenanters. His reputation amongst the Whigs was unsavoury and he earned the soubriquet, 'Bloody Clavers'.

During Graham's time in the south-west he was responsible for the shooting of John Brown of Priesthill in front of his wife and family in 1685. He also ordered the executions of many others, his name appearing with disgust on many a martyr's grave in the south of Scotland. On Sunday 1 April 1679 he appeared at a conventicle, or field meeting, at Drumclog in Lanarkshire where the Covenanters rose up in arms against him. His dragoons were defeated, the Covenanters chasing them as far as Strathaven, where the scuffles continued up the closes of the small burgh town. Three weeks later Claverhouse turned the tables and defeated the Covenanters at the Battle of Bothwell Bridge.

Word reached Graham that William, Prince of Orange, was proposing to land in England and to begin what was to become known as the 'Glorious Revolution'. On 27 September 1688 James VII ordered the Scots soldiers to march into England to prevent this and Graham was among them. For his support, on 12 November the king created him Viscount Dundee and Lord Graham of Claverhouse. The king only remained in the country for a few weeks after that, fleeing to France on 18 December.

With the new royal household in place, Graham realised that he was out of favour and he returned to Dundee, residing at Dudhope Castle. He played a part in the town council, for he had been appointed Provost in 1688 and on 14 March 1689 attended a meeting of the Convention in Edinburgh. He was caught in discussion with the Duke of Gordon, a known Jacobite who had been outlawed. Word spread back to the Estates and they immediately feared that some form of coup was being proposed. Dundee protested that his life was in danger and with 50 men retired to Dudhope. On 30 March 1689 he was denounced a 'fugitive and rebel'.

On his descent from Dundee Law, Bonnie Dundee headed for the safety of the Highlands, though not before saying goodbye to his wife and infant son at Glenogilvie. His supporters, who had been with him in the Scots army, hastily made their way across the Sidlaw Hills and Strathmore to the Mearns. He then headed north over the Grampian plateau to Kincardine o'Neil, Alford, Huntly, Keith and thence to the Duke of Gordon's seat, Gordon Castle. All the way he was trying to raise the support of the neighbourhood for the exiled king. On his way to

Inverness, at Forres, he received word that the dragoons based in Dundee were inclined to support him, so he decided to head back south and raise the whole of Dundee for the exiled James VII.

Parliament, however, had already been notified of the rising on Dundee Law and had sent soldiers under Major-General Hugh Mackay of Scourie off in pursuit. Mackay was a veteran of the continental wars and like Dundee was a highly rated soldier. He soon had bases established in Stirling, Perth and Dundee and he himself took command of the group that pursued Dundee into the Highlands. For some of the time he had his headquarters at Coulnakyle house, in Abernethy.

The two armies nearly met at Fettercairn, at the foot of the Cairn o'Mount hill road. However, Dundee had found out that Mackay was nearby and decided to return to the hills. He crossed the Dee and made his way north to Huntly once more, spending the night at Huntly Castle. He then moved on to Inverness where it was expected that many of the Highland clans would come out in support.

At Inverness Dundee met Coll MacDonell of Keppoch and his clansmen camped outside the town. MacDonell was something of a celebrity for his exploits in battle and the clans of Lochaber had selected him to lead the men raised on behalf of King James. MacDonell was supposed to be ready to guide Dundee and his men westward into Lochaber, where the clans were expected to join the rebellion. However, MacDonell claimed that the people of Inverness owed him money and he and his men threatened the inhabitants with burning them out of their homes if they did not pay up. Seven years previously the magistrates of Inverness had imprisoned Keppoch over an incident arising from a dispute with Mackintosh of that Ilk and there was little love lost between them. The magistrates sent out four burghers to discuss the situation with Keppoch, who immediately kidnapped them. He sent word back that he wanted £300 and a 'Rich suit of scarlet cloaths', failing which he would hang his prisoners and then attack the town. Keppoch kept the town terrorised for three days until the arrival of Dundee.

Dundee would have none of this and warned Keppoch about his behaviour, telling him that history would see him as a common robber and not a hero patriot. MacDonald seems to have acquiesced, though not before the burgh was persuaded by Dundee to pay Keppoch the sum of £2,700 Scots. This was to be repaid on the restoration of James VII. Keppoch still had the last laugh though, for when Dundee's men needed feeding, his men robbed Mackintosh of his cattle, taking more than was required, the extra finding their way back to Lochaber.

The Keppoch MacDonells numbered around 700, adding greatly to Dundee's total. However, the cattle-stealing blood in their veins was too strong and within a day or so left Dundee behind and returned to Lochaber with sheep and cattle lifted from the Mackintosh homelands. Dundee was left with just 200 or so men once more.

Dundee and General Mackay almost met in battle on a second occasion near Elgin, but with the departure of the MacDonells, Dundee decided to give Elgin a miss and head south once more. He made his way through the Great Glen, heading for Invergarry Castle and what was to become Fort Augustus. He then headed east, to Dalwhinnie and Glen Garry and arrived at Blair Castle. The Marquis of Atholl was absent, but his factor, Patrick Steuart of Ballechin, was present and pledged his allegiance. Dundee continued on through the Pass of Killiecrankie and into Dunkeld.

Dunkeld is a small cathedral town, built at a fording point across the great River Tay. In the small community was a Hanoverian captain of horse, collecting taxes and other dues. Dundee surprised him by his appearance, for word was spreading that his was a spent force and that Mackay was hot on his tail. The captain was tortured into passing over his money.

From Dunkeld Dundee headed south to Perth. This was a daring move, for some of Mackay's soldiers were garrisoned there. Dundee handpicked 70 men and then used the local knowledge of Thomas Crichton, chamberlain to the Earl of Perth, in order to make an assault on the town during the hours of darkness. The soldiers in charge of the garrison, William Blair of that Ilk and Lieutenant Robert Pollock, had been sleeping soundly in bed when Dundee's men awoke them and took them prisoner. Blair protested against this, but Dundee retorted, 'You take prisoners for the Prince of Orange and we take prisoners for King James and there's an end to it.' Forty horses were requisitioned, as well as some money from the public purse, but Dundee made sure that there was no looting. The next morning they left the town, arriving at Scone Palace where Dundee dined with Lord Stormont, who later claimed to the Scots parliament that Dundee had forced him to feed him!

The successful attack on Perth was a brilliant piece of publicity for Dundee. The Royalists in Edinburgh had been expecting news of his capture at any time, whereupon the news they received was of his success in taking a major town. The accomplishment also brought out others who were now willing to stand up for King James.

Dundee then made his way through Strathmore to Glamis Castle and then across the Sidlaw Hills back towards Dundee itself. He returned to the summit of the Law, from where he could look down over the town. The residents were aware of his coming and the authorities had armed guards around it. Viscount Dundee sent four troopers towards the town but they were fired on and one was left for dead.

Dundee made his way back to the Grampians, crossing Rannoch Moor and arriving in Lochaber where he was expecting all the clans he had notified now to be ready to rally to the cause. Foremost among these was Sir Ewen Cameron of Lochiel, who had actually been approached by Mackay to join the Royalist side. He had been offered money, the governorship of Inverlochy Castle and the command of his own regiment, but Lochiel was behind the Jacobites. He had 400 men behind him and offered Dundee the use of Moy or Strone House at Glen Loy.

Within a few days the clans made their way to Gairlochy, where they were to gather on 18 May 1689. The meeting place was known as Dalcomera, or Dalmuccomer, where the River Spean meets the River Lochy, half a mile from where it leaves Loch Lochy. On modern maps this is shown as Mucomir. First to arrive was Alasdair Dubh MacDonell of Glengarry (d.1721), with 300 men in tow. Ailean MacDonald of Clanranald (1673-1715) brought 200 Clanranald MacDonalds, whereas Alasdair MacIain MacDonald (1633-92) brought 100 MacDonalds from Glencoe. There were 200 MacDonalds from Keppoch and a further 200 Stewarts from Appin. In all there were around 2,000 men gathered at Strone, ready to face the Williamites.

Within a week other clans came out in support. These were the MacDonalds of Sleat on Skye, Sir John MacLean of Duart with 200 clansmen, more MacLeans from Morvern, Coll and Torloisk, the MacLeods of Raasay and the MacGregors. Dundee kept them at Glenroy, drilling and training them as best he could. He also came to accept that the clansmen were skilled in their own method of fighting and he was willing to use this in battle.

On 28 May Dundee led his army eastward from Mucomir. They made their way up Glen Roy and into the valley of the infant Spey to Garbhamor and across to Raitts Castle, near Kingussie, the site of which is now occupied by Balavil House. The next day around 60 of them arrived at Ruthven Castle, on the other side of the River Spey from Raitts, which was held by Captain John Forbes (a brother of Lord Forbes of Culloden) for King William. Dundee gave him the chance to surrender and join them, but he refused. MacDonell of Keppoch then began filling the moat with timber, announcing to the garrison that he intended burning them out. Forbes then surrendered and Dundee allowed them to leave the castle and disappear. The Jacobites then set the castle alight, to prevent it from being used by the government forces once more.

MacDonell of Keppoch and his men marched on in front and arrived at the Mackintosh seat of Dunachton Castle, near to Kincraig. Keppoch thought that the owner was an enemy of James VII and so he set the castle alight; he was really working to his own agenda. When Dundee arrived and discovered what he had done he was soundly rebuked, ordering him to leave the army and take his men with him. Keppoch apologised, stating that he would only follow instructions in the future, so he was allowed to remain.

Another advance party under Captain Alexander Bruce came across some of Mackay's men at Alvie. They were asked if they would like to join Dundee's army, but the reply was gunfire. After returning a few volleys, Bruce returned to the main force and gave the news that Mackay was nearby.

Mackay had problems with some of his men and it was thought that a few of his officers were ready to abandon him in favour of the Jacobite cause. Discovering that there was treachery about and that the great force of Dundee was so near, he retreated as fast as he could to Castle Grant. Dundee pursued him and for a number of days they outmanoeuvred each other as they continued in an easterly direction.

Dundee arrived at Edinglassie Castle on 4 June, but the privations of the travelling and food conditions meant that he was weak and he fell ill. Meanwhile Mackay was joined by 1,000 men under Colonel Barclay and Sir James Leslie, meaning that he was now in a position to face Dundee's men. Mackay then turned around and set off in pursuit. They arrived at Edinglassie Castle only to find it abandoned, the contents stolen and the surroundings plundered. A few Cameron men were still in the act of stealing what they could and following their capture were hanged from a tree.

Mackay by this time had also worked out who of his officers were suspects. Among these were Lieutenant Colonel Sir Thomas Livingstone and Captain-Lieutenant John Creichton. They were court-martialled and sent off to Edinburgh where they were held prisoner. Mackay's recommendation that they be executed was not carried out.

Mackay's advance party under Sir Thomas Livingstone came across a group of MacLeans looking for meal. Livingstone's men attacked, managing to take a few prisoners. Others fled, but most of the MacLeans gathered themselves together on the slopes of Knockbrecht Hill. Firing their muskets and rolling boulders down the hill they managed to keep the soldiers at bay. They then followed this with a traditional Highland charge, killing Livingstone and many of his men. The rest fled and when Dundee came to find out what the noise had been, he found the MacLeans gathering spoil, which included horses and armour, from the little battlefield.

The followers of Dundee were now becoming a bit restless and recognizing this he led them back west into Lochaber. They were given orders to stand down, but were to be ready to return at 24 hours notice. Dundee then spent much of his time at Moy, near Gairlochy. On 18 July the Privy Council in Edinburgh offered a reward of 18,000 Scots merks (about £12,000 Sterling) for the capture of Dundee. A second reward was later offered of £20,000 Sterling.

Dundee remained in Lochaber for some time, sending letters to various clan chiefs asking for their support. Most of the letters seem to have fallen on deaf ears, for the support got no better. Eventually, on Monday 22 July, he led a force of just 1,800 men out of Lochaber. They made their way eastward through Glen Spean to Badenoch, before heading south into Atholl. They camped near Calvine, three miles from Blair Castle.

On 26 July Dundee's men entered Blair Castle, which was still held by Steuart of Ballechin. By now his force was around 2,000 strong, some MacLeans and Farquharsons having joined him. MacKay's forces were based at Dunkeld. He had 4,000 men ready for battle, which was something of a problem for Dundee. He was expecting reinforcements three days later, but MacKay was too close to hang around waiting for them. The Jacobites held a council of war in Blair Castle, where Dundee related the facts to them. The leaders of the Lowland regiments were in favour of awaiting the arrival of reinforcements. The chiefs of the Highland clans preferred to fight straight away. Alasdair MacDonell of Glengarry was first to speak. 'Highlanders are different to other soldiers. They relish fighting, despite their hunger and tiredness.' Others echoed his sentiments and when the old campaigner, Sir Ewen Cameron of Lochiel (1629-1719), agreed, Dundee was in no doubt – they would fight immediately.

CHAPTER TWO

Battle of Killiecrankie

On Saturday 27 July 1689 MacKay led his men north from Dunkeld. They travelled quickly, arriving at Moulin, which was a small clachan now incorporated into Pitlochry. Here they met Lord Murray and his 300 men who had abandoned Blair Castle as Dundee approached. Lieutenant-Colonel George Lauder had been sent in front and he gradually made his way north through the Pass of Killiecrankie. His men saw no sign of the enemy and word was sent back to MacKay that the coast was clear. MacKay thought things were proceeding too easily and did not believe Lauder. He sent another 200 men from Leven's regiment to scout through the pass, but again the word sent back was that there was no sign of the enemy.

MacKay ordered his men to have a rest; they hung around for two hours, basking in the pleasant summer sun. Still there was no sign of the enemy, so the army was ordered to advance. The narrow defile meant that it took time for the large number of soldiers to pass through and all the time they were wary of attack. At one point a soldier, traditionally thought to have been a MacLean, an Atholl hunter who had made his way alone from Dundee's army, fired across the River Garry and killed one of MacKay's cavalry officers. This took place near to the mouth of the Allt Eachainn. Tensions were high, for the Royalists thought that this was the first volley of battle, but nothing else happened. With heavy hearts and in a less boisterous mood, the soldiers continued through the pass.

MacKay's men emerged from the pass and spread out on the flat floodplain of the Garry at the foot of Allt Girnaig. Whilst they awaited the arrival of the last of the supplies, Lauder and 200 men were sent out in front once more. Near to Aldclune they spotted some Highlanders on the opposite side of the Allt Chluain. Word was sent back to MacKay, who gave the orders that all the men should be armed. As this was taking place, the Royalists suddenly spotted a greater force away to the right. Dundee had left Blair Castle and instead of taking a direct route alongside the river, he had led his men along the higher ground behind the Hill of Lude, dropping down on Killiecrankie from Loch Moraig and the Allt Chluain.

The panic was intense. MacKay ordered his men to execute a 'quart de conversion', or suddenly turn to the right. They advanced as fast as they could up over the low banking above the flood plain, arriving on the higher ground at Urrard House. This last move was important, for if they had not gained the higher ground they would have been trapped in the vulnerable position on the floodplain with Dundee's forces on the higher ground and the summer spates of the River Garry behind.

The two forces stood facing each other about 1500 yards apart. The Jacobite force was arranged along the foot of Creag Eallaich, from Lettoch farm to Orchilmore farm. At the western end were the MacLeans of Duart under the chief, 19-year-old Sir John. Next were the Irish soldiers, under Colonel James Purcell, followed by the MacDonalds of Clanranald. They were under the control of their chief, Alan Dearg MacDonald, again a youthful chief, aged 16 years, but with his tutor for guidance. The MacDonells of Glengarry under their chief, the MacDonalds of Glencoe under chief Alasdair MacIain and the Grants of Glenmoriston followed. All of these battalions were under the command of Colonel Alexander Cannon. In the centre was his cavalry, comprising 180 horses, under the command of Sir William Wallace of Craigie. Dundee commanded the left flank, which comprised the Camerons of Lochiel at the centre, under their chief, the MacLeans of Otter, under Sir Alexander MacLean, the MacDonalds of Kintyre and the MacNeils of Barra, both commanded by John MacDonald of Largie, and MacDonalds of Sleat, again commanded by a young chief, Sir Donald. In all the Jacobites numbered between 1,800 to 2,000 strong.

On the Jacobite side was Sir Ewen Cameron of Lochiel, whereas his second son, Donald Cameron, was an officer in MacKay's army. Before the battle General MacKay is said to have spoken to Donald, 'There's your father, with his wild savages; how would you like to be with them?'

Donald Cameron replied, 'It signifies little what I would like, but I recommend you to be prepared, or perhaps my father and his wild savages may be nearer to you than you would like before nightfall.'

The forces under MacKay were more numerous, being around 3,500 in total. At the west end were Lauder's Fusiliers, followed by Balfour's Foot. Ramsay's Foot followed, then Kenmure's Foot. In the centre were the 100 cavalry under the control of Lord Belhaven and here also were four small cannon, known as 'Sandy Stoups'. On the eastern or right side were Leven's Foot, MacKay's Foot and Hastings' Foot. MacKay took control of the right flank, leaving the left to Balfour.

The two sides stood and faced each other for some time. MacKay rode back and forth along the line, giving directions. He was surprised that the Jacobites did not attack quicker, so he spent some time addressing his men. He was not very inspiring in his speech, asking them to fight for their country and warning that should they fail to stand up to the enemy, they would be chased by Highlanders who were fleet of foot and who could outrun them easily. As MacKay was making his way back and forth he signalled to the enemy who he was. Now and again single gunshots fired down towards him and though none hit him, one or two shots injured or killed soldiers in his ranks.

Dundee was similarly able to make his way along the ranks. He gave a rousing speech, one that was later published. This had more spirit in it than MacKay's and he told the clans that the king would reward them if they won. To sum up he said that they were fighting for 'King James and the Church of Scotland'.

Dundee, who was used to wearing his long red coat, was advised not to wear it that day, for he would stand out like a sore thumb in the ranks. Instead, he agreed to dress down and wear a drabber outfit, but he did wear a white-coloured helmet. This and the fact that, like MacKay, he made his way up and down the ranks, pinpointed him for the enemy. He was advised to keep to the rear, for if he was killed, the Jacobites had no real leader left. Dundee refused, claiming that he was desperate to do a day's '*darg*' (work) for the king.

MacKay was impatient to start fighting. He ordered his four cannon to fire. One of these burst in firing, rendering it useless. The other three might well have been so, for other than creating a loud noise and belching smoke the projectiles did no damage.

Dundee was unwilling to attack just yet. The sun was setting in the west, but it was still high enough in the sky to shine directly into the eyes of his men. Patiently he held them back until the strong light faded as the sun dropped behind the hills. At eight o'clock in the evening the order to charge was given.

The Jacobites ran at speed down the slopes of the hill, yelling and screaming as they went. The sight was awesome and the soldiers under MacKay were taken aback to some extent. The Royalists fired too early, despite being warned to wait until the Jacobites were close enough and most of their shot fell short of the advancing hordes.

The MacDonalds and Camerons, who were on Dundee's left flank, were the quicker in running down the hill, aided by the steeper slope. They came face to face with Leven's, MacKay's and Hastings' men, who awaited the order to fire, given by Lieutenant-Colonel James MacKay, MacKay's brother. The shots killed a number of Jacobites, but those who were still running came together and charged the government soldiers. MacKay's men, having fired their muskets, had no time to reload and were in the process of fixing bayonets when the Highlanders arrived. Armed with their broadswords, the Highlanders hacked their way through the troops with devastating effect.

The troops were only three deep, having been stretched along the hillside to create an illusion of greater numbers. Once the clansmen had fought through, the soldiers reacted to the ferocity of the attack and most of them turned about and ran away. Those who stayed to face the enemy, which included a number of officers, were killed and left lying on the field.

The only real mistake the left flank had made was when the slope forced the Camerons towards the east as they were running down the hill, so that they merged with the MacLeans, MacNeils and MacDonalds. This meant that instead of running at Leven's Foot, they passed through to the side of them. Leven's men were therefore left relatively unscathed and they were able to turn to the right and shoot into the mêlée. The Camerons were to suffer more casualties than the rest of the Jacobites as a result of this.

On the right flank the charge was just as effective. The MacDonalds of Glengarry ran towards Kenmure's Foot, who fired their muskets as the charge came towards them. These shots were fatal, for a number of MacDonalds were killed, including Glengarry's brother, Donald Gorm MacDonell. In the fighting he had killed no fewer than 18 of the enemy with his own hands and when surrounded by the Redcoats he took a dozen pike heads in his targe (a small circular shield made of wood, often covered with deerskin and adorned with red material taken from killed Redcoats). Other deaths included Archibald MacDonald of Largie and his uncle, the Tutor of Largie. In all, it is reckoned that the gunfire claimed around 600 Jacobites.

Kenmure's men also had another problem to deal with. The cavalry under Belhaven had advanced, but suddenly turned to the left and began to retreat. As they galloped back they had to force their way through Kenmure's men, adding to the confusion. Balfour's Foot soldiers had to face the MacLeans, but they too were forced into retreat, trying to find hiding places around Urrard House. The MacLeans pursued them, hacking and wounding with swipes of their swords.

MacKay ordered the cavalry to follow him and he set off forward. A number of others went with him, but many were killed and on passing through the Jacobite ranks he turned round to find that he was alone. Many of MacKay's soldiers had turned around and fled. He later reported, 'in the twinkling of an eye, our men as well as the enemy were out of sight, being gone down pell-mell to the river where our baggage stood.' Most of his left flank forced their way across the River Garry at a ford from Haugh of Urrard towards Balrobbie. Others made their way back towards the Pass of Killiecrankie, crossing the Allt Girnaig and escaping where they could. The swollen waters claimed many more lives than were lost on the field.

One of the Williamite soldiers was Donald MacBean. He escaped from the battlefield and was able to acquire one of the horses used by MacKay for the baggage train. He proposed fording the Garry with this, but one of the Jacobites was hot on his tail, firing his pistol at him. MacBean left the horse behind and ran as fast as he could, over the rocks in the narrow defile. Eventually he came across a narrow part of the river, where a high rock on his side allowed him to jump the turbulent waters. MacBean survived and was able to recount his tale at a later date. The exact point of his escape is not known, but there is a traditional spot known as The Soldier's Leap within the pass where MacBean would have had to jump 18 feet in order to escape.

The Jacobites had lost one significant man however – Bonnie Dundee. Once the Highlanders had begun their charge he and the cavalry galloped down behind. Unfortunately Wallace's horse veered to the right – no one seems to know why, leaving Dundee and around a dozen other riders isolated. He raised his arm as he shouted at the rest to join him, but that was his downfall. A shot from a musket had hit him somewhere below the skirt of his armour and he fell to the ground. Perhaps if he had not raised his arm the sheets of armour would not have opened and he would have survived. Local tradition claims that the shot came from within Urrard House and a family tradition claims that Ringan Oliver of Smallcleuchfoot, near Jedwater, was the man who fired the shot. Dundee was not dead, but his final hours were looming.

A soldier named Johnston tried to make Dundee comfortable. Lying on the ground, the leader could not see what was happening. 'How goes the day?' he asked.

'The day went weel for the king,' replied Johnston, 'but I am sorry for your Lordship.'

Dundee replied, 'It is the less matter for me, seeing that the day goes well for my master.'

The Earl of Dunfermline rallied a group of clansmen and they attacked Hastings' Foot, which had been relatively unscathed. As they advanced, the forces under Leven joined Hastings. The greater number frightened the clansmen, who decided to abandon the fight. Dunfermline made his way back towards the centre of the field, at which point he noticed Dundee lying flat out on the ground. As he approached, Leven's men managed to kill Dunfermline's horse and David Halyburton of Pitcur was wounded. He was to die of his injuries two days later.

The Jacobites regrouped and began to advance further. They were able to take possession of Urrard House and fired shots at any of MacKay's men who were still around.

MacKay managed to rally around 400 of his troops, just over one tenth of his original total and they forded the Garry before making a cross-country route to Weem Castle, which stood near to Aberfeldy, the seat of Robert Menzies. MacKay had lost around 1,200 men, perhaps more, which was around one third of the total he had started with. The Jacobites were also able to take 500 prisoners, but the ordinary soldiers were quickly released; only the officers were held onto longer. Three of MacKay's senior officers lost their lives – Brigadier-General Balfour, Colonel Fergusson and Lieutenant-Colonel MacKay, MacKay's brother.

The Jacobites lost around 700 men and a further 200 were taken prisoner. A considerable number of their officers were killed, including Alexander MacDonald of Largie and Sir Donald MacDonald of Sleat. Cameron of Lochiel was wounded. Officers from both sides were interred in a common burial plot near to Urrard House. Where the other hundreds of corpses were buried is not known. Near Urrard is a mound known as Tomb Clavers and on the floodplain below Urrard House is a boulder known as Claverhouse's Stone, traditionally marking the spot where the leader fell.

The clansmen spent much of the evening looting the bodies of the slain. One of them even robbed Dundee of his belongings, for his near naked body was found the next day by one of his soldiers. He lifted him up and covered him in a plaid.

The corpse of Dundee was carried back to the inn at Blair, where it was laid out in a makeshift coffin. It stayed there overnight and was laid to rest on 29 July in the nearby church. A few artefacts, such as his breastplate, were later recovered. The breastplate is on show in Blair Castle, the 'bullet hole' in it being drilled at the behest of the 4th Duke of Atholl, as he thought this made it look more warlike. In 1869 a tablet was erected in Blair Church to mark Dundee's last resting place.

Despite the loss of their leader, it was a victory for the Jacobites. MacKay was unaware of Dundee's death and spent all of his retreat as far south as Stirling awaiting his return with clansmen behind him, ready for another battle. Word reached Edinburgh of the battle and the city was beset by alarm. It was thought that all of Scotland north of the Forth was now in Jacobite hands and soldiers from the castle were sent to Stirling to try to prevent the Jacobites from coming further south.

CHAPTER THREE

Fight Against Madmen

Colonel Alexander Cannon took control of the Jacobite soldiers after Killiecrankie. He was no Dundee, as many of the Jacobites were soon to find out. Colonel Cannon did not have the same charisma as Dundee and it was claimed that he spent too much time drinking whisky to have had any inspirational affect over his men. Nevertheless, he soon found himself in charge of a force greater than that which had fought at Killiecrankie.

MacKay sent the newly raised regiment known as the Cameronians to hold Dunkeld, the important village at the southern entrance of the Highlands. The Cameronians were under the command of the young Colonel William Cleland (born 1661) and though they only numbered 800, they were a determined force.

On 21 August 1689 Cannon led the Jacobites down Strath Tay towards the village. The Cameronian lookouts spotted the men approaching and sent word back to Cleland, warning him that they numbered around 5,000. He was advised to make a retreat as soon as possible, in order to save their lives. Cleland would hear none of it. 'I have been bidden to hold Dunkeld,' he replied, 'and for me, I shall stay here although every man leaves me.'

The men were still unhappy, thinking that they were at a disadvantage. 'The officers have horses, whereas we cannot ride for it, if things turn out for the worst.'

Cleland replied, 'Then let the horses be led out and shot. Then you will know that we shall stand by you, if you will stand by us.'

This seems to have placated the men and they responded by stating that they now trusted him and would stand by him.

The Cameronians arranged a number of outposts around the village and kept the rest of the soldiers in the centre, to await the charge. This was not long in coming. At seven o'clock in the morning the Jacobites charged at speed, their swords flashing. The Cameronians retaliated with their pikes and halberds. The Jacobites were repelled, but again and again they attacked.

The Cameronians managed to resist each attack, but each one brought more deaths. They had to reduce the size of the area they held, until at last all they had was Dunkeld House and the old cathedral. The Jacobites moved in and occupied the houses in the village. Although the battle was only to last around five hours, tradition claims that the Jacobites had both the time and the need to take lead from the roof of Dunkeld House and melt it down to make ammunition, for they had no shot left.

Small groups of Cameronians managed to weave their way from their strongholds into the village. They tied the doors of the houses closed before setting them alight. Many of the Jacobites were burned alive and the village was left with only three houses still standing. A contemporary account noted that, 'It was a terrible sight. Half the town was in a blaze, while with the incessant roaring of guns was mingled with the piercing shrieks of the wretches perishing in the flames.'

The Jacobites gave up at around midday, making a retreat back towards Blair. Cannon claimed the battle as a victory, though he had lost 300 men in the fight. The Cameronians, who acted with great valour, lost only 15 to 30 men.

Lieutenant-Colonel Cleland was one of those who had died, however. He had been making his way victoriously through the village when shots from a window hit him on the head and body; a Jacobite had survived in one of the houses and the chance to kill the opponent's leader had been too great a chance to miss. Cleland was wounded and his men rushed to his aid. He gave the order to carry him to one of the houses so that he was out of sight, in case the Cameronians lost heart on seeing him wounded. He died within minutes; afterwards his corpse was interred in the nave of the cathedral. His second-in-command, Captain Munro, was also killed.

A Cameronian was later to record some of Colonel Cannon thoughts. Cannon 'was heard to say when he saw our men fight so bravely that his men were not able to stand before them, that he thought it better to fly for it than to stand and fight against madmen, for such he esteemed them who fought so valiantly, being so few in number, against such a multitude of enemies.'

Many of the clansmen decided that they had had enough and were unwilling to fight for Cannon; most of them returned to their homelands, taking what booty they could find. However, a number of chiefs and their men returned to Blair Castle, where on 24 August they formed a Bond of Association, in which they agreed to protect each other against any retribution, as well as pledge their support for King James. In March 1690 William of Orange offered a peerage of any rank below an earldom and up to £2000 in cash, to Glengarry, Clanranald, Sleat, Duart, Lochiel and MacKenzie if they would swap their allegiance to him. Not one of them accepted.

The Jacobite forces that survived continued to move around the Highlands. The Irishman, General Thomas Buchan, replaced Colonel Cannon as officer in charge. Buchan, however, was to be no greater than Cannon in rallying the troops.

Buchan's Jacobites carried on fighting guerrilla fashion throughout the winter. They were left very much alone and all the time his followers depleted in number. By the spring he was supported only by a number of Camerons, Grants of Invermoriston, MacDonalds, MacLeans and MacPhersons. In total they numbered around 800.

At one point the Jacobites held Kildrummy Castle in Aberdeenshire. When they retreated in 1690 they deliberately left the structure in a bad condition, so that the government soldiers would find the defence of little use. John Erskine, 6th Earl of Mar, a noted Jacobite himself, seems to have had no qualms in putting in a claim for compensation to the Hanoverian government, amounting to £900, for a building that was 'being from the most part totally burnt and destroyed.'

Colonel Sir Thomas Livingstone, commander of the Inverness garrison, was given orders to take his men and go in search of Buchan's force. In Strathspey he was joined by the Grants.

The Jacobites were camped at Lethendry in the lea of the Cromdale Hills on the night of 30 April 1690. Early in the morning of 1 May their lookouts spotted Livingstone's troops crossing the River Spey at a ford below Dallachapple. Word was sent back to Buchan's camp that the enemy was nearby, but many of the Jacobites did not have time to get out of bed and put on their clothes before Livingstone surprised them. The Jacobites retreated to the slopes of the hills before facing the government troops. A bloody battle ensued and the Jacobites were defeated; 300 were slain and around 100 taken prisoner by the Hanoverians.

The depleted Jacobite forces wandered westward once more. They attacked various castles, robbing and looting. As the Grants of Strathspey had fought against them at Cromdale, the Jacobites decided to attack one of their seats, Loch an Eilean Castle; this fortress occupies an islet within the loch of that name, to the south of Aviemore. Within was the lady of the house, Grizzel Mhór, wife of James Grant of Rothiemurchus. The Jacobites under MacDonell of Keppoch tried to make an entry, but Grizzel thwarted them and they were forced to give up.

Shortly after King James's defeat at the Battle of the Boyne in Ireland on 1 July 1690, General Buchan disbanded what remained of his army. He, Sir George Barclay, Lieutenant David Graham and a few other officers went to Invergarry Castle, at the invitation of Alasdair MacDonell of Glengarry. They remained there for some time.

Glengarry was a notorious chief. On 14 July 1690 a Decree of Forfeiture was passed by the Scots parliament removing his possessions as a punishment for his part in the rising. He seems to have ignored this and remained at Invergarry Castle. The following year he was still in possession of his lands and he was still fortifying Invergarry in May 1691 in expectation of a siege.

Invergarry was surrounded by signs of the government making sure that the Jacobites would have little chance of rising once more. At Inverlochy a new fort was being erected, named Fort William in honour of the king.

Many of the Jacobite supporters went into hiding. Among these was John Grant of Glenmoriston (1657-1736). He had been active at

Killiecrankie and in retribution his home at Invermoriston was burned to the ground. Grant hid on the rocky hill north of his home, Creag nan Eun. After Sheriffmuir, Invermoriston house was burned again and by this time Grant was so well known for hiding amongst the rocks that he earned the name, 'Iain a' chreagain', or John of the rocks.

    With the Highland clans dispersed and no effective leader to rally them, the hopes of the Jacobites withered and were not to bud again for a number of years.

CHAPTER FOUR
Bobbin' John

John Erskine, 23rd Earl of Mar (1675-1732), succeeded at the age of fourteen. He became active in national politics, being noted in parliament as early as 1696 and was involved in helping to formulate the early stages of the Treaty of Union between Scotland and England. For his part in this, in 1705 he was appointed Secretary of State for Scotland. At the Union, he was one of the sixteen Representative Peers chosen to represent Scotland.

However, in August 1715 Mar was stripped of his office as Secretary of State following the accession of George I to the throne. He was also dismissed as Governor of Stirling Castle. Mar appealed to the new king, but he refused to speak to him. Mar had been a Hanoverian, but these acts made him change his allegiance and so far to the Jacobite side did he swing that he earned the nick-name, 'Bobbin' John'.

Mar left London in early August 1715, disguised as a workman on board a coal vessel. With him were General Hamilton and Colonel John Hay. They landed in Fife, from where Mar made a journey north, visiting many lairds en route. He spoke with these landowners and on his departure, having surmised whether they would support a rising or not, he invited them to a *tinchell*, or great hunting party, that was to be held on his estate of Mar. This was no real hunting party, but rather a euphemism to let them know to meet him there.

Mar seems to have arrived at Invercauld House on 21 or 22 August 1715. This was the home of John Farquharson, chieftain of the clan and a vassal of Mar's. At Invercauld the chiefs of the loyal clans came to discuss the plans and the contemporary records indicate that the following were present: Alexander Gordon, Marquis of Huntly, heir of the 1st Duke of Gordon; William Murray, Marquis of Tullibardine, heir of the 1st Duke of Atholl; John Campbell, 1st Earl of Breadalbane; George Keith, 10th Earl Marischal; Charles Hay, 13th Earl of Errol; Robert Dalzell, 6th Earl of Carnwath; James Livingstone, 5th Earl of Linlithgow; James Carnegie, 5th Earl of Southesk; William Maxwell, 5th Earl of Nithsdale; William MacKenzie, 5th Earl of Seaforth; Charles Stewart, 4th Earl of Traquair; William Livingston, 3rd Viscount Kilsyth; William Gordon, 6th Viscount Kenmure; William Drummond, 4th Viscount Strathallan; James Seton, 3rd Viscount Kingston; David Murray, 5th Viscount Stormont; Robert Rollo, 4th Lord Rollo; Kenneth Sutherland, 3rd Lord Duffus; William Murray, 2nd Lord Nairn; James, Lord Ogilvy, heir of the 3rd Earl of Airlie; and Alasdair Dubh MacDonell of Glengarry 11th Chief. There were also a further 26 Highland chiefs or chieftains of various clans, including Rob Roy MacGregor.

It was significant that one person was missing from the gathering; John Farquharson of Invercauld was either uninvited, which is unlikely, or else he made a timely exit, not wishing to associate himself with the cause. He was drawn into it, however, for being Mar's vassal he had little choice but to follow his orders and supply armed men, or else lose his estate.

Farquharson was keen to preserve his title to the estate and various other legal documents that he owned. At the first sign of trouble in 1715 he removed the family charter chest from Invercauld and had it hidden in a rock fissure on the face of Creag Clunie, on the opposite side of the River Dee from Invercauld. The chest was kept there during all the troubles and only when things had settled was it returned to Invercauld. From that date onward, the hole in the rock has become known as Invercauld's Charter Chest.

The men who had gathered at Invercauld spent some time hunting in the forest of Mar and it is said that on the evening before the standard was raised they ended their hunt by the side of the Quoich Water. A great feast followed and a massive bowl of punch was brewed in a natural stone depression in the riverbed. This bowl has been known as the Earl of Mar's Punchbowl ever since.

The council of chiefs met on and off over the next few days. They met at Aboyne on 3 September, at which point they resolved to call the nation to arms.

The Jacobite peers and the Highland chiefs decided to raise the standard on behalf of King James VIII at Castleton of Braemar on 6 September 1715. The men gathered around a low knoll and there planted the standard of the Chevalier de St George. This had the royal arms of Scotland on one side, the Scots thistle on the other. Streamers were adorned with the mottoes 'For our Lives and Liberties' and 'For our King and oppressed Country.' The ceremony was a solemn one, with various prayers being said and other religious rituals.

There was one insignificant incident that took place, but one that was to affect the superstitions of the Celtic minds. As the standard was being raised, the gilded ball finial on the flagstaff fell off. This was regarded as a bad omen and was to be remembered as such later.

John Forbes lived at Inverernan House, which stands at the foot of the Ernan Water in Strathdon, Aberdeenshire. He was employed as a tacksman, or baillie, for the Earl of Mar's Kildrummy estates. 'Black Jock' as he was known, was a keen supporter of the Jacobite movement and followed Mar. He was responsible for organising the rising in the Strathdon area.

Mar wrote to Forbes:

Invercauld, Sept. 9 (at night) 1715

Jocke, Ye was right not to come to me with the hundred
men ye sent up tonight, when I expected four times that
number. It is a pretty thing, when all the Highlands of
Scotland are now rising upon the King and the country's
account, as I have accounts from them since they were with
me and the gentlemen of the neighbouring Lowlands
expecting us down to join them, that my men should only
be refractory. Is not this the thing we are now about which
they have been wishing these twenty-six years? And now,
when it is come and the King and the country's cause is at

stake, will they for ever sit and see all perish? I have used gentle means too long and shall be forced to put other means into execution. I have sent you enclosed an order for the Lordship of Kildrummy, which you are immediately to intimate to all my vassals; if they give ready obedience, it will make some amends and if not, ye may tell them from me, it will not be in my power to save them (were I willing) from being treated as enemies by those who are ready soon to join me; and they may depend on it that I will be the first to propose and order their being so. Particularly let my own tenants in Kildrummy know that if they come not forth with their best arms, that I shall send a party immediately to burn what they shall miss taking from them. And they may believe this only a threat, but by all that's sacred, I'll put it into execution, let my loss be what it will, that it may be an example to others. You are to tell the gentlemen that I expect them in their best accoutrements, on horseback and no excuse to be accepted of. Go about this with diligence and come yourself and let me know your having done so. All this is not only as ye will be answerable to me, but to your King and country.

Your assured friend and servant

MAR.

To John Forbes of Inverernan,
Baillie of Kildrummy

Forbes was later taken prisoner after Sheriffmuir and transported to Carlisle Castle, where he was held prisoner. He was sentenced to be hanged, but he died the night before this was due to take place.

After the standard had been raised at Braemar, the Jacobites marched southward, up Glen Clunie and down Gleann Beag to the Spittal of Glenshee. Mar led the Jacobites into Perth on 16 September 1715, the town being taken by Colonel John Hay and there they set up a camp. This became the Jacobite headquarters for the immediate future.

A number of clans appeared in support over the following weeks and soon the force greatly outnumbered the government forces. From here he marched around the countryside, travelling as far as Dunblane and back.

Lieutenant-General Alexander Gordon of Auchintoul (1669-1751) had attended the rising at Braemar where he was given the job of raising the clans of the West Highlands. He gathered together 4,000 men, which he used to try and attack Fort William without success, before heading south towards Inveraray where he hoped more men would join the ranks. He then made his way towards Auchterarder, camping in the neighbourhood with his men.

Mar's dallying at Perth was probably his greatest mistake, for having a greater force he could have quite easily taken Stirling and thus be south of the all-important line of the Forth. He would then have been in a position to assist Lord Drummond, whose plans to seize Edinburgh Castle and there take the £400,000 grant payable by England at the Union, which lay in the castle safes. Drummond was defeated by drink and loose talk, for his men spent too long in a city inn and one of them spoke too freely to his wife, who passed on the information to Adam Cockburn, a Lord of Session and formerly Lord Justice Clerk.

Lord Cockburn (1657-1735) was noted for his zeal in suppressing the rebellion and became quite hated in Scotland as a result, being styled 'the Curse of Scotland'. It was said that at the time, when ladies were playing cards and the nine of diamonds came up, a card known as 'the curse of Scotland', they termed it 'the Justice Clerk.' The nine of diamonds was styled the 'curse' from it representing the arms of John Dalrymple, 1st Earl of Stair, who was responsible for sanctioning the Massacre of Glencoe in 1692, when the Campbells slaughtered a number of MacDonalds who had failed to swear their allegiance to the crown in the designated time. Lord Cockburn was in fact one of the commissioners who was appointed at the inquiry into the massacre in 1695.

Mar sent men out from Perth with orders to collect cash, which he regarded as taxes due to the Jacobite crown. Major Grahame was sent to Dunfermline in Fife along with a detachment of horse and foot. Grahame quartered most of his troops in the abbey, the remainder in surrounding properties. He seems not to have been too concerned about their safety and only had one sentry posted, on the bridge over the Tower Burn. Charles Cathcart, later Lord Cathcart, arrived on the outskirts of the town with a detachment of government troops and found access to the town centre rather easy. The sentry was killed and, in the mêlée that followed, the Jacobites made a hasty escape, running as fast as they could north towards Perth. A few were killed in the chase and others wounded.

As part of the scheme for defence against the Jacobites, the Bridge of Teith at Doune was partially destroyed to prevent them from making their way southward easily.

Mar left Perth on 16 October and made his way towards Stirling. He had become aware of the absence of the Earl of Argyll, who was head of the government troops. Consequently Mar thought that now would be a good time to try and take the town. However, he only travelled as far as Auchterarder on the first day and then to Ardoch on the following. The infantry reached Dunblane the same day and remained until the 18 October. Lord Drummond proclaimed the Chevalier as King at Dunblane, before the troops pulled back to Auchterarder.

On 30 October Mar sent a messenger known as John MacLean from Perth to Stirling, where he was to hand over a letter to Argyll. At Stirling Bridge he sounded his trumpet twice, attracting the attention of the guards. He was asked what he wanted and on showing the letter was escorted from the bridge to Argyll's Lodging. He was locked up in the building for some time, before being questioned on Mar's army and its leaders. MacLean was not allowed to leave and Mar was left ignorant of Argyll's reply.

On 9 November the Jacobite leaders held a council of war in Perth. It was determined that the army would be made ready for a march over the Forth. They numbered around 12,000 men. It was decided that 3,000 men should be sent to Dunblane, where they would confuse Argyll's men, which were similar in number; the remaining 9,000 were to march further west and cross the Forth at a quiet spot, before heading south to England.

Mar led his troops to Auchterarder, where they were reviewed.

Here also the western clans arrived, under General Alexander Gordon. Some dispute arose over the position of the troops, which delayed the advance. After resting on 11 November, the Jacobites left the following day. John, the Master of Sinclair, noted in his memoirs that they were marching to someplace, but no-one knew where. They had planned to take Dunblane, but discovered that due to their procrastinations, the Royalists had beaten them to it, so instead halted at the ancient Roman camp at Ardoch. The Jacobites then moved slowly forward and camped at Naggyfauld farm, near Kinbuck, by the side of Allan Water.

CHAPTER FIVE
Some Say That We Wan

The Battle of Sheriffmuir, or Battle of Dunblane as it was also known, took place on Sunday 13 November 1715. The Jacobite forces are thought to have numbered around 7,000, although some accounts place this figure as high as 12,000. On the morning of the battle Mar arranged his men in two lines in the fields of Kinbuck Moor, at Nether, or Lower Whiteston farm. They faced south and soon many of them became aware of an advance party of Argyll's soldiers on the higher ground to the south, near to the Gathering Stone.

Argyll's Royalist troops were about 3,500 strong, of which 1000 were cavalrymen. On the night before the battle the men camped out in the open on the ground between Dunblane and the Stoney Hill, mostly on the farm of Dykedale. Argyll is said to have slept in a sheep-shelter near Dykedale, but on word of the enemy position from his scouts, Argyll went up to the high point on the moor to have a look. He could see the Jacobites below, lined up in battle formation.

Both sides were too close to each other to prevent any conflict. To stop the battle from taking place, one side would have had to turn about and fled, which would have been embarrassing for them at this stage. Mar called a council of war at around 11 o'clock in the morning. He gave a speech that was regarded as one of his best and proposed that the enemy should be attacked. The only person who disagreed was Alexander, Marquis of Huntly, who questioned what was to be gained by fighting. A vote took place, at which everyone bar Huntly sided with

Mar. Accordingly, the commanders were sent back to their men to prepare for battle. When they told the soldiers what the proposals were, the cheers could be heard throughout lower Strathallan.

General Hamilton made a mistake in planning the advance. He sent the right wing first, which comprised the Stewarts of Appin, MacKinnons, MacGregors, Robertsons, Camerons and others; they had the shortest distance to travel before squaring with the enemy. The left wing went last, the final group to form up being Sinclair's Fife Horse; they had the furthest to advance, which meant that by the time they had reached their positions the right wing had long ago reached the front.

Argyll watched as the Jacobites made their way onto Sheriff Muir. He was surprised at the tactics, for he reckoned that it would have been more sensible if they had made their way along the road towards Dunblane, rather than wheel around and march uphill towards his position. He sent word back to the bulk of his army to march up the hill as far as possible in order to gain the advantage of the higher ground. His men marched in two lines up Stoney Hill towards Lairhill. The right flank of his army advanced firstly and like Mar's force, reached the front before the left. Thus it was that when battle commenced, both armies' right wings were in place, their left still trying to reach their position and form up.

In the advance, the Jacobite forces had to travel around two miles. The squadrons seem to have become mixed up during this and the front and rear lines crossed. The infantry also seems to have marched too much to the right, leaving the left flank much weakened by their absence.

The battle took place on the flat moor around the Gathering Stone; the forces extended around one mile or so in a north-west – south-easterly direction to either side of the stone. The shape of the ground meant that the opposite flanks were unable to see what the other was doing and as a result were unaware of the outcome.

The Jacobites are said to have raised their standard on the Gathering Stone. The battle started when the clansmen attacked Argyll's left wing; they had watched as the Royalists passed by a couple of hundred yards in front of them. Captain Livingstone was desperate to attack and called upon General Gordon to give the command. However, he hesitated, awaiting word from Mar, but he was out of sight. In the delay, the chiefs on the Jacobite right decided to take the initiative and led the charge. They fired their guns into the enemy, before jumping to the ground whilst the enemy returned their fire. The men then threw off their plaids and ran forward, brandishing their broadswords. The government troops were taken aback at the strength of this, but they did manage to gain some success, especially with the death of one of the clan's main leaders, Allan MacDonald of Clanranald.

Being the only leader mounted on horseback, MacDonald was an obvious target for attack. A musket ball struck him and he fell from his horse, mortally wounded. His men ran to his aid and were for abandoning the fight, but he yelled at them in Gaelic, 'Revenge! Revenge today and mourning tomorrow, Clan Donald.' This seems to have inspired his men and they fought with even more gusto.

Although he was not yet 30 years of age, MacDonald had been a keen supporter of the Jacobites and prior to the rising had travelled around the islands and West Highlands gathering support in cash, arms and bodies for the cause. He may have had a premonition of his death, for prior to leaving his homelands he ordered that his fortress, Castle Tioram in Moidart, should be set alight so that the enemy could not use it. On the day of battle another of his homes, in Ormiclate, was also burned to the ground.

The government troops were thrown into confusion at the strength of the clans' advance and soon they were trying to escape as quickly as possible. Some of the accounts related later by the clansmen on the right flank claim that they had virtually defeated Argyll's left flank within seven or eight minutes. Some shepherds who were high on Little Hunt Hill to the east witnessed the battle and reported seeing a diamond of red-coated troops, surrounded by Highlanders. As the fight went on, the diamond got smaller and smaller, until at last there were no redcoats left.

The farmwife at Lynns farm found her midden was the centre of a battle and Jacobites killed eleven redcoats within it. Another dozen or so Jacobites pursued a government soldier as far as the Wharry Burn, where he became trapped. He was able to fight so ably that he killed ten Highlanders before his strength gave way and he himself was killed.

The Highlanders on the right flank pursued the government troops for some considerable distance, killing those with whom they caught up. Some of these were chased as far as Cornton, as they tried to make their way back to the safety of Stirling Castle, a distance of four or more miles from the battlefield. Three Jacobites, who had only joined the army the previous day, chased seven redcoats towards the Pendreich Glen. The three men cornered the redcoats and a fight ensued in which all were killed, save for the Jacobite shepherd from Braco. The nine men are said to be buried where they fell, next to the Wharry Burn.

The Jacobite left flank was not so lucky; they were late in forming up, having had the furthest to travel. Nevertheless, they made the first attack, but soon they found themselves in a poorly protected position. This was not lost on Argyll, who sent additional troops there. Argyll and his infantry pursued the Jacobites as they made their way backward and Major-General Joseph Wightman, previously commander-in-chief of the government troops in Scotland, marched behind with his infantry. The government troops pushed the Jacobites back downhill towards the River Allan, taking three hours to do so.

It is recorded that the MacDonalds and the Perth and Angus Horse were particularly good in the battle for the Jacobite side. The Camerons, Gordons, MacKenzies and Stewarts of Appin were regarded as being rather poor on the field. For whatever reason, the MacIntoshes are reckoned not to have taken part and their swords never left their sheaths.

Both leaders seem to have made serious misjudgements during the battle. Argyll was unaware of his left flank's defeat; otherwise he would probably have not pursued the Jacobites on his right so far. It would have been better for him to have taken his men to the assistance of the left. Mar also erred in that whilst some of his men were pursuing the government troops as far as Stirling, there were still around 3,000 men left on the moor, virtually redundant. With hindsight, they would have been better off pursuing Argyll from the rear, as they were chasing the Jacobites northwards.

John Gordon of Glenbuchat was keen to attack the returning soldiers under Argyll and looked to Mar for the command to charge. This was not forthcoming and it was at this point he is reckoned to have shouted, 'Oh, for one hour of Dundee!' in reference to Claverhouse's bravery.

The folk of Dunblane did not go to church on the day of the battle. There was too much of a buzz in the locality for them to think of kirk services and many of them climbed Hillside to the west of the town, from where they could look eastward over the community towards the heights of Sheriff Muir.

Argyll was to return to the moor, but at nightfall he led his men down to Dunblane, crossed the Allan Water and set up camp at Hillside. Mar remained on the moor, but his supply train was poor and there was little for his men to eat. He therefore descended to the north, towards Ardoch.

Argyll's men returned to Sheriff Muir the following day. They were armed in case the Jacobites should return, but they did not. Instead they spent most of their time collecting the bodies of the dead and carrying any wounded that were still lying on the moor down into Dunblane. They also managed to capture the Royal Standard of the Chevalier, an important trophy.

The battle was inconclusive, both sides claiming that they had won. The traditional song describes the doubt:

There's some say that we wan,
And some say that they wan,
And some say that nane wan at a', man;
But ae thing I'm sure,
That at Sherra-muir,
A battle there was, that I saw, man;
And we ran and they ran,
And they ran and we ran,
But Florence ran fastest of a', man.

The Florence referred to was a horse that was ridden by the Marquis of Huntly and had a reputation for great speed.

In reality, the Royalists perhaps had the better claim of a victory, for they were successful in preventing the Jacobites from crossing the Forth, which was an important boundary. Argyll lost 477 officers and men and a further 133 were taken as prisoners. Mar claimed that the Jacobites lost no more than 60 men, but a further 82 are known to have been captured and taken to Stirling Castle and held prisoner. The Jacobites lost Lord Strathmore and Lord Strathallan was taken prisoner.

On the Monday, many of the Jacobites made sure that Argyll was making his way back towards Stirling. They then marched back to Auchterarder, where they spent the whole of Tuesday resting. The provisions stored at the Tullibardine magazine were distributed amongst the men, for fear of looting. A few men were paid to thresh corn taken from Dalreoch and to graze some sheep in the parks of Gleneagles, so that food was nearby for the army. However, many of the clansmen decided to abandon the cause at this point and disappeared north into the Highlands.

A number of Jacobite troops under the Earl of Mar remained together and headed north once more. At Peterhead they made it possible for James Francis Edward Stewart, Pretender to the throne, to land, whereupon Mar was given the Jacobite peerage Duke of Mar. On 19 January 1716 the Hanoverian authorities removed Mar's title and his estates fell forfeit to the Crown.

James arrived in Scotland on 22 December 1715. He soon joined the Jacobite forces, but he failed to bring with him the expected and much needed French back-up, there being only three others in his party. He had failed to congeal the disparate forces and his Roman Catholic sympathies also resulted in him not gaining as much support as he may have expected.

From Peterhead, James made his way south along the coast, heading for Perth. He made his way to Dundee, before heading along the north shore of the Firth of Tay towards Perth. On the way he passed the house of Fingask, where he spent the night of 7 January 1716 in the company of Sir David and Dame Catherine Threipland. The Threiplands were long supporters of the Jacobite house and they made ready the state room at their home in which to feed and entertain the king. An old ballad recounted the visit:

> When the king cam to Fingask
> To see Sir David and his Lady,

> A cod's head weel made wi' sauce
> Took a hunder pund to mak' it ready.

Among the prisoners taken at Sheriffmuir was Colin MacKenzie of Kildun in Lewis. He was sent to Carlisle Castle where he was held for a time. However, he managed to affect an escape by dressing up as his niece, Phoebe. He survived some time after this, but was dead by the time Prince Charles was in the Western Isles in 1746. His widow, however, later welcomed Charlie into her home prior to the abandoned attempt to sail to France from Stornoway.

Alexander Irvine of Drum in Aberdeenshire was wounded at Sheriffmuir. He suffered a blow to the head and though he was able to escape to the continent, he became mentally ill and died insane in 1735. He had no direct heir and the castle passed to a distant cousin.

CHAPTER SIX

Several Losses and Sufferings

King James thought that it would be desirable to lay waste much of the countryside between Stirling and Perth, reckoning that it would be difficult for the government soldiers to cross if there was no shelter or supplies. Accordingly, on 17 January 1716 Mar gave the orders to Colonel Patrick Graham:

> Whereas it is absolutely necessary for our service and the
> publick safety that the enemy should be as much
> incommoded as possible, especially on their march towards
> us, if they should attempt anything against us or our forces
> and being this, can by no means be better effected than by
> destroying all the corn and forage, which may serve to
> support them on their march and burning the houses and
> villages which may be necessary for quartering the enemy,
> which nevertheless it is our meaning should only be done in
> case of absolute necessity, concerning which we have given
> our full instructions to James Graham, younger of Braco.
> These are therefore, ordering and requiring you, how soon
> this order shall be put into your hands by the said James
> Graham, forthwith with the garrison under your command,
> to burn and destroy the village of Auchterarder and all the
> houses, corn and forage, whatsoever within the said town, so
> as they might be rendered entirely useless to the enemy. For

doing whereof this shall be to you and all you emply a sufficient warrant. Given at our Court of Scoon, this 17th day of January, in the fifteenth year of our reign, 1715-16.

By His Majesty's Command,
Mar

The Jacobites seem to have taken to this task with some degree of satisfaction and many of the Highlanders found the authorised looting and destruction of property an enjoyable experience.

At around nine o' clock in the evening of Tuesday 24 January 1716 around 500 clansmen marched from their head-quarters in Perth. They were mainly composed of MacDonalds, Camerons, Stewarts and MacLeans and were under the command of Ranald MacDonald of Clan Ranald, brother of the chief who had been slain at Sheriffmuir. He may have taken great enjoyment out of avenging his brother's death. It had been a stormy night and the snow lay thick on the ground.

As the Jacobites made their way south westwards towards Auchterarder, one of their number, Andrew Taylor in Strageath, who was serving under Lord Drummond, wanted to warn some of his friends there. He rode out as fast as he was able, but Ludovic Drummond and his son, James, caught him on the way. They warned him within an inch of his life not to continue, or else he would find himself shot.

The Jacobites arrived in the old town at around four o'clock in the morning. They marched into the centre of the main street and sentries were posted around the outskirts of the town, so that anyone trying to enter would be prevented from doing so and also to stop anyone leaving and warning the government forces, which were thought to be within two miles or so.

The Jacobite soldiers were ordered to force an entry into every house. They were not to allow any of the residents to leave and each house was to be searched, in case there were any of the government soldiers hiding within. The Jacobites would not allow the residents time to get out of bed and put on their clothes. In each house the clansmen searched through all the chests and cupboards and if they found anything that they liked, then they took it for themselves. The Jacobites were incensed at the amount of food, including meat and liquor, that they found within the houses and they claimed that the householders were storing this to feed the Royalists, should they arrive.

The Jacobites discovered that the Royalists were not as close by as was originally thought – in fact they were around fourteen miles away at Dunblane. They then acquiesced and allowed the residents to leave their homes. Fired up in a rage, many of these folk went to Clanranald to complain bitterly of the treatment they had endured. The chief listened to their complaints and promised that he would redress them all before they were to leave.

One of the older residents, William Davidson, a merchant in the town, complained to Clanranald that his house had been plundered when the soldiers stayed there en route to Sheriffmuir, as well as on the way back. He also told him that the soldiers had beaten his sons and son-in-law. Clanranald apologised for this treatment and assured the old man that his goods would be searched for among the men and duly returned. He also told Davidson that he would not suffer any harm whilst he was leader. At that he kissed each member of the family and left.

Clanranald ordered all his men to gather in the street. Loudly, he told his men to, 'Go and burn all the houses in the town. Spare none, except the church and Mrs Paterson's.'

Mrs Paterson had been singled out for special treatment because she was a known supporter and it was in her house that the Jacobites had held a number of meetings prior to the rebellion. Her house, which stood two storeys in height, was known as The Abbey, being on ground owned at one time by the Abbot of Inchaffrey.

The orders were heard by many of the residents, who ran in terror to their homes. They gathered as many of their belongings as they could and threw them out into the street, so that they could gather them up later. As they did this, the Jacobites ran after them, gathering up anything of value.

The houses were quickly set alight and the number of soldiers present was sufficient to enable the task to be completed quickly. Janet Miller was unable to save anything and, realising her children were still inside, ran into the house where she perished in the flames. Others tried to run for the safety of the church, but the deep snow prevented them from doing this quickly and many of the Highlanders pursued them. They stripped them of their clothes and stole any money and goods that they may have been able to carry. Without clothes to keep them warm, many of these folks perished in the snows.

The old William Davidson, who had been promised by Clanranald that he would be okay, was treated just as badly as the rest. The Jacobites set his house on fire and his daughter and daughter-in-law had to force their way through the smoke and carry the sick man from the house. They were fortunate in making it to the church, where Davidson had to remain for the next few days.

Davidson's son-in-law, James Shearer, had been captured by the Jacobites on their march south towards Sheriffmuir. In the heat of the battle he managed to escape and returned home. However, when the Jacobites arrived in Auchterarder he knew that he would be in danger, so hid behind a large chest, remaining there for some hours. When the clansmen set the house on fire, he was forced to make an escape and ran as fast as he could in his nightclothes to a small wood one mile away.

The local schoolmaster, William Davidson, tried to make an escape, for he was known locally for being a staunch Hanoverian. He was caught by the rebels, who stripped him of his clothes and robbed him of his money. He eventually managed to get away and hide in the same wood as Shearer, who was his brother-in-law. The Jacobites went back to his house, where they found his expectant wife. When she complained when the men began plundering her belongings, they knocked her to the ground using the butt of a gun. She was left dead on the floor, the blood flowing from her mouth and nose.

Similar tales could be recounted throughout every household in the town. The Jacobites at length went to the church and many of those taking refuge there were searched and any money they had managed to escape with was taken from them.

At around half past nine in the morning about two or three hundred Jacobites left Auchterarder and marched on foot to Blackford. A few men accompanied them on horseback, including William Maitland, whose father was the innkeeper in Blackford. He was to guide them through the snows. However, half a mile from Auchterarder the Jacobites kidnapped another guide, John Rebron, of Greenwells. He guided them into Blackford, which they reached at around half past twelve.

The Jacobites fed their horses at Maitland's Inn, after which they set out into the village. They arrived at one of the larger houses, occupied by a widow, Jane Edie. She boarded all the windows and closed the door and from within shouted out to ask what they wanted. She told them they could come in if only they would spare her and her property. The soldiers threatened to shoot in through the windows and began breaking down the door. They stole what they could from the house and then used corn and straw from the stable to set it alight.

Other men went to James Brice's house, at the west end of the village. His wife was in the house at the time, but she managed to effect an escape and fled to the hills. The soldiers set the house on fire, commenting, 'What a pity that such a bonny farm and houses should be destroyed, as it is really by much the best in the place.'

More houses followed. Isobel Brice's cottage was burned, despite the fact that there were still young children within. It was with considerable difficulty that they were rescued. Alexander Gibson's house and shop followed. The goods were stolen and the building set on fire. Gibson himself was beaten and robbed of cash and his wife fainted at the sight. A little child of theirs was left lying in the snow and was lifted by a Jacobite and taken back to Maitland's Inn. He yelled at the rest of the men that such a treatment was so cruel that no king in Christendom should have had a hand in such barbarity. The remonstrations brought a tear to many of the Jacobites' eyes.

James Maitland had been advised that his house would be spared, but it was later determined that the inn should be burned, to give the impression that there had been no favouritism. However, the fire was poorly lit and basically only piles of straw were burned, so that when the men had left, Maitland's family were able to dowse the flames and the building was saved.

Blackford Manse lay to the west of the village, at Ogilvie. The minister had been forced at a previous date to flee to the hills, but his wife remained. When she saw the flames and smoke over the village she sent a servant to run as fact as she could to Stirling to inform the garrison of what was happening. However, his story seemed so extraordinary and unbelievable that they classed him as a mad man and it was not until the following day, when more reports reached them of the atrocities perpetrated that they decided to head there to find out more.

The Jacobites arrived in Crieff on 26 January, but the residents pleaded with the men to save their property, fearing the same fate would befall them as the residents of Auchterarder. The Jacobites swore to them that they had no orders for burning Crieff. The inhabitants were taken in by this and the Jacobites resided there for a few days. On 28 January Captain Cameron was staying at the home of Thomas Caw when their conversation turned to argument. Cameron left the house and ordered his men to, 'Fire the house!' The signal was acted upon instantly and within minutes the rest of the Highlanders were setting the other houses alight. Ludovic Drummond had been known to dislike Thomas Caw and at one time had been heard at an inn saying that he 'hoped to gett a fitt season for Glencoing the Caws of Crieff.' Thomas's 80-year old father lived next door, but the soldiers would not allow Thomas to awaken him, saying, 'let all burn together.' Only a few died in the flames, but more died of the cold and lack of clothing and food afterwards.

Afterwards Marion Caw applied for compensation, her account including the following items:

		£ s. d.
Item,	2 lairge chists, a bead furnished, a press and a bink amrie	26 0 0
Item,	A lairge Bibell, 2 chairs an armed chair and pan	7 10 0
Item,	A pair shits 2 pair of bead plaids a dubel plaid a goold ring 2 hokes	25 0 0
Item,	A tub, a dison & ? od spoons, 5 pleats, 5 winchies, 2 bots, 7 bottals	6 0 0
Item,	2 pair Kardes, a chopin stop, a pint stop, a little ghill and mikoll, 2 canabatos, 2 broad chadleis	12 0 0
Item,	A weight amand, 2 grot skopts a caf bed	3 0 0

The Bridge over the River Earn, to the south of Crieff, was also partially destroyed as part of the Jacobian plan to prevent Hanoverian advances. The Jacobites broke the southern arch of the bridge, rendering it useless for crossing.

James soon realised that his attempt at burning the countryside was a political disaster and issued a proclamation explaining his actions and promising damages.

William Maitland returned to Auchterarder on Friday 27 January and handed out a number of printed handbills. These were sent at the order of King James, the Old Pretender, who explained that the circumstances of his campaign meant that he had to burn the villages of Blackford and Auchterarder:

By the King a Declaration.
JAMES R.

Whereas it was absolutely necessary for our service and the publick safety, that the villages of Auchterarder and Blackford should be burned and destroyed, to prevent the far greater inconveniences and hardships which must have ensued to our subjects had our clemency and tenderness prevailed upon us to preserve these places, we were therefore at last induced, from the strongest motives, tho' with the greatest reluctancy and unwillingness, to give our orders for the effect above mentioned, which we understand since have been put in execution. And in regard we came into this our ancient kingdom, with a sincere and fixed intention to ease and relieve all our subjects in general of the hardships and calamities which they have laboured under for these several years past; and being, therefore, most sensibly affected with the losses and sufferings of our good subjects by the devastation of these villages, which justly moves our compassion and tenderness towards them; and being, therefore, resolved to make them suitable reparation for the damages they have sustained on this occasion and to the end they may be no losers thereby, it is, therefore, our will and pleasure, that all and sundry persons concerned do immediately prepare estimates of their several losses and sufferings and that they deliver the same in writing to their several masters, so as we may order relief and reparation to be made to them for what losses and

damages they have sustained in their houses, goods, furniture
and corns, or any other manner of way whatsoever. This we
hope will be sufficient to convince them and all the world of
the tender regard we have for our subjects and of the part we
bear in all their sufferings. And we hereby charge and
command the ministers of the several Parish Churches of
Auchterarder and Blackford publickly to read this our
declaration to their several congregations immediately after
Divine service, the two Sundays next after the date hereof to
be affixed on the church doors, so as all the people concerned
may have due notice of this our intention towards them and
may accordingly reap the benefit thereof. Given at our Court
of Scoon, this 26th day of January, 1716 and in the fifteenth
year of our reign.

By His Majesty's command,
MAR.

During the hours of darkness, at about one o'clock in the morning of
the 28th, Colonel Patrick Graham and soldiers from the garrison at
Tullibardine arrived in Auchterarder and set fire to a small house that
had survived at the west end of the town. The sound of the flames and
the bright light created sent terror throughout the community. Again
the residents fled, mothers lifting young children and running with them
naked through the streets, heading for the open countryside. Andrew
Mailor, with his wife and five children, was one who was making an
escape when he came upon Graham. He pleaded with him to let him
save as much straw as would feed his cow, so that his children could have
milk, but Graham burned it before his eyes.

   Graham gave orders to Robert Menzies to make sure that all that
had survived was to be burned to the ground. Graham even shouted to
the residents that he reckoned they should also be burned, for failing to
come out in support of James. He then moved on to the nearby village
of Milltown, where he burned all the houses belonging to the Duke of
Montrose, but saved all those belonging to Lord Drummond. Graham
then moved on to Aberuthven House, where the laird and his family

were absent. He is said to have told the servants who remained that all he desired was that the roof be removed, so that the building would be useless in enemy hands. Thinking that they were being let off lightly, the servants got ladders and began to remove the thatch, whereupon the soldiers stole the ladders and set fire to the building. As the flames climbed up around them, the servants had to jump from the eaves.

Graham then moved on to Damside House, home of the Duke of Montrose's factor, David Clow. He was absent, but his aged mother was still there. She begged the soldiers to save the house and her son's papers and offered them money as a bribe. This was readily taken, but the building was torched, Graham telling his men, 'Do your work and be damned.'

Back in Auchterarder, Robert Menzies, once Graham had left, seems to have been less ruthless and saved what he could of the village. He was later sent to Aberuthven, with orders to burn a barn that had been missed, but finding it full of corn, he let it go. The residents also had a fair word for Lieutenant James Campbell, brother of Campbell of Glen Lyon, who, though present, refused to carry out any act of destruction.

It was reckoned that Auchterarder lost 142 houses in the attack. There were countless others which were set on fire, but which the residents managed to save. Much of the winter stock was destroyed, leaving the people insufficient food to live on and little with which to feed their cattle.

At five o'clock on the evening of Saturday 28 January 1716 Lord George Murray and 300 Jacobites arrived in Dunning. It was the property of Lord Rollo, whose estate of Duncrub lay to the north west of the village. Rollo was a supporter of the Royalists and so the Jacobites regarded his property as suitable for destruction. They spent four hours at Duncrub, feeding their horses and refreshing themselves. At nine in the evening they marched into Dunning with beating drums and arrived at the cross. The colonel read a proclamation stating that he had orders to destroy the village, whereupon his men set the houses alight.

The same spectacle of crying children and mothers trying to escape through the snows could be seen. Three weak adults are known to have succumbed to the shock and it is surprising that no more corpses resulted. There were thirty-three homes burned in Dunning, which was virtually the whole village. This included the home of William Reid, the minister, who died within hours of the manse being set alight. The residents managed to bury him before the Jacobites knew of this and their leader is said to have declared that he 'was sorry they did not get the old dog's flames to birsle in the flames of the house.' At a later date a thorn tree was planted in the village, commemorating the burning.

Many of the Jacobites were quartered in Drummond Castle and on 28 January made their way into Muthill at around nine o'clock at night. Again the houses were set alight and people forced to flee their homes without being given the chance to rescue any belongings. One merchant's shop was separated from his house by a stone wall, but the thatch covered the whole building. The merchant's sons tried to remove some of the thatch to prevent the flames from travelling into the shop, but the Jacobites spotted them and aimed their guns at them, warning them not to proceed and to allow the flames to burn the shop.

Rev William Hally's grandmother-in-law was in the manse when the Jacobites arrived. He pleaded with them to save the building, but the men would have none of it. They set fire to straw around it and soon the building was alight. The old woman had to be brought out of the house quickly on a blanket. She died in the moving and when she was laid out on the ground, the soldiers pushed her off the blanket and took it with them.

A man tried to bribe the soldiers to prevent them from burning his corn, but the soldiers beat him up for his attempt. In another house the Highlanders set a bed on fire, with a child still in it and had not the mother been quick enough to rescue it, the child would have died in the flames. In total, it was reckoned that the poor folk of Dunning lost £500 Sterling worth of goods.

The lands and farm at Dalreoch, north of Dunning, were burned on Sunday 29 January. On the same day the government troops marched north. Arriving at Braco Castle, they found the Jacobites had abandoned it. The next day they marched to Tullibardine and removed the last of the Jacobites from there and thence to Auchterarder. There being nowhere to stay, the men had to camp.

Argyll by this time had reinforced his army and was making his way north towards Perth. The Jacobites met to decide whether to face this army, but on 31 January they decided to withdraw from Perth. So cold was the weather that the Tay was frozen and most of Mar's men walked across it and headed north.

Mar and his leader, James Francis Edward, headed north for Montrose. In the town they, the Earl of Melfort, Lord Drummond and a few others boarded a ship and set sail for France on 4 February. The rebellion had passed. The treatment of fellow Scots left the Jacobites with a poor reputation that would take some time to rebuild.

The Jacobite royal household never paid the losses suffered by the residents of Strathearn. They may have proposed doing so on return to power, but this was not to be. Eventually the Hanoverian government agreed to compensate the victims and accordingly sums of money were paid to numerous individuals. In 1721 the sum of £4,453 was paid from the forfeited estates, a further £2,502 was paid in 1722 and more in 1723 and 1777.

The clansmen were left wondering what to do after Mar and the Pretender left the country. They marched through the winter snows to Ruthven Castle in Badenoch, where they decided to split up and each returned their own separate way to their home glens.

A number of prisoners had been taken to Stirling or Edinburgh, where they were held for a time. Sir Robert Walpole, the Chancellor of the Exchequer, was of a mind to execute them, but was persuaded against this. Most men of little standing were eventually released, especially those who submitted to the Hanoverian government.

Those who failed to accept the sitting regime were marched south from their prisons to Carlisle Castle, where they were held. A total of 74 arrived at Carlisle, of which 34 were released without trial. A further 32 were tried. One of these was acquitted, for he was an elderly man and claimed that he was forced into joining the Jacobites. Although most of the remainder were found guilty, no sentences were passed. In 1717 an Act of Grace was passed by which they gained their freedom.

The peers, which included the Marquis of Huntly, Lords Rollo, Stormont and Strathallan, were kept in Edinburgh. After some time they were released, Huntly being freed on the condition that he used his influence in the north east to convert the district into supporting the Hanoverians.

CHAPTER SEVEN
Northumberland Rising

Prior to Sheriffmuir, 2,500 Jacobites from Mar's headquarters at Perth left under the command of Brigadier General William Mackintosh of Borlum (1662-1743). The plan was to join the Jacobites who were rising in the Borders and then to march on Glasgow. Borlum took his men across Fife and on the night of 11 October 1715 set sail in small vessels across the Firth of Forth to East Lothian, landing at Aberlady, Gullane and North Berwick. Over 1,200 men were transported in the daring feat. They managed to dodge the government ships that patrolled the firth and only lost 40 men, who were captured.

Landing in Lothian, they marched towards Haddington where they camped for a few hours. During that time Borlum made his way to the burgh cross and there proclaimed the Chevalier de St George as James VIII. At Haddington Borlum changed his plans. He decided not to head for the Borders but instead to march on Edinburgh and take the capital. Word of the Jacobite arrival reached Argyll at Stirling. To get as many men into Edinburgh as quickly as possible, he sent two men on a horse cross-country and arrived in the capital just before Borlum. Borlum's men were too weak to force an attack, so made a quick retreat and hid in the countryside.

Borlum's men joined with a number of Jacobite supporters in the south of Scotland. They made their way south, being joined by the Jacobite supporters of the north of England.

In August 1715 a group of soldiers had begun to organise an

armed rising in the north-east of England; they included Captain John Shafto and Captain John Hunter. Entering Newcastle, they began to collect support and soon had a small number of men willing to support the Jacobite forces.

In Newcastle was James Radcliffe, 3rd Earl of Derwentwater (1689-1716), an illegitimate grandson of Charles II and the actress Moll Davis on his mother's side. He and his brother Francis had been sent to St Germains in 1702, where they were brought up in the company of James Francis Edward (James VIII and III). He first took action for the Jacobites in 1708 but was unfortunate to be captured at sea in a French ship. At the time of the 1715 Rising he was living on his estate at Dilston Hall, a mile south west of Corbridge. The Secretary of State issued a warrant for his arrest on 22 September, but word reached him of this. Three men were to take the warrant to Dilston and three bailiffs of the Sheriff of Northumberland accompanied them. The men watched Derwentwater enter Dilston at seven o'clock in the evening. They planned how to capture him, reckoning that they would have an easier job if they took the hall early in the morning. Their plans were made and they settled down for a rest.

At six o'clock in the morning the seven men forced an entry into Dilston Hall, but found that the lord had gone. Derwentwater had escaped during nightfall and had crossed the Tyne and travelled the four miles to his neighbour's house at Styford Hall. The owner, Mr Bacon, was a Justice of the Peace, but he did nothing to report on Derwentwater's whereabouts. From Styford, Lord Derwentwater moved into more remote countryside and spent a few nights at Mr Lambert's of Newbrough. The men at Dilston took the earl's horses and passed them over to Sir William Cotesworth, a staunch Whig magistrate.

For two weeks Derwentwater and his brother went into hiding. There are numerous local tales of their exploits and a number of hideouts where they stayed are known. One of these was a cave at Shafto Crags, near to Wallington. They used a number of local women, including Mary Hodgson of Tone and two Swinburne sisters from Capheaton, to pass messages between themselves and other Jacobites and a few 'post boxes' where this mail was left are known; one of these was a standing stone at Fourstones and another was in some old holly bushes near to Dilston.

Others in Northumberland were to come out for James III and the list included Thomas Forster MP, Younger of Edderston. He was a High Anglican and Tory and was seen as being an important player in that he was not a Roman Catholic. Forster also went into hiding and the warrant for his arrest was less than complementary in its description of him, stating that he was 'of middle stature, inclining to be fat, fair complexioned, his mouth wide, his nose pretty large, speaking the Northern dialect.' Forster hid with Mr Fenwick at Bywell, before moving on.

On 5 October the Jacobites met at Nafferton Tower, two miles north-west of Prudhoe, where they openly declared their adherence to James. The meeting was organised as a race event, but this was only a cover. They resolved to gather once again the following day, complete with arms, at Green Rigg, near Sweethope Lough, twelve miles north of Corbridge on Dere Street.

On 6 October the Jacobite forces made their way to Green Rigg. Derwentwater had managed to purchase his horses back from their keeper and had persuaded others to join him. There were around 60 supporters gathered there, including Thomas Forster MP, Derwentwater's cousin, Thomas Errington of Beaufront, Sir John Fenwick and Swinburne of Capheaton Hall.

A quick council of war was held at Green Rigg and it was determined that the force should move to Plainfield Moor, north of the River Coquet, east of Sharperton. More supporters joined them there, including William, 4th Lord Widdrington and his friends and 'Mad' Jack Hall of Otterburn.

The Widdrington family had a long Royalist and Catholic history. William was a brother-in-law of Richard Townely of Townely in Lancashire, who kept him up to date with the Jacobite movement there. Widdrington Castle stands near to the coast of Northumberland, six miles north east of Morpeth and had been proposed as one of the places where the Jacobites would land in 1715. Noted for his strong Jacobite adherence, Widdrington's other seat of Stella Hall was closely watched. Widdrington was captured and imprisoned in the Tower of London, under the sentence of death. He was reprieved on the very morning of his execution, but lost his title, fortune and estates for his part in the rising. He retired to Bath where he died in 1743.

Mad Jack was something of a character, for he was a Justice of the Peace. He was caught later and tried for treason, but he claimed that he was insane. He also claimed that he had been surrounded by Jacobites and compelled to accompany them. However, at his trial it was discovered that on hearing that the Jacobites proposed meeting at Plainfield Moor, he had hastily left the Quarter Sessions at Alnwick, leaving his hat behind, and made his way to the moor.

Mad Jack wanted the Jacobite forces to ride into Alnwick and take the town, but he was out-voted and instead they made their way to Rothbury, five miles east of Plainfield Moor, where they spent the night. The next day they continued their ride down Coquet Dale as far as Warkworth. On the evening of 6 October the Jacobite leaders feasted in the village's Mason's Arms. The men camped on Lesbury Common further north.

It being a Sunday, Rev Buxton, the Jacobite chaplain, entered Warkworth church and delivered a short service, in which he prayed for King James, Mary the Queen Mother and all the other members of the Royal Family. At the burgh cross, Thomas Forster sounded his trumpet and proclaimed James III as king.

The government forces in Newcastle were quick to respond. They secured Newcastle by posting soldiers around the town walls, assisted by 700 volunteers and 700 keelmen. Many of the inhabitants signed a bond of allegiance to King George. In the town those who were suspected of being Jacobite adherents were arrested and held in gaol. Throughout the area houses belonging to Catholics were raided and their arms and horses confiscated.

Nephews Lancelot and Mark Errington captured Holy Island Castle on 10 October and held it for the Jacobites; this was achieved without any bloodshed. They were anticipating reinforcements from Forster and the arrival of French troops by sea, but these did not arrive. Soldiers from Berwick garrison arrived first and the Erringtons had to surrender. They were taken north to Berwick where they were held in gaol. The French ships arrived on 14 October and signalled to the soldiers on Holy Island, unaware that they were Hanoverians; when there was no response, they sailed north to Scotland.

The Jacobite force was growing all the time and was soon 300 strong. Reinforcements had joined them at Felton and others came south from Alnwick. The numbers would have been even greater if they had allowed footmen to join, but they restricted membership only to those on horseback. At Felton Park the Jacobites are said to have stabled their horses in the mansion. From Warkworth they made their way south and entered Morpeth. From there they made their way further south, intending to enter Newcastle.

The city gates were locked and entry was not to be obtained. One of the number, Robert Lisle, an agent of Derwentwater, who had advanced into Newcastle before the rest of the party, was found out and arrested at Pandon Gate. He was captured and forced into telling the authorities of the planned attack on Tynemouth Castle.

The Jacobite force then made its way up the Tyne towards Hexham, camping on a moor near to Dilston Hall on 15 October; since that time the spot has been known as Rebel Hill. It was thought that a good number of reinforcements would join the men there, but the Hanoverian authorities were thick on the ground and Sheriff Officers were keeping Sir William Blackett of Wallington Hall, who was expected to bring his mining employees, under observation.

The Jacobites remained at Hexham for three days. On the night before leaving, Thomas Forster made his way to Hexham cross and again proclaimed James III as king. The written document, which was left behind, remained on the cross shaft for three days, indicative of the local support.

The Scottish Jacobites under Lord Kenmure had by this time made a difficult march across the Cheviot Hills and were camped at Rothbury. They had travelled through Kelso, where a local militia was raised under the command of Sir William Bennet of Grubbet and Sir John Pringle of Stichil to defend the town. They had erected a number of barricades across the main entries into the community, but as word of the approach of the Jacobites came they abandoned their posts and fled, allowing the Jacobites to enter the town unopposed. The Jacobites were making their way through the Borders and those already at Kelso went out to meet them at Ednam Bridge. The larger army then marched back into Kelso, their bagpipes skirling in the rain.

The next day, Sunday 23 October 1715, the soldiers made their

way into the 'great kirk' or abbey for a church service, taken by Robert Patten, Vicar of Allendale, who preached from Deuteronomy xxi 17, 'The right of the first-born is his.' On the following day the Jacobites paraded in Kelso Square and the Earl of Dunfermline proclaimed the Chevalier as the rightful King.

Derwentwater and his men rode north to join the Scots Jacobites at Rothbury. On the way, Rev Patten, who was Forster's chaplain, trailed behind and came upon a group of keelmen near to Rothbury Forest. They were Scots and one of them took his bonnet and lifted water from the stream. He declared to Patten, 'We are Scotsmen going to our homes to join our countrymen, now in arms for King James. I'll drink hi health just now!' The other men joined him in the toast, exclaiming 'Here is King James's health!' Seeing that they were fellow Jacobite Patten gave each of them a shilling and signed them up f Derwentwater's troop.

The Jacobites made their way into Rothbury, where they captu the head-constable, just in case he was going to report them; he was up and kept prisoner in his own home. The next day the Jacobites northwards to Wooler, from where they rode across the Cheviot and into Kelso. There they joined the clansmen who had made thei south from Perth. By this time the Jacobite forces numbered 600 o and 1,400 foot.

Thomas Forster was appointed General of the Jacobite fo England. This was a ploy to try and attract other Protestants to th and thus spread the support base, but it failed to work; only Craster and two others were influenced into joining this way.

From Kelso, the Jacobite army made its way southwa were divided over what to do and were unsure whether Carpenter's army or else try to take Newcastle. Others wish Dumfries, or else head north to try and trap Argyll's army. F had their own agenda and with no information coming from what to do they were left without an overall strategy. A delivered to them at Longtown, which promised consider from Lancashire. It was decided to march south, but no Highlanders who did not wish to take part in a rising ov had deserted.

CHAPTER EIGHT
Battle of Preston

The Jacobites marched into Brampton on 1 November 1715. Letters with instructions from Mar finally reached them, requesting that if they were unable to take Newcastle then they should head north to Perth. His letter was ten days old by the time it arrived, so the Jacobites decided to ignore his instructions and continue southwards. They were expecting a number of Cumbrian Jacobites to join them, but few did. However, on 3 November they came upon the Cumbrian Militia at Penrith Moor. The militiamen had heard of the Highlanders' skills in combat and decided that it was prudent to flee, leaving considerable amounts of arms and food behind. Feeling better after this, the Jacobites continued south through Appleby, Kendal and Kirby Lonsdale.

Charles Widdrington arrived with news that the Lancashire Catholics were ready to rise and that Manchester had already come out in support of King James. They marched on to Lancaster, taking the town on 7 November without having to resort to arms. They were also able to take a ship that lay in the harbour with six cannon and copious amounts of brandy in the borough. Despite their success, the Jacobites were divided as to what to do next; the Scots wished to camp there for the winter, using it as a garrison with supplies brought in by ship and the English Jacobites wished to push further south, suggesting Liverpool as a more readily defendable port. Word reached them that the government soldiers at Preston had withdrawn and this was the information that was to decide their actions. They marched south on 9 November.

The Jacobites reached Preston that night and were camped throughout the burgh. They remained for two days, by which time word reached them that the government soldiers under General Sir Charles Wills from Chester were making their way north. They held a council of war and decided to face them on the south side of the town. General Wills was in charge of an army of six regiments of cavalry and one of foot and had the support of a considerable number of militiamen.

The battle took place on 12 November. General Wills's men crossed the Ribble Bridge at around two o'clock and entered the town from the south. The fighting took place throughout the streets of the borough until nightfall, the Jacobites successfully fending off all assaults and inflicting heavy casualties among the Hanoverians whilst losing only 17 of their own.

During the hours of darkness the flow of battle changed. Lieutenant-General George Carpenter arrived from the north with three regiments of dragoons and some infantry, resulting in the Jacobites being surrounded in the town. Infighting amongst the Jacobite leaders took place and eventually the Jacobites had little option but to surrender. On the morning of 14 November they laid down their arms.

The Jacobites were held prisoner in Preston for a period of time before being sent for trial. The leaders were held in decent houses in the borough, whereas the officers were held in various inns, including the Mitre, White Bull and Windmill. The common foot soldiers, in particular the Highlanders, were locked up in a large church building with little clothing or food. Some of these men ripped the cloth covers from the pews to make themselves items to wear.

Many of the Jacobite leaders were later transported to Chester, Lancaster, or Liverpool. A few were lucky enough to escape. The organisers were sent south to London where they were held in either the Tower of London, Newgate gaol or the Fleet prison ships, according to rank.

Many of the Jacobite leaders were executed. Captain John Shafto was shot on 2 December along with three Scots officers. The lords Carnwath, Derwentwater, Kenmure, Nairn, Nithsdale, Widdrington and Wintoun were found guilty of high treason on 9 January 1716. Other leaders, including Thomas Forster, Thomas Errington and William

Shafto, were impeached for inciting the people and raising them in rebellion against church and state.

In the weeks before the executions were due to take place a number of appeals were made to the government. Eventually lords Carnwath, Nairn and Widdrington were reprieved and lords Nithsdale and Wintoun escaped from the Tower. Lords Derwentwater and Kenmure were executed on Tower Hill on 24 February 1716.

George Collingwood of Eslington and 'Mad' John Hall of Otterburn were also executed. 'Mad' Jack tried to plead that he was insane, but this was not accepted. On the scaffold he swore his allegiance to the Stuart crown and that he was 'not a traitor but a martyr'.

Thomas Forster was luckier due to his connections. His cousin, Lady Cowper, was the wife of the Lord Chancellor and so Lord Bernstoff offered to let Forster escape. Dorothy Forster, Thomas's sister, rode to London where she was able to obtain a wax impression of the master key for Newgate. A copy was soon made, with which she managed to open the door and let Forster out on 11 April 1716, a week before he was due to stand trial. He then escaped across the Channel to Paris.

Charles Radcliffe, brother of Lord Derwentwater also escaped from Newgate. He disguised himself as a visitor and managed to walk free.

A number of Jacobites were held at Chester, from where William Sanderson of Highlaws and John Talbot of Cartington managed to effect an escape.

On 4 May 1716 old Mackintosh of Borlum led around a dozen prisoners to freedom from Newgate. They had been exercising in the yard when they took their chance. Most of the escapees were recaptured, but Borlum managed to flee back to Scotland, from where he headed to France. Unfortunately he was to return to Scotland at a later date, whereupon he was arrested and locked up in Edinburgh Castle. He was held there for many years, spending his time writing a valuable book on arboriculture. He died in 1743.

Many of the Jacobites of lower standing were banished abroad, where they were to work as slaves in the plantations for a period of seven years. Over 650 men were thus sent to America where they later settled and thousands of American citizens can trace their ancestry back to settlers who were sent there at this time.

CHAPTER NINE
Battle of Glenshiel

As a result of the Treaty of Utrecht and the Anglo-French alliance of 1717, King James and his court were obliged to move from St Germains in France to Spain. There they worked with the Spanish authorities in an attempt at persuading them to assist in an attack on Britain. The authorities in Spain decided that an invasion of Great Britain would be fruitful in that it would hope to return the Stewarts to power and allow them to run their country without the influence of the Hanoverian monarch. On 19 March 1719 a large fleet of warships, containing 5,000 soldiers, arms and other supplies, sailed from the port of Cadiz. They were under the command of the Duke of Ormond.

The Spanish fleet had proposed landing in England, but prolonged storms blew up off Cape Finisterre and so severely damaged the flotilla that they were obliged to limp back to the Iberian Peninsula. At the same time as the main fleet left Spain, two frigates left the port of San Sebastian, complete with around 350 Spanish infantry under Don Alonso al Santarem. The ships were loaded with 5,000 pistoles in money and 2,000 stands of arms. They had been sent by Cardinal Alberoni, First Minister of Philip V of Spain and virtual ruler of the country. On board was the Scots leader, George Keith, 10th Earl Marischal, with the Earl of Seaforth, Marquis of Tullibardine, MacKenzie of Coul, Campbell of Glendaruel and others.

Unlike the main flotilla, the two frigates arrived safely in Scotland, touching down at Lewis in the Western Isles on 2 April. A dispute over the leadership broke out between the Marquis of Tullibardine and the Earl Marischal, with the result that the latter decided to return to Spain. In the middle of May the Jacobites sailed from Lewis and landed on the west coast of Scotland.

A number of other prominent leaders and clansmen joined the Jacobites, including Lord George Murray, Clanranald MacDonalds, MacDougall of Lorn and Cameron of Locheil. They gathered together as many supporters as they could, but could only muster 1,000 or so men.

The Jacobites took Eilean Donan Castle and converted it into their garrison and supply base. Forty-eight Spanish soldiers under a captain and a lieutenant were used as guards. A second powder magazine was established in Strath Croe at the head of Loch Duich. The soldiers then moved further east and set up a camp in the lower reaches of Glen Shiel. Word of the failure of the main attack on England had by this time reached them and the company became very much disillusioned, realising that their paltry number was insufficient to create any major rising.

On 10 May a squadron of three Royal Navy frigates, the *Enterprise, Flamborough* and *Worcester* sailed up the west coast of Scotland and anchored at Loch Alsh under the command of Captain Boyle. From the sea they pounded Eilean Donan with mortar shells. The Spaniards in the castle surrendered and were taken prisoner; placed on board the frigates, they were taken back to Leith.

The rest of the Jacobites left the west coast and were heading for Inverness, when they were stopped in their tracks by the government forces on 10 June.

General Joseph Wightman, with around 1,100 government troops, made his way west from the base at Inverness towards the Jacobite forces. His force comprised two regiments, one battalion, four dragoon companies, Dutch auxiliaries and 146 grenadiers. He was unsure of the country and relied on Hanoverian clansmen, such as the Munros, Frasers and Sutherlands, for guidance. On 10 June 1719 they made their way west by Loch Cluanie and into the headwaters of the River Shiel. The mountains rise steeply from the side of the river, leaving little room for the track to make its way through the glen.

Descending the glen, the Hanoverian troops came upon the Jacobites posted across the throat of the glen, at a spot known as the Pass of Glenshiel. The Spanish forces had been positioned high up the hillside, which afforded them a clear view of the glen below. The MacKenzies, Murrays and MacRaes were positioned along the bottom of the glen. The MacGregors under Rob Roy were located on the hillside to the north, ready to form a counter-attack.

The two sides squared up to each other for some time, neither willing to make the first move. However, by five o'clock at night General Wightman ordered an attack, his mortar bombs landing on Murray's men. The Spaniards met this with an effective volley of shots. The MacGregors then made an attack, but the Hanoverians managed to repel this to some extent by shots. A number of Hanoverians scaled the hillsides and overpowered the Spaniards from above. They gave in too readily, probably unwilling to fight for a cause that they had little passion for. Many of them were captured and taken prisoner.

The Highland Jacobites kept fighting for much longer, launching numerous attacks. These were a success in that they prevented the enemy from making an advance, but with the loss of the Spaniards the Jacobites were now considerably outnumbered.

A number of the Jacobite leaders were badly wounded in the fray, including Seaforth, Tullibardine and Lord George Murray. A musket ball had shattered Seaforth's arm. Lord George's leg was hit by shrapnel, resulting in him walking with difficulty. Tullibardine's injuries were less serious. The battle had raged for three hours, but by nightfall the Jacobites realised that they were beaten. The order was given to make a getaway.

The Highlanders melted into the darkness, carrying their wounded over the mountain ranges and disappearing home. Rob Roy is reckoned to have crossed the peaks of Kintail and descended into Gleann Lichd. From there he dropped to Strath Croe, where he blew up the gunpowder magazine in order to prevent it from getting into government hands.

The Jacobite leaders advised the Spaniards to surrender to the government troops, but many of them were unwilling to do so and tried to make an escape over the hills. Many of them ascended a mountain thereafter known as *Sgurr nan Spainteach* ('peak of the Spaniards') and dropped into *Coirein nan Spainteach* ('hollow of the Spaniards').

The Hanoverian forces lost 21 men and 121 were wounded. General Wightman then led his men down Glen Shiel and alongside Loch Duich to Eilean Donan Castle. There was still a considerable amount of gunpowder and arms in the stronghold, but Wightman ordered that it should be blown up, leaving it in ruins.

The largest majority of Spaniards actually surrendered and were taken prisoner; among these was their leader, Don Alonso de Santarem. A total of 275 Spaniards were held as prisoners of war. They were expected to pay for their own food, but they had no funds to do this. Eventually their keeper, Brigadier Preston, gave them food, but he found difficulty in being reimbursed by the authorities. At length all the Spaniards had to sign IOUs which covered the cost of their keep and transport back home. Spain refused to recompense Britain, even though their commander had been held as hostage to ensure payment.

Seaforth, Tullibardine, Lochiel and George Murray wandered around Kintail and the West Highlands for a time before they managed to escape back to France.

CHAPTER TEN

Alexander Robertson
of Struan

One of the greatest supporters of the Jacobites was Alexander Robertson, 13th Chief of the Struan Robertsons. He was born around 1670 and succeeded to the chiefship of the clan in November 1688 on the death of his father and elder brother.

Robertson was educated at St Salvator's College at St Andrews University. He was studying religion with the expectation that he would become a minister, but on succeeding to the estate he did not follow that career.

When the Rising of 1689 commenced, Alexander threw his lot in behind the Jacobites. His mother was totally against this and tried to persuade him against joining Viscount Dundee. She even tried to get his uncle to convince him against joining the insurgents, citing the possible loss of his estates as a likely outcome. His mother wrote to his uncle from Carie, by the side of Loch Rannoch, 'He is going to Badenoch just now. For Christ's sake come in all haste and stop him, for he will not be advised by me.'

Joining Dundee, he allowed the viscount to use Struan as his headquarters for a time. Robertson himself was not active at Killiecrankie, having been sent with the Menzies down to Perth with a band of King James's troops. However, MacKay's men were in the town and managed to repel them.

Being a wanted man, Robertson escaped to Holland in 1690 where he lived in exile for some time. At first he was in Rotterdam, where he lived in poverty, but later moved to France where he entered the service of the king. His estates in Perthshire were attainted. Robertson remained abroad until 1703 when an act of remission was passed against those who had risen against the government.

When Mar led the Jacobite rebellion of 1715 Robertson came out in support once more. He is supposed to have lifted the Robertson talisman, the *Clach na Brataich*, or stone of the standard, and looked into its clear surface to see how he would fare. He was shocked to discover that it had an internal crack within it, claimed to be an omen of defeat. Nevertheless, Robertson raised 500 men and took part in the Battle of Sheriffmuir.

Keen to fight, he was somewhat dismayed by how quickly the Hanoverians fled on his side of the field. As a result he ran out in front of the Jacobite line, brandishing banknotes at the foe and shouting, 'Turn, caitliff, turn! Fight with me for money, if not for honour!'

Robertson was on the left wing in the battle and was captured by the Hanoverian troops. A kinsman, Robertson of Invervack, managed to rescue him from the foe, but somehow he was captured once more.

The soldiers kept Robertson tied up and sent him southwards towards Edinburgh. However, his sister Margaret came up with a scheme and managed to spring his release.

Robertson headed for France once more, where he remained for eleven years; there he became a Colonel in the Scots Brigade. His estate fell on hard times and was taken over by the government. In 1723 George I granted the estates to Margaret Robertson, but she wished only to look after them until her brother's return.

In 1726 Robertson was able to return to Scotland, where he claimed the Struan estates once more. Margaret Robertson had passed them back to their rightful owner, but there were numerous arguments over the ownership thereafter. Robertson, who described his sister as 'both an imperious and a wretched woman', at one point had her held a virtual prisoner on a little island in Loch Rannoch. He then sent her to the Western Isles, where she died in 1727.

On the arrival of Prince Charles in 1745, old Struan Robertson was ready to throw his lot in behind the Jacobite cause once more. Despite now being 75 years of age, he raised around 140 men and set off south to join the Prince at Perth. It is claimed that Charles 'wept as he embraced the aged chief of Clan Donnachaidh.' Robertson followed the Prince as far as Prestonpans, after which it was realised that he was now too old to be of any use to the movement. Nevertheless, the Jacobites wished him to return home in style.

Sir John Cope's carriage was taken at the battle and it was decided that Robertson should be sent home in it. Dressed in Cope's fur-lined jacket and wearing his chain, Robertson was taken back north to his home by Loch Rannoch-side. He stopped off in Dunblane, where he lodged with Rev William Simson. Robertson had actually stayed with the minister on his march south and, though they were at opposite ends of the spectrum politically, they had spent a pleasant evening discussing the merits of either side. On his return north, dressed in Cope's best clothing and riding in his carriage, Simson is reputed to have said, 'Struan, you come back in better order than you went.' Struan responded, 'Oh, all the effects of *your* prayers, Mr Simson.' The post road ran out short of Robertson's home, but, undaunted, his men hoisted the carriage up and carried it the last few miles to his home.

Despite his part in the '45 Rising, the government seems to have turned a blind eye to Robertson, perhaps because of his age. They did take revenge on his property, however, for The Hermitage, or Mount Alexander, above Dunalastair Water was burned in 1746; so too was Carie and a third house in Kinloch Rannoch. Robertson rebuilt Carie, where he lived for four years more, dying there on 18 April 1749.

About two years after his death, a single octavo volume of Robertson's poems was published. These were fairly popular at the time of printing, but have no real merit. Among the verses are a couple of epitaphs, including an 'Epitaph upon the Captain of Clanrannald, who was killed at Sheriffmuir, 1715'. This includes the lines:

He fell supporting his true Prince's Cause,
To raise his Country and restore her Laws.

His coffin was taken to the family burial plot at Dunalastair, at Strathtummel in Perthshire. Having never married, he was succeeded in the chiefship by his cousin, Duncan Robertson of Drumachune.

CHAPTER ELEVEN
Prince's Strand

Prince Charles (1720-1788), son of the exiled King James VIII and III (1688-1766) and Clementina Sobieska (1702-35), first landed on Scottish soil on 23 July 1745. He was just 25 years of age and was here to claim the throne for his father. Charles's vessel, the *Du Teillay* or *Doutelle*, hit the western shore of the Outer Hebridean island of Eriskay. The sandy beach where the vessel landed has ever since been known as *Coilleag a' Phrionnsa*, which translates from the Gaelic as 'the Prince's strand'.

Charles had left France one month earlier. Before embarking he laid a false trail in France, writing letters to various officials requesting that they should lead an attack on England. Meanwhile, he was heading across country using assumed names and wearing disguises, to the port of St Nazaire at the foot of the River Loire, on the west coast of the country. On the morning of 4 July the ship was loaded with goods and set sail for Scotland, in a contrary wind.

Accompanying the *Du Teillay* was the *Elisabeth*, another vessel loaded with arms and ammunition; the *Du Teillay* was captained by Mr. Darbe or Durbe whereas the *Elisabeth* was in Captain D'Au's charge. Charles was on the former, disguised as an Irish priest, so that the crew knew not whom they were ferrying.

En route the ships came into conflict with an English vessel, the *Lion*, on 9 July. For five hours the vessels engaged in pistol shooting, the result of which left the *Lion* with tattered rigging and broken masts. The

French vessels then made a mad dash for safety, leaving the *Lion* limping behind. The English vessel had lost 45 men, another 107 were wounded and of these a further seven were to die soon after.

The *Elisabeth* suffered more. She lost her captain, as well as 140 soldiers. A further 160 were wounded, leaving the vessel with little option but to return to France. The *Du Teillay* was unable to have some of the soldiers or arms transferred to it and so it continued alone, lacking any real clout. The sailors came close to further battles, but each time either managed to sail off into safety or else lose the enemy ship in the mist and storms that they had to endure.

At four o'clock in the morning of Saturday 20 July the sailors' spirits rose when they spotted land. They sailed slowly past the headlands, working out where they were. Spirits fell quickly when it was realised that it was not Scotland that they were viewing, but the north coast of Ireland. The ship was steered onto a new course, although the captain admitted it was 'not promising.' After a further two days of sailing the sailors spotted land once more. Barra Head, the massive headland on the southern tip of the Western Isles, came into view and the ship was steered for Barra.

Duncan Cameron and Aeneas MacDonald left the vessel in the small rowing boat that was used to ferry passengers to the shore. On Barra they met with the MacNeil of Barra's piper, Calum MacNeil, who was willing to guide the vessel. A second pilot was acquired from a passing boat, on which had been a horse, a calf, a woman and children.

The *Du Teillay* was then steered for Canna, but as it was making its way there a large man-of-war appeared on the horizon. Captain Darbe turned the vessel as quickly as he could, but the warship pursued them. Back at the Western Isles, Antoine Walsh decided that it would be best if Charles and his companions were sent off the ship on the ship's boat. Accordingly they disembarked just off the coast of Eriskay. The *Du Teillay* sailed on, still pursued by the larger vessel. However, the warship was unable to anchor at the same place as the French ship and had to sail a mile further on to find a suitable place to halt.

Landing with the Prince was the Marquis of Tullibardine, heir of the 1st Duke of Atholl. He had been active with Lord Mar and had fought at Sheriffmuir and Glenshiel. In the Jacobite peerage he had been created Duke of Rannoch in 1717. After Glenshiel he had lived in France, where he was imprisoned for debt for a time, before returning to Scotland with the Prince.

As the vessel was heading towards the shore, a large eagle hovered overhead. Tullibardine was the first man to spot it, but was frightened to mention it lest the sailors regarded it as a bad omen. Eventually he could ignore it no longer and spoke to the Prince. 'Sir, I hope that this is an excellent omen and promises good things to us. The king of birds has come to welcome your Royal Highness upon your arrival to Scotland.'

On the shore at Eriskay grows a little pink convolvulus (*calystegia soldanella*), known also as sea-bindweed, which became known as the Prince's flower. Tradition claims that prior to leaving France, Charles gathered a few seeds from flowers growing on the French shores; on his arrival in Scotland he scattered the seeds and they took root. The flower has often been transported elsewhere, but for some reason it only grows on the island of Eriskay.

Prince Charles spent his first night in Scotland sleeping in a tiny croft house, the home of Angus MacDonald.

The chiefs of Scotland's Highland clans were not enthusiastic at the arrival of the Prince. They warned him that there were insufficient men ready to rise for the cause and those that were ready had too few arms. 'Go home,' was their advice, 'and await a more suitable time.'

'I am come *home*,' replied Charles, 'and can entertain no notion of turning back. I am persuaded that my faithful Highlanders will stand by me.'

Alexander MacDonald of Boisdale told Charles that neither Sir Alexander MacDonald of Sleat nor Norman MacLeod of MacLeod would come out in support and as John O'Sullivan recorded, 'Everybody was strock as with a thunder boult, as you may believe, to hear yt sentence.'

The arguments against a rising continued for some time, until at length an exasperated Charles turned to Ranald MacDonald of Clanranald. 'Will you not aid me?' he asked.

'I will! I will!' he responded, 'and though not another man in the whole Highlands should draw a sword, I will die for you!'

Soon the other chiefs acquiesced and the rising was underway.

Charles spent a second night on Eriskay. The island, which lies in the Sound of Barra, between Barra and South Uist, extends to only 1,737 acres. The MacNeils of Barra owned it at the time of Charles's visit. Captain Darbe arrived back and picked up Charles and his party, but the man-of-war also appeared back on the horizon and this time it was accompanied by a frigate. Fortunately the winds were such that these vessels were not able to reach the shore and had to wait further out to sea. It was decided that the only means of escape for Charles and his party was to sail during the night.

During the night of 24-25 July Prince Charles set sail across the Minch for the mainland of Scotland. They passed the islands of Rum, Canna and Eigg and arrived at Loch nan Uamh, in Morar on the west coast of the Scottish mainland. At four o'clock in the evening the small boat was lowered over the side of the *Du Teillay* and Charles and his men rowed ashore.

On the following days a number of local clan chiefs came to visit Charles, offering their allegiance. Many of them were still of the opinion that it would be better for him to return to France, as he had no troops to back his claim. But Charles would have none of it. Eventually he was able to win over the main MacDonald chiefs of the district to support him and a major bonus for the cause was when Donald Cameron of Lochiel (1695-1748) was persuaded to join in.

CHAPTER TWELVE
The Seven Men
of Moidart

At Kinlochmoidart, on the road between Acharacle and Glenuig, along the remote western shores of Moidart, are seven beech trees representing the 'seven men of Moidart' who landed with Prince Charles in July 1745. The trees were originally planted around 1820 by David and Margarita Robertson-MacDonald, but one has succumbed to age and the elements and has had to be replaced. Within the estate is 'The Prince's Walk', a quiet lane where Charles wandered for some fresh air.

On his arrival on the mainland of Scotland on 25 July 1745 Prince Charles had a company of seven close friends. One of these was William Murray, the Marquis of Tullibardine; he is regarded by Jacobites as the 2nd Duke of Atholl, though he did not actually succeed due to his attainder and the title passed to his brother, James. The second was Sir Thomas Sheridan, an Irish native, who had acted as the preceptor to Prince Charles. The third was Sir John MacDonald, or MacDonnell, another Irishman who was an officer in the French cavalry. The fourth was Aeneas MacDonald, the younger brother of the laird of Kinlochmoidart and a banker in Paris. The fifth was John William O'Sullivan, another Irish officer in the French army. The sixth was Rev George Kelly, an Irish minister and servant to the Prince. The seventh was Francis Strickland, an English gentleman who belonged to Westmorland.

On 11 August 1745 Charles and his men sailed from Borrodale across the Sound of Arisaig to Moidart, landing at Glenuig Bay. There he was greeted by a crowd of locals, some of whom were so excited at his presence that they danced a reel on the shore; this dance was later to become known as the 'Eight Men of Moidart,' for Prince Charles was counted in this instance. The Prince and his men crossed the headland of Moidart by way of the little Glen Uig and they boarded a small boat on the shores at Caolas; this took them eastward, up through the channel between the mainland and Shona Beag and across Loch Moidart, landing them once more at Kinlochmoidart.

Donald MacDonald, who had five brothers, owned the estate here and the Prince spent a full week in their company. This time was spent in arranging supplies and planning his next move. He wrote numerous letters, one of them noting that he intended raising the standard at Glenfinnan. On 18 August he was joined at Kinlochmoidart by John Murray of Broughton, who was appointed as his secretary. Donald MacDonald was aware of the danger his property was under and it is said that he took most of the valuables from the house and hid them beneath a large rock, known thereafter as the Plate Rock, which lies by the shore of Loch Moidart.

During this time, the clans in the district were rising for the Prince. Word was spreading that Prince Charles had landed on Scottish shores and the messengers were sent out to the chiefs of the neighbouring clans. Cameron of Lochiel raised 1,200 men or more. MacDonell of Glengarry raised 700 men; MacPherson of Cluny brought 600 and Colonel Alexander MacGillivray of Dunmaglass brought 700 of the Clan Mackintosh. The Clanranald MacDonald contingent was weaker in number, for some members of the clan were against the rising and only 300 came out in support.

Not all of the clans who were expected to support the Prince came out in his favour. Allan MacDonald of Clanranald was sent to Skye, where he was to raise the MacDonalds of Sleat and the MacLeods of Dunvegan. After hearing of the Prince's arrival, these two chiefs colluded in sending word to President Forbes of Culloden to inform him of the impending rising and who and how many people were taking part. In the letter they write:

> You may believe, my Lord, our spirits are in a great deal of
> agitation and that we are much at a loss how to behave in so

extraordinary an occurrence. That we will have no
connection with these madmen is certain, but we are
bewildered in every other respect till we hear from you.

When word came back to Charles that the clans were rising in his
support and that they would attend the raising of the standard at the
head of Loch Shiel, he set off to join them. Leaving Kinlochmoidart
behind on 18 August, accompanied by fifty Clanranald men, he crossed
the hill of Torr a' Bhreitheimh to Dalelia, at the south-western end of
Loch Shiel. He boarded a vessel and sailed seven miles north eastwards
up the loch to Glenaladale, where he landed again.

Glenaladale was the home of Alexander MacDonald, a keen
Jacobite. Here the Prince spent the night. On 14 August Captain John
Gordon of Glenbuchat arrived at the house, bringing with him Captain
Swetenham, a Hanoverian soldier from Guise's Regiment who had
been captured in the Braes of Lochaber by Donald MacDonell of
Lochgarry.

The following morning the Prince and his party boarded their
boat once more, sailing the final six or seven miles up Loch Shiel to
Glenfinnan. The party halted for a rest at a rocky promontory known
ever since as Torr a' Phrionsa, or 'the Prince's Rock,' which lies at the
foot of Beinn Odhar Mhor on the north side of the loch. At mid-
morning on 19 August the party arrived at Glenfinnan, where they
alighted from their vessel, ready to meet the supporters. However, there
were none to be seen. Only two shepherds were found, who greeted the
Prince in Gaelic and wished him 'God speed.' Dejected by the lack of
support, Prince Charles retired to a local hut, or inn, where he awaited
something happening.

CHAPTER THIRTEEN

The Rout of
the High Bridge

With word of the arrival of the Prince in the west, soldiers from all over Scotland were mobilised in an attempt to capture him. Two companies of the Royal Scots, numbering about 80 or 90 men and under the command of Captain John Scott of Balcomie, were sent south from Fort Augustus towards Fort William, following the military road which took them alongside lochs Oich and Lochy. As they left the heights of Stronenaba behind and descended towards the River Spean, the men became complacent about nearing Fort William, which was just another seven miles to the south west.

The River Spean makes its way through a deep gorge hereabouts, as it leaves Glen Spean and drops to the lower levels of Glen More. The military road has to drop steeply into the glen and it crosses the river by a narrow bridge over a rocky gorge, usually known as the High Bridge, but also known in Gaelic as *An Drochaid Bhan*, the white bridge.

Word of the movement of troops had reached MacDonell of Keppoch, who decided that this was an ideal place to attack. Although he had few men at his disposal, he managed to gather a small company. There were 13 men in total and he sent them to the inn on the south side of the High Bridge, to await the arrival of the soldiers; his cousin Donald MacDonell of Tirnadris led the small band and among their number was a piper.

MacDonell of Tirnadris hid his men behind the small hostelry. They gazed northwards to the other side of the river and awaited the arrival of the soldiers. When the soldiers appeared, the command was given for the piper to strike up a tune. The men rushed out from behind the inn, making as much noise as they could and darting about from tree to tree, hiding behind the trunks. The soldiers were confused as to how many rebels there were and were terrified by the noise and piping. Scott ordered his sergeant and a servant to advance, to try to find out how strong the force was. They were allowed to cross the bridge, but when they arrived on the southern bank of the river MacDonell's men jumped out on them and dragged them both away as prisoners.

The sight of this brought terror to the other soldiers and they were ready for abandoning the fight and running. Captain Scott was for none of this and was keen to try to force a way across the bridge. The other officers in the party, Captain James Thomson and Lieutenants Fergusson and Rose, had less mettle and pleaded with Scott that they should turn around. They explained that the men were tired, their morale was low and that it would be prudent to turn back. Eventually Scott agreed and gave the command.

The soldiers took to their heels and made their way back up the hillside as fast as they could. MacDonell watched from the bridge and once he was sure that the men were indeed retreating, he ordered his men to pursue them. He was eager that the soldiers would not notice just how small his force was, for if they did so then they could quite easily turn on them.

MacDonell followed the soldiers for some distance. MacDonald of Keppoch had been busy in the meantime; he had gathered as many clansmen as he was able and led them to the site of the skirmish. At the Low Bridge he joined Tirnadris and a number of Camerons of Dochanasie also came from the west to swell the Jacobite numbers. By this time the soldiers had run five or six miles. The Jacobites now numbered around 50 men and felt that there were sufficient numbers of them to shoot at the redcoats. The Royal Scots fired back, but in the panic their aim was indiscriminate and no Jacobites were killed.

The soldiers arrived at Laggan Achadrom, which is located near to the head of Loch Lochy. In front they found their way blocked by another 50 Jacobites, under the command of Glengarry. He ordered his men to fire and a few shots were successful in killing some of the soldiers. One of the bullets hit Captain Scott, wounding him on the shoulder. Over a dozen redcoats were wounded.

MacDonell of Keppoch then drew his sword and marched alone towards the Royal Scots. He yelled an order to lay down their arms and surrender, for if they did not then he would have them all killed. Scott realised that he meant this and passed on the order to his men.

The Jacobites rounded up the soldiers and took their arms from them. As this was taking place, Cameron of Lochiel arrived from the west with a few men and it was decided to take the prisoners back to Achnacarry. The regular soldiers were held in an inn there, but Captain Scott was taken into the house and looked after, 'treated more like a friend and a brother than an enemy and a prisoner,' according to his own account. A message was sent to the garrison at Fort William to inform them of the prisoners and to request a surgeon to attend Captain Scott. The request was refused, so Lady Lochiel dressed it herself. Lochiel was so shocked at the commander's lack of assistance that he released the captain and had him taken to Fort William. His white horse, however, was kept and renamed Tirnadris. It was later presented to the Prince who kept it thereafter.

Lieutenant Ferguson of the Royal Scots had in his possession at the time of the capture a number of bank notes to the value of £59. He was obviously concerned about the safety of this and decided it would be prudent to rip off the serial numbers on each banknote. These he stuffed into the lining of his coat. The remainder of the notes were passed to Sergeant Johnstone who decided that it would be better to throw them away rather than let them get into enemy hands.

On the following day the prisoners were taken by Cameron's men and marched to Glenfinnan, where they were forced to watch the raising of the standard. After having witnessed the event, Prince Charles gave the order that they should be released on parole. Lieutenant Fergusson and Sergeant Johnstone both survived the incident and Fergusson later appealed to the Bank of Scotland to have his money refunded, on proof of the serial numbers. The bank was unwilling to refund him, but after Sergeant Johnstone was able to corroborate his story, the bank eventually paid up.

CHAPTER FOURTEEN
Raising the Standard in Glenfinnan

Bonnie Prince Charlie remained for two hours at the hut in Glen Finnan, all the while his spirits becoming more dejected. Suddenly, at around four o'clock, he heard a noise from outside and he made his way from the building to see what it was. In the distance, high on the ridge, he could hear the faint sound of the bagpipes playing. His spirits rose slightly, realising that they were being played for him. As he gazed up at the hillside, he scanned the slopes for a sight of anyone. Suddenly he spotted a movement and his heart leaped a bound when he saw the array of men before him.

Cameron of Lochiel and around seven or eight hundred men were coming to the head of Loch Shiel, where the standard of King James was to be raised at the appointed time. The Camerons were an impressive sight, coming in two distinct directions – some from Loch Eil to the east, the others making their way down Glen Finnan from the head of Loch Arkaig. The raising of the Camerons had not been entirely easy for the chief; he had been a reluctant adherent himself, for with the Prince's lack of support he had at first advised him that he should return to France. His brother had been of the same opinion. Charles, however, was clever enough to persuade Lochiel to join him.

A considerable number of Camerons lived by the side of Loch Rannoch, on land belonging to the chief of the Menzies and Struan Robertson. A group of two dozen Cameron men from the west travelled amongst these distant clansmen and warned them that 'if they do not forthwith go alongst with them, they would that instant proceed to burn all their houses and haugh their cattle. Whereupon they carried off of the Rannoch men about one hundred mostly of the name Cameron, amongst which there were nine recruits that were listed by him, the informer, for Captain Murray's Company.'

Among them was Miss Jenny Cameron, riding at the head of the Camerons of Morvern and Sunart. Jenny, or Jean, was the daughter of Hugh Cameron of Glendessarry. She came with the men, probably just to catch a glimpse of the Prince and afterwards returned home, where she looked after her brother's affairs. As she was the first woman to come out in support of Charles, the Hanoverian propaganda merchants claimed that she became Charles's mistress and remained with him for the remainder of the campaign, but this is untrue.

Jenny Cameron had married an Irishman named O'Neil, but had left him due to his cruelty. She later moved to Lanarkshire and died in 1772 at East Kilbride, where her grave is still marked. It is said that she wished to be buried back in Lochaber, but her family were unable to afford the cost of transporting her corpse there.

Prince Charles was delighted at the support from the Camerons and resolved to go ahead and raise the standard without waiting for anyone else. Only 150 men under the Laird of Morar were there in addition to the Camerons when William, Marquis of Tullibardine, the Jacobite Duke of Atholl and two supporters marched up onto a rock outcrop and unfurled the banner of the Chevalier de St George. The silk flag was white and red in colour and it fluttered in the wind. It had been sewn by the ladies of Kinlochmoidart.

Joining the rising were 300 men under MacDonell of Keppoch and 300 men under Clanranald MacDonald. Around 1300 men had gathered in the glen by this time and they remained camped there for two days.

On 21 August the Jacobite forces began their march eastward. They headed direct for Loch Eil, where word reached Charles that the King had placed a ransom of £30,000 on his head. Not to be outdone by this, Charles immediately issued a proclamation in which he offered a similar sum for the Hanoverian 'elector'.

At Fassifern, or Fassfern, House, the party halted and spent the night. The Prince stayed in the house, which was the home of John Cameron, brother of the clan chief, who was absent at the time as he was a supporter of the Royalist household. It is claimed that it was at Fassifern that the white rose was first used as a symbol of Jacobite support; Prince Charles is said to have leaned from his bedroom window and plucked a rose from the climbing bush that grew there. This was of the *rosa alba maxima* variety, although it is also thought that the *rosa semi-plena* was used at times, the latter being plucked at Ardblair in Perthshire.

On the following day, to avoid capture by the Hanoverian soldiers at Fort William and to confuse the enemy as to the size of the army, the Jacobites separated their number. The baggage train and some of the men were sent by way of Corpach to Moy, by the side of the River Lochy. The main army took a more remote route from Fassifern, up Gleann Suileag and down Glen Loy on the opposite side.

The soldiers taking the lower route, by way of Corpach, had the Prince and Lochiel amongst their number. Lochiel arrived at a thatched cottage at Annat, west of Corpach, where he and two others entered the house. An elderly lady was inside and recognised Lochiel. He asked to speak with her husband and she responded by telling him that he was working out the back. He was quickly notified and entered the house.

Lochiel asked the man if he could recommend someone to guide him and the army over the hill to Moy, thus avoiding a route by way of Corpach and Banavie that would be too dangerous, being almost within sight of the fort at Inverlochy. The old man replied, 'My son is in your army, but he does not know the route as well as myself. I will lead your men over the hill, for I know every inch of the way.'

Lochiel thanked the man and at that point introduced him to the gentleman sitting on their armchair, saying, 'This is your Prince.' At that the Prince stood up and shook hands with the man, thanking him for his assistance.

The army then made its way up the slopes of the hillside behind Annat farm, following the Allt Dogha. From Loch Kilmallie the route was then made down through Gleann Laragain towards Muirshearleach and thence to Moy, where the rest of the army was rejoined. The baggage train, however, had too much of a load with them and at one point a number of cannon had to be buried in a peat bog.

From Moy the Jacobite force made its way across the Fords of Lochy to Mucomir and thence up the east side of Loch Lochy. At Letterfinlay a halt was called. The men later proceeded to Laggan and Loch Garry, the Prince spending the night in Invergarry Castle.

On the following morning, Bonnie Prince Charlie and his men decided to head southwards. Word had reached them that Sir John Cope and his troops were positioned on the south side of the Monadhliath Mountains at Garbhamor, near the headwaters of the Spey. The Prince was keen to engage in battle, so it was decided to make a route as quickly as possible over the hills to Garbhamor. The most direct route from Invergarry would be by way of a military road that General Wade had forced over the mountains in 1731, a route that climbed to 2,500 feet above sea level known as the Corrieyairack Pass.

As Prince Charles got himself ready at Invergarry, putting on a new pair of brogues, he is known to have said, 'Before I throw these off, I shall meet with Mr Cope.'

Leaving Invergarry, the route taken went by way of Aberchalder and Culachy to the foot of Glen Tarff. From Culachy the military road begins its route, winding ever upwards towards the heights to the south east. As the Prince's men were steadily climbing up the ridge, Charles sent on two officers as scouts, to see if the enemy was in sight. They reached the watershed at the head of Corrieyairack, but on looking down into the valley below could see no one.

Word had reached Cope that the Jacobites were heading his way and he decided that it would be better to make a tactical retreat to Ruthven Barracks. Therefore, at a spot ever since known as 'Cope's Turn', near to Dalchully House, west of Laggan, he turned his men around and made for the safety of the barracks. Not all of his men were in agreement, however and 40 of them are known to have deserted at this time. They were later spotted by Charles's lookouts ascending the zigzag route up through Corrieyairack and were easily persuaded to join the Prince's side.

Whilst camped in the Corrieyairack vicinity, Prince Charles's force was increased in number with the arrival of 250 Stewarts of Appin under the command of Charles Stewart of Ardshiel, the MacDonells of Glengarry, the Grants of Glenmoriston and 150 MacDonalds of Glencoe.

CHAPTER FIFTEEN
Over the Corrieyairack

From the Corrieyairack Pass, Prince Charles led his men down through the upper reaches of the Spey valley, crossing the Garbha Bridge and arriving at Garbhamor inn, a Kingshouse established by the government when the military roads were being constructed to try to pacify and civilise the Highlands. Charles had heard that Cope was in the vicinity and he was keen to engage him in battle. But Cope had cold feet and was heading further north, hoping to prevent the Jacobites from blocking the Slochd Mor and thus isolating Inverness and Fort Augustus from the south. Instead the Jacobites camped there for the night.

On 29 August 1745, which was a fine summer's day, the Jacobites began their march southward. A group of men left the party to raid Ruthven. After the 1715 Rising a series of barracks had been erected across the Highlands. One of these was Ruthven Barracks, built on the site of Ruthven Castle, which had been a Comyn stronghold but which was burned to the ground by Claverhouse and his followers. In 1718 the remains of the castle were removed and a new barracks erected on the green mound, which lies south of Kingussie in Strathspey.

The barracks were under the command of Sergeant Terence Molloy, who had 14 privates below him. Sergeant Molloy was warned by one of the guards that there was a large band of men coming towards the barracks. When he went to the lookout post to see who was approaching, he found that there were around 300 Jacobites making their way across the plain towards the garrison. They were under the command of MacDonell of Lochgarry, Dr Archibald Cameron and John William O'Sullivan.

The Jacobites came to the gate and insisted on speaking to someone within. They demanded that Molloy should surrender the barracks to them and should he readily agree to this, then they would guarantee that no harm would be inflicted on the soldiers within and that they would be free to take their possessions with them. Molloy was defiant, however, warning them that, 'I am too old a soldier to surrender such a strong garrison without bloody noses.' The Jacobites were incensed at this retort and warned Molloy that they would attack the barracks and hang both Molloy and his men. Molloy responded by saying that he would take his chance.

The Jacobites retreated some distance, but as nightfall came they began to make preparations for assault. At midnight around 150 Jacobites returned to Ruthven and attacked the building. They assailed the fore-gate with guns and rams, trying to force it. At the sally port, which was smaller, a number of old barrels and other combustible materials were piled up against it and set alight. The fire quickly caught and soon the flames were charring the door. The men inside the fortress managed to get barrels and buckets of water and douse the flames from above. The man responsible for setting the fire and keeping the infant flames going was spotted as he did so and became an early victim.

At around half past three in the morning the Jacobites withdrew and all went quiet for a time. Two hours later word was sent to the barracks that two of the Jacobite leaders wished to talk with Molloy. The sergeant agreed, but he spoke to them from the safety of the parapet. The Jacobites played their hand as though they were winning and offered Molloy conditions for surrender. He refused their demands. A further request was made, asking that they be allowed to remove their dead, to which Molloy agreed. There had been two casualties in the Jacobite forces and a number of others were wounded; these were taken back to Ruthven village. The government soldiers lost only one man, who had been foolish enough to raise his head above the parapet, despite orders to keep down.

The Jacobites later left Ruthven village, though not before stealing many of the provisions available to the residents. A merchant in the village, Mrs MacPherson, was also the barrack-wife and she had her shop ransacked. She exaggerated to Molloy that there were around 3,000 men in the Jacobite force and that they were camped in the fields west of the village.

In a letter written by Sergeant Molloy to his Lieutenant General, Sir John Cope, he noted that:

> I expect another visit this night, I am informed, with their pateraroes [small cannon], but I shall give them the warmest reception my weak party can afford. I shall hold out as long as possible. I conclude, Honourable General, with great respect,
>
> Your most obedient and humble servant,
> Molloy, Sergeant.

Sergeant Molloy was immediately promoted to the rank of Lieutenant. The expected attack did not materialise for some months, until 10 February 1746. Around 300 Jacobites, under the command of John Gordon of Glenbuchat, surrounded the building and they had the advantage of cannon.

John Gordon was born around 1673. At the Jacobite Rising of 1689 he joined the Jacobite forces when he was still only 16 years of age. Nevertheless, he rode with the soldiers to Killiecrankie where he took part in the battle.

At Mar's rising, Glenbuchat joined the Jacobites once more. He fought at Sheriffmuir, but was captured and taken prisoner. Held at Carlisle Castle, he was able to arrange his release in 1716 by bribing General George Carpenter. During the 1719 Rising, Glenbuchat supplied Carpenter with intelligence reports on the Jacobite support; on that occasion the forces in the barracks managed to hold out for three days but eventually were forced to capitulate.

The Jacobites offered Molloy terms for surrender, which he had no option but to accept. As he left the barracks, the Jacobites made their way in and set the barrack blocks and stable building alight. They have remained in ruins ever since.

Another raid was more successful. The local laird, Ewen

MacPherson of Cluny, lived at Cluny Castle in Strathspey. A party of Camerons made their way to his home and took him hostage. He was brought back to Prince Charles who managed to persuade him to change his allegiance and throw his lot behind the cause. Cluny, as will be seen, became a devoted Jacobite, but the fact that he was arrested under the threat of 'be burnt or join' became important at a later date when he had to answer to the government.

The main party of Jacobites headed south, crossing the moors of Dalwhinnie by way of Wade's road. They camped on 30 August at Dalnacardoch, where a wayside inn had been established in the 1730s.

Having entered Atholl their spirits began to rise, for the locals rushed out to greet them. Men, women and children left their homes to join the marching soldiers, for the Duke of Atholl was of their number. He had not been seen in his home country for thirty years, having lived in exile since the 1715 Rising. News of the arrival of the Prince reached Lady Lude, who was told to make her way to Blair Castle in order to receive the Prince and act as hostess. She found the castle abandoned, the Hanoverian Duke of Atholl (the Jacobite Duke's younger brother) having fled.

Charlotte Robertson, Lady Lude, was the widow of John Robertson of Lude (d.1732); only in her thirties, she was a daughter of Lady Nairne and a cousin of the Duke of Atholl. She was somewhat overcome by the Prince's arrival and seems to have gone over the top in making him welcome. The factor, Thomas Bisset, recorded that 'Lady Lude is here with [the Jacobites] and behaves like a light giglet and hath taken upon her to be the sole mistress of the house.' She gave the Prince a pineapple to eat, the first time he had ever tasted the fruit.

Soon the Jacobite army reached Blair Castle, arriving on 31 August. A camp was set up in the ground, the Prince and his officers staying in the castle. They remained there for three days.

On 2 September Charles ordered his men to parade in the castle grounds, so that he could review them. He was annoyed to discover that a number of men who had been upset that they had not been able to engage Cope had fled from the party. Charles sent a number of his officers out into Strathspey to round them up and indeed most came back to join the force.

Charles relaxed at Blair Castle for a time. He took a walk in the grounds with Lady Lude. At one point he came upon the manicured lawn of the bowling green, which he found interesting, having never seen one before. Lady Lude sent to the castle for a set of bowls to show him; these he recognised, for a set had been presented to him in Rome as a curiosity.

It is thought that whilst camped at Blair, Prince Charles spent the night of 2 September at Lude House, seat of Lady Lude. On that night a ball had been organised for a few of the Prince's officers and the Prince himself delighted the family by wearing a jacket of Robertson tartan. He is known to have enjoyed himself at the dance, taking part in various reels and minuets. The first dance he called for was 'This is not mine ain hoose.'

The ball was presided over by Lady Lude. A keen supporter of the Prince, she had her own company of soldiers in the Atholl Brigade. She warned them that if any of them should desert the Prince, then she would have them hanged should they return to the area. Lady Lude was to be later arrested for her Jacobite sympathies in 1746 but she was not prosecuted.

The following day the Jacobite forces continued on their march south. They left Blair and headed through the Pass of Killiecrankie and down Tayside towards Dunkeld. They camped at the village, the Prince staying in Dunkeld House. Cameron of Lochiel had been in front and had proclaimed King James at the village cross. On the following day they continued towards Perth. On 4 September they reached the House of Nairne, which stood at Loak, six and a half miles north of Perth. The seat of the 2nd Lord Nairne, the house was a grand classical edifice, the main block four storeys in height. Prince Charles remained there, being entertained by Lord Nairne and his mother, the Dowager Lady Nairne. Lord Nairne's involvement was to result in the later forfeiture of his mansion and estate, which were eventually sold to the Duke of Atholl who demolished the house in 1764.

Lochiel led 400 of his soldiers into the city of Perth. They occupied a number of houses, as well as the old Cromwellian citadel. The standard of James was hoisted and he was proclaimed king, with Charles proclaimed Regent.

That evening Prince Charles and his immediate followers made their way from the House of Nairne into Perth. He made a grand entry, riding the white horse he had been given. The residents gave him a mixed reception; some cheered enthusiastically as he made his way through the streets and others kept their mouths closed, for the Jacobites had taken £500 from the city purse to support their cause, the Prince having by this time just one guinea to his name. That night the Prince stayed at an inn owned by John Hickson, later known as the Salutation Hotel, which still stands. Other accounts state that he stayed, perhaps only for part of the time, at Lord Stormont's town house, which was located in the High Street. There Stormont's sisters entertained the Prince.

One of those who was with Charles in Perth was Colonel Bower of Kingoldrum. He was later captured and tried at York as a Jacobite, but 'the only charge that could be brought against him was that he had worn a white cockade in his bonnet and had been seen shaking hands with Prince Charles Edward at the Salutation inn in Perth.'

At Perth many more men joined Charles's Highland soldiers. Many of the local gentry joined the cause, including Lord George Murray, who brought his followers, and Lord Ogilvy, son of the Earl of Airlie, who brought almost 600 of his clan. Lord Strathallan joined, as did the titular Duke of Perth, whose followers may have numbered around 150.

One local laird failed to join the Prince due to the wily actions of his wife. John Gray, 12th Lord Gray (1716-82), had been in Dundee where it was his intention to offer his support to the Hanoverian cause. However, the Duke of Cumberland was slow in acknowledging this, so he took the huff and set off back to his home at Kinfauns Castle, east of Perth. He told his wife, Margaret Blair, of his intentions to join Prince Charles instead, proposals that horrified her. She told her husband to have a seat and she would get him a basin of water in which to soothe his feet after such a long journey from Dundee. Lord Gray sat in front of the fire, but the water that Lady Gray poured over his feet was boiling, scalding him so badly that he was unable to walk for weeks. A local ballad recounts the tale:

I'm brint! I'm brint! How came it this way?
I feat I'll no' ride for mony a day.

Send aff the men and tae Prince Chairlie say:
'My hert is wi' him, but I'm tie by the tae.'

The wily wife flushed, but the laird didnae see
The smile on her face through the tear in her e'e.
'Had I kent the guid man wad hae had siccan pain,
The kettle for me sud hae coupit its lane.'

The actions of his wife probably saved the family lands from forfeiture at a later date.

In total, Charles and the Jacobite army spent ten days in Perth. Lord George Murray drilled the men, improving their standard immensely. William Lindsay, a wright in the town, was employed to make targes for the Prince's army.

From Perth the Jacobites spread out to neighbouring towns and cities. On 5 September a group of soldiers marched into Dundee and proclaimed James as king. Charles also began collecting taxes he claimed were due to him and sent various members of his support to surrounding places to collect these. John Murray of Broughton was sent to Dundee, Montrose and other communities to collect them.

On Sunday 8 September Prince Charles went to church. He was keen to demonstrate his religious tolerance and thus increase cross-religious support. Although a Roman Catholic, he decided to attend an Episcopal service. This took place in the Scottish Episcopal Church in Perth, where Rev Armstrong preached to him from Isaiah 14: 1-2:

For the Lord will have mercy on Jacob and yet choose Israel
and set them in their own land: and the strangers shall be
joined with them and they shall cleave to the house of Jacob.
And the people shall take them and bring them to their
place: and the house of Israel shall possess them in the land
of the Lord for servants and handmaids: and they shall take
them captives, whose captives they were; and they shall rule
over their oppressors.

CHAPTER SIXTEEN

Great Disturbance in the Country

News that Sir John Cope's army was now at Aberdeen and was heading southwards prompted the Jacobites into advancing. It was decided to make haste for Edinburgh and take the city before Cope returned there, which he was considering doing by sea. There were still a few problems to tidy up in Perth, however. Colonel O'Sullivan had arrested the provost and one of the bailies of the town for no apparent reason and was still holding them captive. Lord George Murray heard of this and it was reported to the Prince. Charles had to intervene and the two men were released.

On 11 September the Jacobite soldiers got themselves ready and began their march out of Perth. Taking the Stirling road, the force was by this time 2,000 strong and it was an impressive sight. They arrived at Auchterarder where they halted, the troops being lined up for a review. Charles left them behind, advancing himself to Dunblane where he lodged two nights with Alexander MacGregor or Drummond of Balhaldie, an elderly man of 70 years but a veteran of Sheriffmuir. That night various locals paid the Prince a visit and Mrs Russell, wife of the bailie, is said to have given the prince a purse of gold sovereigns to assist in the campaign. On the following night, the Prince lodged at Newton House, near Doune.

At Dunblane the minister complained in the session book that the income had dropped:

... the smallness of the collections now and afterwards which
may be observed, is owing to the uncertainty of public
worship in regard that the young Pretender came to this
place on Thursday last with an army of Highlanders and
others his adherents, marching southwards and parties passing
continually to join them, which created great disturbance in
the country.

The Jacobites captured Doune Castle and Gregor MacGregor of
Glengyle was appointed as its governor by Bonnie Prince Charlie.
MacGregor held the castle for months afterwards.

By the evening of 12 September the Jacobite army had caught up
with the Prince and camped for the night in the grounds of Keir House.
James Stirling of Keir was a willing host, for he was still a keen supporter
of the Prince despite his forfeiture.

The way to Stirling could have caused the Prince and his men
some difficulty, for the Forth was a major natural obstacle on the north
side of the town and it would have been fairly easy for the Hanoverians
to guard Stirling Bridge. However, the Jacobites made west for the Fords
of Frew, near Kippen, and crossed the river with little trouble.

Moir of Leckie was a known supporter and the Jacobites headed
for his home, where they had been promised food and refreshments.
However, the Hanoverian soldiers had arrived at the house the day
before and had arrested Moir for his adherences. Taking him back to
Stirling, they forgot about the provisions that Moir had laid in, resulting
in the Jacobites enjoying Moir's hospitality, but without the benefit of
his company.

The Jacobites were billeted throughout the area. Some lodged in
the village of Thornhill, where the soldiers took a horse from a Mr
Ballantyne of Piper's Cottage. This horse was later to throw its rider and
make its way back to its rightful owner.

Prince Charles spent the night in Touch House. Whilst there, a
Highlander in his army was so hungry that he killed a sheep from one
of the tenants on the estate. Unfortunately he picked one belonging to
an elderly widow who complained to the leaders of the army. An
argument erupted between Cameron of Lochiel and the chief of

MacGregor over which clan the miscreant belonged to, but eventually it was discovered that it had been a Cameron who was responsible. When he was brought before the chief, Lochiel was so angry that he shot him. The man died of his wound the following day and was to be buried within the estate. The estate joiner, however, had Hanoverian sympathies and refused to make a coffin for him, so the clansman was interred near to Old Touch Bridge in a coffin made by another man of the name Mellies; the spot has since become known as the Highlander's Grave. When Elizabeth Seton, the owner of the estate, returned home and heard this story, she had the estate joiner sacked and offered the job to Mellies.

It was from Leckie that Prince Charles sent a letter to the Provost of Glasgow, demanding that he supply the army with £1,500 towards their costs. The city was thrown into confusion by the demand and the authorities were unsure what to do. However, it was soon realised that the Jacobites were set for Edinburgh, so the magistrates in the city decided to ignore the demand.

On 14 September the Jacobites left Leckie behind and made their way along the southern side of Stirling. The soldiers in the castle could see the force in the distance and aimed a few shots in their direction. No damage was done, though it was noted that a few balls landed close to the Prince.

The march continued towards Falkirk, where the men camped in the grounds to the east of Callendar House. Prince Charles had the benefit of staying within the fine mansion, the guest of Lord and Lady Kilmarnock. Lord Kilmarnock had only that day entertained some of Gardiner's Dragoons in his home and had managed to get some information from them regarding the Hanoverian position. With this news, Charles decided that it would be worth attacking Gardiner's camp, which was located nearer Linlithgow.

The Jacobites set off at speed, keen to engage with the enemy, but on arriving where the soldiers had been based, found the camp abandoned. Gardiner's men had headed off towards Edinburgh as fast as they could, having heard of the Prince's advance.

It was a Sunday morning (15 September) when the Jacobites arrived at Linlithgow's West Port. Most of the residents were making their way to church, but the arrival of the troops diverted their attentions from the sermon. Prince Charles is supposed to have sent a letter to Rev Robert Dalgleish requesting that he continue with his planned service, but as no-one wanted to miss any excitement the pews were empty and he had the morning off. The Prince spent the night in Kingscavil House, a couple of miles east of the town. The people of Linlithgow were fairly supportive of his movement, but the soldiers had a tendency to rob shops and steal things. Knowing this, Charles ordered his men to camp east of the town at Threemiletown, on the road to Winchburgh. On the following morning (16 September), the Jacobite force marched eastward to Corstorphine, on the outskirts of Edinburgh. The soldiers were diverted slightly to Slateford, where they camped for the night. The Prince stayed in Gray's Mill.

From Gray's Mill the Prince wrote a letter to Archibald Stewart, the Lord Provost, demanding that he surrender the city. The capital had been expecting an attack for days and plans had been made for strengthening the defences. The town guard was to be assisted by a further 1,000 recruits and the old town walls were to be rebuilt. Little of these plans seem to have been done when the Jacobites took the city and some blamed this on Archibald Stewart, claiming that he was in fact a secret supporter of the Prince.

The soldiers based in Edinburgh sent out scouts to see where the Jacobites were. At Corstorphine the two groups came within sight of each other and the Jacobites fired at the enemy. The soldiers took panic and fled back to the city as quickly as they were able. Word spread throughout the city that the Jacobites were surrounding it and that they had already defeated the dragoons in battle at the 'Canter of Coltbrigg', as the non-battle became known. The residents warned the Provost that the government soldiers were retreating eastward towards Musselburgh and, in order to protect lives and property, no resistance should be offered to the Jacobites.

The Hanoverians, however, heard that Cope's forces had been seen out in the Firth and that there was now a chance to defend the city. The dragoons were gathered together at Preston, where they camped and sent word to Cope that he should land not at Leith, but instead at Prestonpans or Dunbar, where he would be of more use to them.

In Edinburgh the authorities met to decide whether or not to try and defend the city. A Mr Alves, Writer to the Signet in the town, started spreading the information that the Prince and his followers were willing to enter the city peaceably, so long as the citizens offered no resistance. Should they try to attack, then the Jacobites would respond by acting in a military fashion. Alves was arrested on a charge of treason for spreading the story. A second man also spread the story that he had seen the Jacobites and that they numbered around 16,000. The 1,000 new recruits who were trying to train in preparation decided that they were not that keen to engage in battle and immediately headed for the castle, where they handed in their weapons and resignations.

In the city panic ensued. The authorities prepared for attack and the financial houses began to send their stocks of cash to the castle for protection.

In the meantime, a letter had been sent to the city authorities that were holding a meeting to try and decide what to do. Written by John Murray, it was signed by the Prince:

From Our Camp
16th September 1745

Being now in a condition to make our way into the capital of his Majesty's ancient kingdom of Scotland, we hereby summon you to receive us, as you are in duty bound to do; and in order to it, we hereby require you, on receipt of this, to summon the Town Council and to take proper measures for securing the peace of the city, which we are very desirous to protect. But if you suffer any of the Usurper's troops to enter the town, or any of the cannon, arms, or ammunition now in it (whether belonging to the public or to private persons) to be carried off, we shall take it as a breach of your duty and a heinous offence against the king and us and shall resent it accordingly. We promise to preserve all the rights and liberties of the city and the particular property of every one of his Majesty's subjects. But if any opposition be made to us, we cannot answer for the consequences, being firmly resolved, at any rate, to enter the city; and in that case, if any of the inhabitants are found in arms against us, they must not be expected to be treated as prisoners of war.

CHARLES P.R.

The letter helped make the decision and four bailies were sent to speak with the Prince, requesting him not to take the city by force. However, word reached the meeting that Cope was within striking distance of the city and the city authorities changed their minds. Another bailie was sent to bring the original deputation back, but he was unable to reach them, resulting in claims that he was a Jacobite. The Prince sent a second letter, warning that if he did not receive a positive answer to his first communication, then he would take relevant measures to attack.

At three o'clock on the morning of 17 September the Jacobites under Lochiel made their way into the Canongate, which lay outside the city walls. Hiding in closes and up stairways, they waited in the darkness for a chance to take the city. A ruse to force the gatekeeper of the Netherbow Port to open the gate failed, but at a later hour they were taken by surprise when the gates were opened and a coach and horses exited the city. The chance was taken by Lochiel and a few men, who forced their way through. The guard was arrested and soon the rest of the Jacobites followed them through. With pipes blaring, they reformed themselves and marched up the High Street to Parliament Close.

Charles and the rest of the Jacobites prepared to enter the city later that day. To avoid the guns on the castle rock, they took a route to the south and east, making their way through Morningside to a position in Holyrood Park known as Hunter's Bog. It was there they set up camp, Charles himself enjoying the luxury of the Palace of Holyrood House. At Duddingston is an old house that was used as an inn at the time of the Jacobite occupation and where the Prince is said to have drunk on occasions.

Ensconced in Holyrood House, the Prince arranged a grand ball to which many of the local dignitaries were invited. It was probably at that time that Laurence Oliphant, Charles's aide-de-camp, had the honour of 'crowning' him with a wreath of laurel; he was later to be rewarded by receiving the Prince's signet ring, on which are engraved the thistle, rose and harp, as well as the letters CPR and the Prince of Wales's feather.

On the following day a proclamation was issued in which all residents were ordered to surrender their arms and ammunition; should they fail so to do, then they would be treated as rebels. At the same time an order went to the council requesting the supply of 1,000 tents, 2,000 targes and 6,000 pairs of shoes, the value of which totalled around £1,500. A levy of two shillings and sixpence was laid on the residents, with promise of it being repaid later.

All the while the Jacobites were in the Edinburgh district, support was growing. Men travelled from various parts of Scotland to join the force, though not without difficulty. On 30 October a group of men were crossing the Forth near Alloa when soldiers on manoeuvre from Stirling Castle stopped them. A scuffle ensued and a few of the men were injured. Most were arrested and their belongings, which included 'cows, horses, baggage, arms, money and letters', were taken back to Stirling Castle.

CHAPTER SEVENTEEN
John Gordon
of Glenbuchat

Glenbuchat Castle stands in ruins on a low hillside above the River Don, fifteen miles by road west of Alford. A particularly fine Z-plan tower-house, the castle was erected in 1590 by the Gordons. The name is often spelled Glenbucket, but the more modern preference is for the guttural 'ch' version.

John Gordon of Glenbuchat was a veteran of the three earlier Jacobite Risings. He sold his estate in 1738 to the Earl of Fife and spent some time in France, persuading the Stuarts that the time was ripe for a rising. He was among the first men from the Grampian area to join Bonnie Prince Charlie in his campaign, even though he was by this time an old man of 72. Nevertheless, he was to lead the Gordons and Farquharsons in the coming months.

On 18 August Old Glenbuchat met Charles at Kinlochmoidart. On his way there he had come upon Captain Swettenham of General Guise's regiment and was able to take him prisoner. He was dutifully handed over to the Prince. Charles awarded him the commission of Major General and instructed him to return to the east where he was to raise the men of the Cabrach, Glenbuchat, Strathavon and Strathbogie.

Although he was now aged 72 and known as 'Old Glenbuchat', he was still able to persuade his followers to rise for the Prince.
In August 1745 he issued orders to his son-in-law, George Forbes of Skellater, that he was to raise all fencible men between the ages of 16 and 60. On 15 September 1745 he wrote from St Bridget, or the Mains

of Camdell, in Strath Avon, to Skellater:

> Dear George,
> I am concerned to see your country so backward to relieve
> yourselves from slavery and poverty. Though no pleasure to
> force, yet necessite obliges. Get your own men ready, march
> down amongst those your order obliges you to raise. Since
> Cushing his health will not allow of his going, he'll concur
> to oblige his tennants and give arms. If Glenkindie is gone,
> you'll raise tennants and take his arms and so goe accordingly
> with the whole. I march from this to Glenlivet this day qhr,
> you'll acquaint me qht your doing. No tyme to be lost. I am
> glad yr uncle is come. How soon this came to yr hand
> acquaint Blelack that I marched and that he may acquaint
> Monaltrie and all our friends to make all possible despatch to
> joyn without loss of time. If absolute necessite, I shall send
> one party over yr ladder on ye Strathbogie and Enzie
> gentrie. I hope they'll be ready, or I can reach them. If I am
> forced to send a partie, it must be Highlanders who, I am
> afraid will not, away from myself, be so agreeable nor so
> regular to the countrie. But since they deserve be made
> examples of, blame yourselves. Your orders are full, therefore
> pray goe dilligently about ym. In all haist, for tomorrow
> night I design to be the length of Auchindoun, in order to
> raise that country. My service to yr uncle, Christiane and the
> Bairns.
>
> John Gordon

By 25 September Glenbuchat had raised around 400 men and they
began to march south to join the other Jacobites in the Lothians. On 14
October he had arrived in Edinburgh where he met up with the Prince.

CHAPTER EIGHTEEN
The Four Minute Battle – Prestonpans

Late at night on 19 September 1745 the Jacobite army left their camp at Duddingston and marched in darkness through Musselburgh towards Tranent.

Cope's forces had by this time landed at Dunbar, but the troops were so run down that they could not march just yet. They spent a day of rest before moving on 19 September westwards, camping to the west of Haddington. On the following day Cope set off, hoping to reach Musselburgh. However, word soon reached him that the Jacobites had moved east and were already at Preston, just a mile or so from his own forces.

Charles's men were ready for fighting. The Prince had led them east from the city with his sword unsheathed, telling the men, 'Gentlemen, I have flung away the scabbard. With God's assistance I don't doubt of making you a free and happy people. Mr Cope shall not escape us as he did in the Highlands.'

From Musselburgh the Jacobites decided to head in a south easterly direction, in order to take the higher ground on Falside Hill. To the west of Tranent, from Birsley Brae, he and his men could look north over the low-lying ground along the coast, where Cope's men were marching west from Seton. The weather was good and in the late summer afternoon the armies gazed at each other.

Cope was delighted with his spot, for he reckoned that it was well protected – by high estate walls to the west, by a low-lying march and ditch to the south and by the sea to the north; only at the east was the line of defence weak. Cope sat there stubbornly, refusing to move from a spot which would prevent the Highlanders' favourite form of attack, the mass charge downhill.

A number of disputes within the Jacobite army now took place. Charles sent a group of men to the west, to guard the roads into Musselburgh and thus prevent Cope's men making a fast exit towards Edinburgh. Lord George Murray disagreed with this and threw his gun to the ground, warning the Prince that he would never fight for the cause again if the men were not brought back. It was only the intervention of Lochiel that calmed the argument. Likewise John William O'Sullivan had sent some men to Tranent kirkyard, only for them to come under fire from Cope's canon. Lochiel ordered them back.

It was then decided that the best way of attacking Cope's men was to do it from the east. A local lad, Robert Anderson, had offered his assistance in leading the men along a pathway through the bog. Accordingly, at three o'clock on the morning of 21 September, the Camerons led off to the south of Tranent, before heading north, passing Blindwells to Riggonhead farm. At daybreak they had arrived on the east side of Cope's army and began lining up. The MacDonalds were on the right, with the Camerons and Stewarts to the left. In the centre were the Duke of Perth's regiment and the MacGregors. The second line comprised of the Atholl men, the Robertsons, MacLachlans and MacDonalds of Glencoe. Prince Charles had planned to stand in the centre of the front line, but his men persuaded him that this was folly; instead he stood between the two lines.

The Royalists soon found out that the Jacobites had moved and in a rush tried to swing their forces around to meet them. From left to right, the Hanoverians had 2,500 men ready to fight. At the rising of the sun the Jacobites attacked, running through the fields towards the enemy. The Camerons were first to engage the opposition, fighting with Gardener's dragoons. The dragoons were so frightened by the sight of the Highlanders that most of them took to their heels and ran, leaving only their commander trying to rally the troops.

Hamilton's dragoons, on the opposite flank, did not wait to engage the MacDonalds who were advancing towards them and turned around before they arrived. The infantry fired at the Jacobites, but as the

Highlanders came among them, they panicked and fled.

Only Gardener and a few men around him seem to have played their part well. They fought with all their might until Gardener was killed, after which the game was over. Accounts of the battle state that it lasted for just four minutes, which was probably an accurate enough time, for the second rank of the Jacobites did not have time to reach the fighting.

The Royalist soldiers were by now in full flight. The Jacobites pursued them and managed to capture 700, who were held prisoner. On the field of battle the Royalists had lost 400, whereas the Jacobites only suffered 30 fatalities and 70 wounded.

Amongst the Jacobite dead was David Stuart, eldest son of Sir David Stuart of Threipland. He had already been active in the 1715 Rising and had been imprisoned in Tolbooth and then Edinburgh castle. He managed to escape from the latter with a number of others using a rope made from sheets knotted together. Young David was part of the 36 Perthshire horsemen that took part in Prestonpans. After the battle had been won, he was foolish enough to follow some of the retiring Hanoverians. At St Clement's Wells Sir John Cope had halted for a rest and was gathering together his remaining men. When they spotted three Jacobites following them, they turned around and killed them. Sir David was one of these and he was later buried where he fell.

Threipland's horse was put up for sale at a cattle fair in Perth by someone who had found it and others on the battlefield. The land-steward of Threipland recognised it and was able to purchase it and bring it back home. It was never asked to do a days work for the rest of its life.

Prince Charles and Lord George spent much time on Prestonpans battlefield offering assistance to the wounded men in Cope's army. An officer in Clanranald's regiment records the scene:

> Whatever notion our Low-country people may entertain of
> the Highlanders, I can attest they gave many proofs this day
> of their humanity and mercy. Not only did I often hear our
> common clansmen ask the soldiers if they wanted quarter
> and not only did we, the officers, exert our utmost pains to
> save those who were stubborn, or who could not make
> themselves understood, but I saw some of our private men,

after the battle, run to Port Seton for ale and other liquors to support the wounded. As one proof for all, of my own particular observation, I saw a Highlander carefully and with patient kindness, carry a poor wounded soldier on his back into a house, where he left him, with a sixpence to pay his charges. In all this, we followed not only the dictates of humanity but also the orders of our prince.

Not all accounts were so glowing. The Hanoverians claimed that many of their men 'were killed in cold blood ... the foot seeing themselves naked and defenceless and the enemy rushing impetuously upon them sword in hand, they threw down their arms and surrendered prisoners. But the merciless enemy would grant no quarters, until they were compelled by their superior officers. The unheard of manner in which the dead were mangled and the wounded disfigured was the great evidence of the truth of this.'

The Jacobites spent some time going through the battlefield collecting booty. The Hanoverians had a supplies depot at Cockenzie and the Highlanders made an attack on the soldiers who guarded it. Within a short time the Royalist troops abandoned their spot and the booty was large. Here they found numerous supplies and more importantly, Cope's military chest in which were his papers and £2-3,000.

Sir John Cope, however, was off like a hare. He left the battlefield behind and rode with haste over the Lammermuir Hills to Lauder, through Greenlaw and Coldstream to Berwick, a distance of 40 miles. At Berwick Barracks he reported the defeat of the Battle of Preston, as the Hanoverians originally called the encounter. Lord Mark Kerr, who was in Berwick at the time, is reported to have said, 'Good God! I have seen some battles, heard of many, but never before of the first news of defeat being brought by the general officers!'

The Jacobites, who named the conflict as the Battle of Gladsmuir, were elated by the victory. They spent some time resting in the area and Bonnie Prince Charlie made his way to Pinkie House, where he spent the night. He wrote letters to his father in France, detailing his exploits thus far. On the following day, a Sunday, there were no sermons in the churches.

CHAPTER NINETEEN
Edinburgh

After the victory at Prestonpans, the Jacobite forces made a grand re-entry into Edinburgh; they marched with pipes playing, drums beating and loud 'hurrahs!' In the parade they carried a number of banners and standards that they had taken from the enemy and in the march were several hundred prisoners.

The occupants of the castle still held for the Hanoverian crown, however. Communication between the garrison and the city continued for some time, with requests being made both ways at the main gate. A week after the battle word came out that the occupants of the garrison were short of supplies, at which news Charles decided to try and starve them into submission. General Guest, who was in charge of the castle, responded by firing his cannon across the city. When it was prudent to do so, some of his men left the castle and made raids on neighbouring houses, after which they set fire to or demolished them. The damage done did not affect the Jacobites, but to stop it affecting the relationship between them and the townsfolk, Charles ordered the blockade to be ended as he did not wish to be blamed for the damage the garrison was inflicting on innocent civilians. It is said that one of the cannonballs fired from the battlements lodged itself in Cannonball House on the Castlehill, where it has remained ever since.

At Holyrood Charles established a more properly constituted council, which met first thing every morning. They discovered that many of their soldiers had deserted after Prestonpans, having gathered so much booty that they felt inclined to return north with it. The muster-master, Henry Patullo, a merchant from Dundee, reckoned that there were now just 1,400 men in the camp at Duddingston, which meant that over 1000 must have deserted and headed off home.

Prince Charles needed to expand his army before planning any more moves. Accordingly he sent men across Scotland to try to raise more clans. Some of those who had pledged their allegiance to him failed to respond, such as the MacLeods of MacLeod and the MacDonalds of Sleat; indeed, they raised men to fight for the Hanoverians instead. In the central Highlands he was more lucky, though some of the clans were split between the two sides, unsure which way to leap. In the far north of the Highlands, in Sutherland and Caithness, the clans were against him. Those who joined the Prince at this stage came from lesser groups or else chiefs sent their sons with a few men, thus keeping a foot in both camps.

John Gordon of Glenbuchat raised 400 men in Aberdeenshire and Lord Ogilvy arrived back from Angus with 600 men. From Banffshire and Strathbogie there came 480 men and more from Aberlour. The Jacobite Duke of Atholl raised a further 600 men in Atholl and Cluny MacPherson 400. Other clans and lairds supplied men, so that by the end of October he had once again a sizeable force behind him, comprising 5,000 foot and 500 horse.

John Hickson, who had joined the Prince at Perth, was sent south to England to spread the news of the Jacobite victory and to prepare the supporters there, for Charles intended marching south fairly soon. Hickson, however, was captured at Newcastle and a search of his clothing produced the letter from Charles to his followers.

The raising of funds was also a serious matter. A group of MacGregors was sent westward to Glasgow where they managed to get £5,000 in cash and a further £500 worth in kind from the Provost and city magistrates. Other towns had their provosts sent for and they were sent back with an order of how much they were required to contribute to the Jacobite purse.

The long-awaited help from France began. There had been no action from the time the Prince landed in the west until word reached them of his victory at Prestonpans. At this point three ships were sent from the French court, landing in Stonehaven and Montrose. On them were cannon, arms and 4,000 guineas, the latter a gift from King Louis XV of France. Later, in November, Lord John Drummond landed with 800 men, cannon and ammunition.

CHAPTER TWENTY

The March
to England

On 1 November 1745 the Jacobites got ready to leave Edinburgh behind. There had been some dubiety as to whether they should march into England, for many of the chiefs had only offered their support to get Charles back on the throne of Scotland. They were quite content with that and had no desire to see him take the throne of England as well. They would have been happy to have had the Union of Crowns annulled and Charles recognised as Regent of Scotland, leaving the Hanoverian royal family to rule south of the Cheviot Hills.

Prince Charles, however, wanted more, having promised his father that he would regain both countries. It took some persuasion to get his men to agree on a march into England, but he was eventually able to convince them that there were many Jacobites south of the border ready to offer their support and that aid from France was ready. Eventually the chiefs agreed on an attack on London.

But the infighting continued. Charles wished to head directly for Newcastle, where Field Marshall Wade was positioned at this time. His advisers reckoned that they should go by the western route, south through Carlisle and Manchester, where there were men ready to support the movement. This would also take them through the Cumbrian Mountains, which were more like the Highlands and thus more suited to their style of fighting. At length, Charles agreed.

The Jacobites set off from Edinburgh in a southerly direction towards Dalkeith, where they spent two nights. It was decided to separate the army into two – one commanded by the Prince and Lord George Murray, the other by Tullibardine and the Duke of Perth. The route taken by Charles's men went by way of Soutra Hill to Lauder. The Prince spent the night of 3 November at Thirlestane Castle, seat of James, 7th Earl of Lauderdale, though at the time unoccupied.

After arriving at Lauder the Prince discovered that a number of his Highland followers were straggling rather far behind and it was thought that they were planning to desert. Rising early in the morning from his bed at Thirlestane, Charles rode back as far as Channelkirk, where he caught up with those trailing their tail and forced them on to Lauder.

The route then crossed country towards Kelso, where the army arrived after dark on 4 November; this route was chosen to fool the enemy into thinking that the plan was to attack Newcastle. The Jacobites spent two nights in the town, trying to raise support, but no-one was willing to join them. In fact, some of the locals did their best to prevent the Prince from gaining anything at all. At Sunlaws, on the banks of the River Teviot, a large cave was used to hide a number of horses, thus preventing them from being requisitioned by the Prince. The Prince actually used the old tower of Sunlaws as his base and he was later to recount that at Kelso he had many drinking friends, but few fighting ones.

As a feint to the enemy, Charles sent one of his cavaliers, Henry Ker of Graden, over the Tweed and across country as far as Wooler, fifteen miles into the English countryside. As Ker was confusing the enemy, the remainder of the Jacobites prepared to head off in the opposite direction.

From Kelso the Jacobites made their way south westwards towards Jedburgh, arriving in the town on a Sunday morning when the residents were in the kirk. A message was sent in advance to the minister informing him that the Jacobites were coming and that he should end his sermon now, to allow the ladies of the town time to prepare food for the arriving forces. When the Prince made his entry, the ladies of the town swooned at the sight of him and rushed forward to kiss his hand. The men of the burgh, however, were less enthusiastic and as at Kelso there were none willing to join him. Indeed, the only recruit in the district was a local farmer, Mr Davidson, who set off after the forces the day after they had left; he was the father of James Davidson of Hyndlee, the original of Sir Walter Scott's character, 'Dandie Dinmont'.

Prince Charles spent the night at a house in Jedburgh known as Blackhalls, now occupied by 9-11 Castlegate. In Jedburgh it was decided that they should make their way towards Carlisle in two columns, as a means of confusing the enemy. One of these was to be led by Prince Charles himself, the other by Lord George Murray. Murray's men went by way of the Wheel Causeway, an ancient route that climbs over the moors and hills south of Bonchester Bridge, before dropping into Liddesdale. The Prince's men took the route further west, crossing the pass known as the Note o' the Gate. A local tradition claims that this pass was named after the fact that Prince Charles ordered his men to 'Take note of the gait [way]' when he was giving them instructions; at a later point on the journey he heard them talk about the 'Note of the Gait' as though it was the name of a place.

Shortly after leaving Jedburgh the cavalry camped at Spittal-on-Rule. During the night a daring Borderer made his way into the camp and stole a bag containing a considerable amount of cash. On discovering its disappearance, the Jacobite soldiers let it be known that they would burn the village of Denholm to the ground if it was not returned. The bag found its way back.

On the moors hereabouts, the soldiers lost all semblance of a military fighting machine and eyewitnesses record the fact that many of them straggled behind, unable to keep up with those in front. The soldiers also plundered any goods that they could find on these remote moors. At Hudhouse they came across some sheep fenced up within a sheepfold. Feeling hungry, some of the men killed a few ewes and cooked them in a large iron pot that they found at the same place. Unfortunately, they had not cleaned the pot and were later to suffer illness; indeed, one of their number supposedly died of food poisoning and had to be buried at a spot known since as the Hielandman's Grave.

Another group of soldiers tried to rob one of the Armstrongs who lived at Whitehaugh Mill. Facing him with a pistol, the Jacobite soldier was taken aback when Armstrong managed to knock it from his grasp, take it from him and then turn the tables!

Another tale from the Jedburgh area is more cordial. As the soldiers were marching along the road near to Ancrum they came upon a little girl. Seeing the soldiers, she did not know whether to hide or run away and as she stood there rooted to the spot, one of the 'bonnie gentlemen' from the army stopped by her, comforted her and stayed with her watching the soldiers pass by. Once they were all out of sight and she was no longer frightened, he rode off and rejoined the army, leaving the girl with a lasting impression.

Down in Liddesdale the army regrouped and settled for the night at Haggiehaugh, now known as Larriston house. The laird was absent when they arrived, but the wife welcomed them. She arranged for the leaders to spend the night in her home and for the soldiers to camp around it. A fine feast of sheep and cattle was supplied at reasonable terms by a local farmer, Charles Scott. He was retained to help with their slaughter, for which he was paid a guinea but, on leaving the encampment that night, Scott was ambushed by some men and forced to give up his earnings.

From there the route went down through Liddesdale towards Canonbie and within two miles the forces crossed the Scots Dike and entered England for the first time. Three miles further south they crossed the River Sark and entered the first real part of England, the village of Longtown.

On crossing the river the Jacobites drew their claymores and held them up into the air, shouting and yelling. Lochiel did likewise, but as he did so he was unfortunate in that he cut his hand in the process; this was later to be regarded as a bad omen, a sign of the defeat on Culloden Moor.

Tullibardine and Perth's half of the Jacobite forces left Dalkeith and headed southwards towards Peebles. From there they took the route up Tweeddale and over the Devil's Beef Tub to Moffat, from where they made their way down Annandale towards Gretna. The soldiers under their command were prone to plundering houses as they passed and one of their number was court-martialled for doing so. At Cairnmuir, in Peeblesshire, the soldiers found the laird absent. His wife was still at home and they demanded that she should give them large quantities of drink and food.

'By what right do you force your way into a lady's room with your bonnets on your heads?' she demanded.

The hats were quickly removed and she offered generous hospitality in return. Unfortunately, later in the same day, the soldiers were to steal a horse from the lady's young son, not realising to whom it belonged.

Throughout the Borders the townsfolk established lookout posts and sentinels to warn of the arrival of the Jacobites. The folk of Darnick established their post on the road to Galashiels. Word was sent back to them that the army was coming, so the folk of the village ran off and hid in the hills south of the community. They were later much affronted when the approaching 'army' turned out to be nothing more than a drover and his cattle.

Protecting the Border cattle seems to have been something of a priority. The cattle from the area around Larriston were taken to a quiet glen, hidden from view. Similarly at Galashiels the laird took the cattle to a remote valley at Neidpath. His wife was left behind at Gala House. On seeing a detachment of soldiers passing, she waved her handkerchief from a window, yelling, 'God save Prince Charlie!' and 'Long live the Prince!' The Jacobites came to her home, where she offered them a hearty welcome and supplied them with food and drink.

The folk of Dumfries had heard a rumour that the Prince and his men were now well over the border and decided that they could muster enough recruits to make an attack on the baggage train, under the command of Tullibardine and Perth, which was still heading south and which was at this time located south of Lockerbie. The recruits made their way east from the town and attacked the train, which had left some equipment at Ecclefechan, managing to take 32 carts worth of goods back to Dumfries.

Whilst the Jacobites were at Carlisle, news of the Dumfries folks' attack reached them and a party of soldiers were sent back to try and have the goods returned. The orders were that should the townsfolk refuse to surrender the goods, then they were to pay an indemnity of £2,000 instead; however, the men sent to Dumfries were recalled before they could carry out their task.

The two groups of Jacobites reformed on 9 November, camping on a waste heath to the north of Carlisle.

CHAPTER TWENTY-ONE
Taking Carlisle

The city of Carlisle was still surrounded by its walls, but these were rather run down by the mid eighteenth century, there having been no cases of fighting for over a century. Even the castle, which was still kept by a Governor, had little more than a small number of invalid soldiers looking after it. When word reached them of the Jacobite arrival, the Cumberland Militia were ordered to prepare for attack, but instead they left their posts during the night and escaped over the city walls.

The Jacobites reckoned that it would be a fairly easy task to take the defences, but from their camp outside the city they could do little due to the thick fog that surrounded them. A few men were sent to reconnoitre as best they could and came back with the good news that an attack was possible. The forces camped at Kingmoor and Moorhouse and rested for a time.

On the night of 9 November, the Jacobites surrounded the town and awaited orders. The Prince himself stayed that night at Blackwell, before heading further east to Brampton. Many of the soldiers employed themselves in preparing siege material, cutting down trees in the Warwick and Corby woods with which to make ladders and other weapons. Charles was invited into the home of Mrs Warwick of Warwick Hall, where he also met Mrs Howard of Corby. Their husbands kept away, for they had been active in the 1715 Rising and did not wish to suffer fines or forfeiture again. Mrs Warwick made the prince most welcome and he noted that 'these were the first Christian people' he had come across since arriving in England.

On Sunday morning the Jacobites began to make their way back towards the edge of Carlisle. They were situated on three fronts and some of them got so close that the soldiers defending the town fired at them from the English and Welsh gates, as well as from the Castle. Despite rumours that Tullibardine had been killed, the action had little effect other than to use up valuable ammunition.

On the afternoon of Sunday 10 November, Prince Charles sent a letter to the mayor of Carlisle, requesting that the city should surrender. If it did, then the Prince would ensure that no harm would befall the inhabitants. Should they fail to capitulate, then he claimed no responsibility for the actions that would follow. Although the council deliberated over the letter, they sent no reply.

Prince Charles retired to Blackwell Hall, the home of Sir Richard Musgrave, where he began planning his next move. Word that Wade was making his way west from Newcastle made up his mind and so he ordered the Jacobites east towards Brampton, where it was expected the two sides would meet. However, Wade was never to appear. In the meantime, Thomas Pattinson, a local grocer and deputy mayor, believed that it was as a result of his actions that the Prince's army had left the town and was even daft enough to send a message by special post to London to inform the authorities of this fact! The locals were not long in composing a rhyme:

> Oh, Pattinson! Ohon! Ohon!
> Thou wonder of a mayor!
> Thou blest thy lot thou wert no Scot
> And blustered like a player.
> What hast thou done with sword and gun
> To baffle the Pretender,
> Of mouldy cheese and bacon grease
> Thou much more fit defender?

The soldiers, once their equipment was ready, attacked the town on Thursday 14 November. The siege lasted for some time and at 5:00 pm the residents of the town hung up the white flag. The castle remained defiant, however, but by early evening on the 15 November had also surrendered. On 16 November the authorities capitulated. The mayor, Joseph Backhouse, went from the city eastward to Brampton, where he kneeled down and ceremonially handed over the burgh keys to the Prince.

Preparations were made for the proclamation of King James VII at the market cross, which took place on 16 November. On Monday 18 November an even more elaborate parade took place, with Bonnie Prince Charlie, riding his white horse, entering the town behind one hundred pipers.

The Jacobites remained in Carlisle until 22 November; during this time the Prince stayed in Highmoor House, which stood in English Street. The Jacobites restocked with provisions, arms and horses. All horses in the town had to be brought to the Castle Yard where the owners had to prove that they rightfully belonged to them. The Jacobites kept any others, which were suspected of being ex militia horses.

Whilst the Jacobites held Carlisle, Joseph Dacre of Kirklinton Hall was taken prisoner and held in the castle. His wife, Catherine Fleming, daughter of the former Bishop of Carlisle, had just given birth to a daughter, Rosemary, at Rose Castle, which stands six miles south of Carlisle. Shortly after the birth, Joseph Dacre sent for the Bishop of Carlisle's chaplain, so that the infant could be baptised as soon as possible. The service was arranged to take place in the castle itself, but as it was about to start, the castle was attacked by a Jacobite force under the command of a Captain MacDonald, who may have been either MacDonald of Kinlochmoidart or MacDonell of Tirnadris. Word had reached the Jacobites that Rose Castle was full of silver plate and other valuables, hence their attack.

An elderly servant of the Dacres ran out of the castle and pleaded with the soldiers not to attack. He explained that there was a young baby and his poorly mother in the castle and that any noise or alarm may result in their deaths. Captain MacDonald inquired, 'When was the child born?'

'Within the hour,' the old retainer replied. 'They are just about to baptise the child.'

The Captain stopped his men and removed his cap; on it was a cockade which he removed. He handed it to the servant, telling him, 'Let her be christened with this cockade in her cap. It will be her protection now and afterwards, should any of our stragglers come this way. We will await the ceremony in silence.'

The Jacobite soldiers then stood in silence to allow the baptismal ceremony to take place. When it was over they were welcomed into the coach yard of the castle, where they were entertained to a fine meal of beef, cheese and ale. After a hearty toast was drunk to the infant Rosemary Dacre, they left the castle without robbing or disturbing it further. The white cockade remained the property of the child thereafter; she later became Lady Rosemary Clerk.

The Jacobites travelled for many miles around Carlisle, gathering provisions. Men were sent to the seats of local lairds demanding that each estate should provide 1,000 bales of hay and ten loads of oats. Those estates where the demand was made were Dalemain, Edna Hall, Greystoke Castle, Hutton Hall, Hutton John and Lowther Hall. The owners feared for their property if they did not comply – only Lowther refused to do so.

On Wednesday 20 November Lord George Murray led a detachment of around 3,000 Jacobites south from Carlisle to Penrith. The town was so small that it could hardly cope with the numbers of soldiers billeted there; indeed, there were reports that up to one hundred men could be lodged in a single house.

CHAPTER TWENTY-TWO
South to Derby

The decision was made to head south. Lancashire was known as being strongly supportive of the Jacobite movement and it was felt that the cause would expand considerably if the rising took in those there. A few men were left behind in Carlisle, holding the castle, but the main body of the army was sent south to follow the vanguard led by Lord George. He was by this time pushing further south, over Shap and into Kendal, arriving there on 21 November at 7pm.

The main body of Jacobites left Carlisle early in the morning of Thursday 21 November. The way to Penrith was tough, but the 16 mile journey was completed by about 3pm. The residents of the burgh were taken aback by the larger force, their number 'swarming in like bees' according to a local. Prince Charles spent that night in the George and Dragon Inn, the rest of the army lodging with the residents.

The way south continued in a like manner, the advance party preparing the town for the arrival of the main army by ordering the preparation of food, beds and other supplies. From Penrith the next stop was Kendal. A day of rest was ordered for Sunday 24 November and Prince Charles remained for most of the day in his accommodation in Stricklandgate. The Jacobites filled the churches, but Charles did not, for fear of offending any particular group of adherents. However, he ordered his officers to contribute well to the collections and the ministers are reported to have been delighted with the sums raised that day.

On the following day, suitably rested, the army followed the advance guard south into Lancaster; the route was easier than that already experienced in crossing the Cumbrian Mountains and the force reached the city centre by around 3pm. One hour later King James was proclaimed at the Market Place.

On Tuesday 26 November it was planned for the whole army to reassemble in Preston. Lord George Murray led his men into the town centre but continued through to the south side of the town, finding places to billet the troops in the villages there. Armed guards were sent to patrol the various routes into the town, for the men were uncomfortable in occupying a place where the Jacobites had been defeated before. Prince Charles and the rest of the army arrived later that day. He made a magnificent entry into the town and again James was proclaimed at the town centre.

Preston seems to have accepted the Jacobites with some delight and the Jacobites found their accommodation the finest they had experienced since leaving home. Thousands of new shoes were ordered from the inhabitants and one local cobbler long took delight in reporting that he was responsible for making Prince Charles's own shoes. The soldiers had a time of rest and some of them made new friends here.

The Hanoverians in the rest of England were taking fright. The Jacobites were thought to be weak and at first folk thought they would not cross the border. When they did, the folk of England reckoned that Carlisle would be enough to halt them in their tracks. However, news that the army had by now reached Lancaster and Preston sent them into a flurry of activity. Not knowing where the army would head and with rumours of Yorkshire, North Wales or Manchester changing by the day, no-one knew how best to deal with them.

Orders were given to prevent the Jacobites from crossing the Mersey and thus entering Wales, where Sir Watkin Williams Wynn was said to have organised a rising in support. As a consequence a number of bridges across the river were demolished or blown up, in order to prevent an easy crossing; the bridges at Barton, Carrington, Holmes, Warrington and Crossford were demolished. In Manchester itself, most of the inhabitants fled, leaving only a number of citizens who had Jacobite tendencies.

On Thursday 28 November the Jacobite forces marched their way along the road to Wigan. There Charles lodged in the Old Manor House in Bishopsgate and the rest of the troops were lodged throughout the town. The route then went by way of the town of Leigh into Manchester, a city that had celebrated when word of the victory at Prestonpans had reached it. First to arrive there were Lord Pitsligo's Horse, led by Major Andrew Hay of Rannes (1713-89).

Rannes was the son of Charles Hay of Rannes and Helen Fraser. He was a supporter of the Jacobite movement and joined Charles shortly after the rising. Throughout the campaign in England he remained close to Charles, becoming friendly with him and being gifted with a portable writing case on the eve of Culloden. He was to survive that battle, but had to go into hiding. He spent six years dodging the Hanoverians and on his father's death was forced to escape abroad. He remained there for eleven years, returning home in 1763. He did not receive a pardon until 1780, by which time he was 67 years of age. This pardon, the only one to survive in private hands, remains at the family seat of Leith Hall in Aberdeenshire, now a National Trust for Scotland property.

Prince Charles arrived in Manchester at around 3pm on the afternoon of 29 November. As he made his way up through the streets there were shouts of 'God bless Prince Charles!' and the church bells rang out. Ladies rushed forward to kiss his hands and Charles was again in his element responding with waves of his sword.

The proclamation in favour of King James was read out at the Cross at four in the afternoon, though not without some reluctance, by the two Manchester constables, one of whom claimed to have forgotten his glasses and the other claiming that he had a speech impediment. This, however, was probably the only real lack of enthusiasm in the support for Charles in the city. One of the local ministers, Rev Thomas Coppoch, or Coppack, had been so keen in his support that he was appointed Royal Chaplain and remained thereafter in the Jacobites force. He was to be executed on 18 October 1746.

Recruitment was more successful in Manchester than it had been in the other towns passed through en route, though still poor; although the town had more than 30,000 inhabitants, there were only 2-300 men willing to sign up for the cause. Nevertheless, they were all welcomed into the army and formed the new 'Manchester Regiment'. The muster place was the Collegiate Church and Francis Townley of Townley Hall in Lancashire, who had joined the Jacobites at Preston, was appointed as the colonel.

From Manchester the army headed south towards Macclesfield. Lord Forbes of Pitsligo and 55 men were given the job of erecting a new timber bridge across the River Mersey at Gatley Ford, using locally felled trees, planks and sods. The army reached the old market town when most of the residents were at church, but on hearing the noise from outside and having been warned previously that the Jacobites would be coming this way, they all ran out of the buildings into the streets to witness the spectacle. The king was proclaimed at the Cross and Charles was lodged in Sir Peter Davenport's town house.

From Macclesfield, where the Jacobites rested for a couple of days, the way southward was by way of Leek. The approach of the Hanoverian soldiers was now imminent and the Jacobites were getting ever more ready to face them in battle. One of the Hanoverian agents was captured and it took some persuasion from Thomas Sheridan to stop him from being hanged. The force split up again, some taking the route through Bosley and Rushton Spencer to Leek, the others heading more to the east and passing through Wincle and Danebridge.

The Jacobites arose early in the morning of 4 December from their billets in the houses of Leek. They set off on their march south eastwards along the road to Ashbourne, the heavy frost making the muddy track way more suitable for the wheeled wagons that they had. They arrived in Ashbourne by breakfast time and rested. The wait was short, however and later that day the army set off once more, heading for Derby.

In the county town the residents were more receptive to the arrival of the soldiers than those of Leek or Ashbourne had been; the church bells were rung out and bonfires were lit in celebration. Again James was proclaimed king. The Jacobites were billeted throughout the town, this time in more salubrious accommodation than they had been used to up till now, for Derby was well-provided with large town houses owned by the local gentry.

A group of 80 soldiers were sent to guard the Swarkestone Bridge, which lay across the River Trent to the south of the town. This bridge had been ordered by Cumberland to be demolished, but the Jacobites seem to have arrived just before this was about to be put into effect. The soldiers held the bridge for the following two days.

The Jacobites stayed in Derby for a couple of days. The high quality of their accommodation was something that they enjoyed and some were known to have commented that the rest made them feel that they could fight an army twice their size. Many of the Jacobites wrote letters home from Derby, but these were later to be intercepted by the Hanoverian forces.

Charles lodged in Exeter House, in Full Street, where a council of war was called on Friday 6 December. He was keen to continue on the march to London, arguing that as they had managed to outwit the Hanoverian forces under Cumberland and Wade so far and being nearer to London than they were, this was the obvious thing to do. Lord George Murray, however, was of the opposite opinion. In Manchester he had agreed to the march south through Derbyshire to see how the locals responded to the appeal for recruits. There being virtually none signing up, he was convinced that there was little support in England for the movement and thus the only choice was to head back for Scotland.

CHAPTER TWENTY-THREE
The Skirmish of Inverurie

In a number of locations throughout the Highlands, the Jacobites and Hanoverians met at times and sparred with each other. Most of these were small-scale affairs that were little more than opposing factions skirmishing in the streets of towns where they lived. One such skirmish, however, was more serious and in some accounts has been grandiosely referred to as the Battle of Inverurie; this took place on 23 December 1745, at the time when the main Jacobite forces under Bonnie Prince Charlie were making their way back from Derby.

A number of Hanoverian soldiers were based around Aberdeen and were in the process of trying to reclaim the Grampian district from the control of the Jacobites. Norman MacLeod of Dunvegan led five of the recently raised Independent Companies through the Highlands from Inverness, eastwards through Fochabers and into Aberdeenshire. He faced no opposition to his march through the Grampian lowlands and was delighted to link with a further two Independent Companies that had been raised amongst the Munros by Captain George Munro of Culcairn. The enlarged force decided to camp around the Aberdeenshire village of Inverurie, a fairly small community located at the confluence of the River Urie with the River Don; little more than a main street, the village was an important market site and historical location.

The Hanoverian troops were dispersed around the district. Around 400 of the soldiers were billeted in and around the village itself and were ready to reform at short notice, should the rumour of a Jacobite attack from Aberdeen come true. A further 300 soldiers were billeted in the adjoining countryside to the north-west of Inverurie, staying in barns and sheds on farms around Balquhain and Harlaw.

In Aberdeen, Lord Lewis Gordon gathered together the Jacobite support and decided to organise the city in case of an attack from the Hanoverians. He arranged soldiers to watch for any advance on the city and it was recorded that he would 'give them a warm reception' should the Hanoverians attempt to enter Aberdeen by either the Bridge of Don or road from Kintore. Gordon was a younger son of the Duke of Gordon, with a long family history connecting him with the north-east, hence Prince Charles appointing him as Lord Lieutenant of Aberdeen and Banff-shires. He had a naval background, being Third Lieutenant on HMS *Dunkirk*.

The rumoured attack on Aberdeen did not materialise and, with growing bravery, a small group of Jacobites under Captain Alexander White and Lieutenant Robert Sinclair decided to make a journey through the Aberdeenshire countryside to find out where the Hanoverians were based. It was during this foray that they came upon John Bartlett, a lawyer in Aberdeen, who had left the city and was making his way to join the Hanoverian forces under MacLeod and Munro and supply them with information. The Jacobites seized Bartlett and a few others and Captain White took them back to Aberdeen, where they were held for some time.

Other information gathered on the reconnaissance mission included the detail that the Earl of Loudoun's Hanoverian company was too busy searching for Lord Lovat to send support to the MacLeods and Munros, who had basically settled at Inverurie and did not seem to have any plans to move on. Accordingly, Lord Lewis Gordon decided that it would be an ideal time to attack.

The Jacobites left Aberdeen on 23 December 1745 and headed up the wide valley of the River Don; there were around 1,200 men in the regiment. Short of Inverurie the company was divided into two groups. The first kept to the right-hand bank of the River Don and was led by Major John Gordon; it would follow the main road towards Inverurie, which could be reached by fording the Don at the southern end of the village, and comprised of around 300 men from Lord Lewis Gordon's

Strathbogie Regiment and a further 200 of Sir James Kinloch's Ogilvy Regiment. The second company would take the left-hand side of the River Don and make its way via Kinmuck and Keith Hall (the seat of the Earl of Kintore), thus fording the Urie and reaching Inverurie from the east; this group was led by Major Lancelot Colbert (or Cuthbert). Overall command was held by Lord Lewis Gordon, although he left the control to his two leaders; he joined Colbert's column.

Major John Gordon's company had a shorter and easier route to take, so they spent some considerable time procrastinating and hiding about the countryside. Some of this was spent at Kinellar church, from where an advance party was sent to Kintore to see how things were placed to the north.

Major Colbert's men comprised a mixture of battalions: Farquharson of Monaltrie's, Moir of Stoneywood's, the Royal Ecossais and a variety of volunteers. They made good progress across the countryside, making their way to Keith Hall, where they halted. A few of their number climbed the low hill of Upper Kinkell, on Keith Hall estate, to view westwards across the Urie into Inverurie and try to determine how the enemy lay; these men were spotted by the Hanoverians and word was reported back to MacLeod and Munro, but they seem to have taken no action.

The Jacobites awaited the setting of the sun and, one hour after it had dropped behind the hills of Bennachie and Menaway, made their advance; both columns of Jacobites crossed the fords and entered Inverurie. At the east side, Colbert crossed the Urie at the Mill of Keith and soon discovered a small outpost of Hanoverian soldiers which was easily captured. One of the soldiers in this had spotted the arriving Jacobites and fired his gun into the air to warn the residents of the village of the impending attack. The Hanoverian leaders, MacLeod and Munro, were still dining with some ministers in the town when the alarm was raised, but soon had their troops mobilised. Most of Colbert's men crossed the ford near to the Bass of Inverurie, an ancient Norman motte hill, and reached the bottom end of the village. Some of the volunteers which had joined the Jacobites feared the worst and at this point many of them 'ran off and skulked.'

The Hanoverians shot at the Jacobites, but it is reckoned that only one man was lost at this point. Colbert led his men onto the ground at the bottom of the village and soon had them lined up – the Royal Ecossais battalion to the right, Stoneywood and the remaining volunteers in the centre and Monaltrie's battalion on the left. The Hanoverians took up what the Jacobites agreed was a strong position, hemmed in with a dike to the west, the River Urie to their east and the town of Inverurie behind them. However, the second column of Jacobites was fording the Don and coming upon the Hanoverians from the west.

The Hanoverian leaders were not willing to fight, having previously issued secret orders to their leaders that they should retreat if attacked. MacLeod and Munro sent off the military chest, containing the money belonging to the battalions, and were soon fleeing behind it. Indeed, it was reported that MacLeod beat such a hasty retreat that he did not even take time to place a bridle on his steed and rode off with a halter on its head.

The Jacobites pursued the retreating Hanoverian soldiers up through the main street of Inverurie; they adopted a method of 'street firing', which involved a rotating group of leaders making its way at the head of a column through the street of a town. The Hanoverians fought back. Indeed, Colbert reckoned that the MacLeods fought like regular troops and had it not been for the return of the volunteers who had skulked off earlier, he may not have been able to defeat them.

The MacLeods and Munros gave in and flew as fast as they were able across the open fields of Blackhall and the Burgh Muir at the north-western end of Inverurie; at one point they fired back, but this was a minor example of resistance. The Hanoverians who had been billeted at farms around the village joined them and together they escaped into the depth of the Aberdeenshire countryside, not halting until they had crossed the River Spey. The Jacobites pursued for as long as they were able, but in the dim moonlight they lost the trail. At one point they are known to have shot at some natural mounds and piles of stubble, the silhouettes looking like crouching soldiers in the gloaming.

The losses at the Jacobite victory of Inverurie were fairly minor. Nine Jacobites lost their lives, most from the Royal Ecossais troops. A further twenty of them were wounded. The Hanoverians lost around five men, two further dying as a result of their wounds. Sixty of their men were taken prisoner, including Gordon, Younger of Ardoch, Forbes of Echt, Maitland of Pitrichie and John Chalmers, Regent of the University of Aberdeen. The victory was quite significant for the Jacobites, however, for the Highland Hanoverians abandoned Aberdeen and Banff-shires to their control, keeping to the west of the River Spey and within the control of their headquarters at Inverness. Word of the victory reached the Jacobites to the south, bringing them comfort.

One of the Hanoverian supporters taken prisoner at Inverurie was Donald Ban MacCrimmon, the piper to the MacLeods of Dunvegan. The MacCrimmons had been hereditary pipers to the Macleods for centuries and Donald Ban followed his chief, playing on his pipes for major events as well as encouraging the MacLeods in battle. The Jacobites at Inverurie were able to take him alive and held him for some time; however, with no gaols in which to keep prisoners, they were gradually let go and MacCrimmon was eventually released on parole. A Hanoverian supporter, he ignored the conditions of his parole and later rejoined his regiment; he was not to be so lucky the second time, for he was killed at the Rout of Moy on 16 February 1746.

CHAPTER TWENTY-FOUR
The Retreat North

The sixth day of December 1745 was termed 'Black Friday' by the supporters of the Jacobite movement. It was the day that the chiefs of the clans had persuaded Charles that their march was now too risky to continue, there being little evidence of any great support in England for the movement. In the morning the Jacobites packed up their belongings and got ready for the long walk home.

Prince Charles had been totally against the retreat, being convinced that the right thing was to continue on their march to London. He expected the assistance from France to arrive and back in Scotland there were more soldiers forming up and getting ready for the cause. However, this latter fact was partly to blame for the decision by the rest of the council to persuade him into retreat – for they thought that it would be better to join this force and thus create a bigger army.

When the Jacobites left Derby Prince Charles kept to the rear and, to show his dissent, he rode solemnly on a horse behind the men, rather than marching in front. The soldiers made their way back to Ashbourne, though not without some incidents. Some of the Jacobites began looting and various arms and goods were stolen from local houses. A local farmer shot two of them.

On the march south the local residents had been impressed by the discipline shown by the soldiers, who paid for their keep and were civil to their hosts. The return journey was different. The Highlanders, who had in previous years been noted for their tendency to empty homes of their belongings when they were billeted there, returned to their old ways.

In a similar way, the residents along the line of the retreat did their best to harry the soldiers. Any stragglers from the army were likely to suffer death. A number were captured by the Hanoverian supporters and either killed or sent to prison.

The route north continued through Leek and Macclesfield to Stockport. Homes were robbed on the way and in Macclesfield the soldiers demanded that the town should subscribe funds to the cause, equivalent to that paid to the Hanoverian troops. The Mayoress claimed that there was no subscription list from which to work, whereupon the Jacobites threatened to burn the town unless she came up with one. The Town Clerk eventually produced one, saving the burgh and the Mayoress's life. In Stockport a few homes were burned and shots fired in the streets.

The retreating army reached Manchester on 9 December. The city had planned forming an army of 'loyal' residents, which was to face the Jacobites and hold them off long enough until General Wade could reach them. Five hundred men signed up and more were raised in neighbouring towns. However, the authorities in Manchester changed their mind and sent word that all these men were to stand down and return home, fearing that a battle in the centre of town would have grave results for the place. As a result, the Jacobites managed to take the town relatively peacefully and lodged there that night.

The Prince and his council demanded a levy of £2,500 from the authorities in Manchester, a sum they had been persuaded to accept instead of the £5,000 originally requested. This figure was paid and a local merchant, James Bailey, who had been held as hostage for surety, was released.

As the army left Manchester, a number of locals fired at the soldiers, resulting in a series of small skirmishes. There were fatalities on both sides and warnings were sent to residents who lived near to the route being taken by the Jacobites to hide themselves away as the army passed. The army made its way through Wigan to Preston, where it lodged for two nights. The locals were forced into supplying all the hay, straw and foodstuffs that they had, both to feed the Jacobite horses and to prevent them from falling into enemy hands.

The Earl of Perth was sent in front to Lancaster; there he found a number of Jacobites held in prison and heard of Henry Bracken's plans to have them locked up onboard a prison ship off the Lancashire coast. This did not take place, however – instead the men were imprisoned in Lancaster Castle. Perth took the castle easily and had the prisoners freed. He added them to his own group of soldiers and together they went to Bracken's home. He was not there, but his wife was issued a demand for 600 guineas as a fine for her husband's behaviour. She, however, managed to escape from their home through a cellar window. On discovering this, the Jacobite men robbed her home of all its furniture and goods before setting it on fire.

The retreat of the Jacobites resulted in many of the Lancashire Protestants coming out of the woodwork, for they thought that the Jacobites were now the losers; shouts of 'No popery' could be heard as the men wandered around the streets and in some cases swords were drawn as arguments became more heated. The Protestants in the town even took the chance to burn down or damage some of the Roman Catholic chapels in the burgh.

The rest of the Jacobites left Preston on 13 December and were closely pursued by Hanoverian troops. There was a slight skirmish on Ellel Moor, when Major-General James Oglethorpe's troops attacked the rear of the Jacobite forces. Oglethorpe's troops suffered four dead and a few injured before retiring once more; the Jacobites continued relatively unscathed on their way to Lancaster.

On the following day, 14 December, the Jacobites in the advance party entered Kendal. Rumours had reached the town before them of a defeat south of Lancaster and the residents were of the opinion that only a few survivors were heading north; this explains their bravery in attacking the first soldiers to arrive, starting a minor battle that resulted in deaths on the Jacobite side. The way north continued through the mountains to Shap, from where it was a moorland route into Penrith. It was not to be a simple journey.

The Jacobites making their way back north had reached Penrith by 18 December. However, Lord George Murray was still trailing behind with much of the baggage and cannon. To the north of Shap he became aware of various soldiers studying his men from surrounding hills and he made arrangements for groups of scouts to spread out and keep him informed of any advancing soldiers.

At Thrimby 200 horsemen appeared on the hill in front of Murray's rearguard. He was at the back of the soldiers and unable to see exactly what was happening up front. However, Lieutenant Brown took command and ordered Perth's and Roy Stewart's men to charge. The Hanoverian soldiers fled at the sight, though not without the loss of a few lives.

Further north a second skirmish took place, this time nearer to Clifton. The Hanoverians attacked Murray again, but he was able to repel the men. The struggle spilled over into various places, with fighting taking place in Clifton village and near to Lowther Castle. Whilst this was going on the Duke of Cumberland arrived on his march north from Shap.

A larger struggle then took place on Clifton Moor. Reinforcements were sent back from Penrith to assist in repelling Cumberland. As darkness fell the battle intensified, with the Highlanders resorting to their infamous charge; this frightened the Hanoverian soldiers who turned about and retreated. Murray then ordered his men to turn around and head north, crossing Lowther Bridge and entering Penrith. The battle had seen around 50 men killed, 40 of whom where from Cumberland's army. Prince Charles later ordered his men to engage in a night march to Carlisle, which they reached at noon on Thursday 19 December. The fight on Clifton Moor was to go down in English history as the last battle on their soil.

The local vicar recorded a few burials within his graveyard:

19th of December 1745. Ten Dragoons to wit, Six of Blands, three of Cobhams and one of Mark Kerrs regiment, buried, who was killed ye evening before by ye rebels in ye skirmish between ye Duke of Cumberland's army and them at ye end of Clifton Moor.

After the battle Cumberland went to the home of Thomas Savage, a local Quaker. He lived right in the midst of the battlefield, but remained at home during all the fighting. He was relieved when the soldiers dispersed and was even more thankful to discover that his cattle had been unharmed. On retiring into his home, he was taken aback by a knock at the door and on answering it to find Cumberland there, requesting a bed. Savage was later to record that 'pleasant agreeable company he was, a man of parts, very friendly and no pride in him.'

In Carlisle a War Council was held, at which letters sent by Lord Drummond and Lord Strathallan were read. These detailed the state of play in Scotland. Some thought that the Jacobite army should remain in Carlisle, whereas others felt it would be prudent to continue north across the border. Many supporters left at this point, in particular those who had signed on in Manchester.

At Carlisle it was decided that the journey north should continue. However, it was agreed that a garrison should be left in Carlisle Castle, which would have two functions. It would send out a message that the Jacobites intended to return south again and when they did so, it would mean that they did not have to retake the town and castle as they had done on the march southwards.

The Manchester Regiment under Colonel Townley was left behind at Carlisle; this comprised of 250 soldiers and a further 100 men with a French background. Cumberland came with his forces and after a few days of bombarding the castle he was able to get it to surrender to his terms on 30 December 1745. The Manchester Regiment were led out of the great sandstone building and all were held captive for some time. Most of the Jacobite prisoners were taken to the cathedral, where they were held in the choir, much to the annoyance of the clergy; to pass the time, many carved their names or pictures on the pews there. After a fortnight had passed, the men were transported south. The officers were given a horse each, but their feet were tied below the horses' bellies and each horse's tail was tied to the horse behind. The foot soldiers were made to walk, their wrists tied together and the whole number tied to each other.

The officers were in the main all executed for High Treason and the men were transported abroad. Francis Townley himself was executed on Kennington Common on 30 July 1746.

CHAPTER TWENTY-FIVE
This Set of Ruffians

The main Jacobite army made its way out of Carlisle along the road to Longtown in the early hours of Friday 20 December; this day was also the twenty-fifth birthday of Prince Charles, but there was no celebrating. The crossing of the River Esk was troublesome due to floods and it was bitterly cold. The horses were sent into the water first of all and they managed to get to the other side. The Highlanders then said they would risk it and after some negotiating all men made it to the Scottish side. There were accounts of women supporters being drowned, but this may only be Whig propaganda. On the other side the men built fires for themselves to dry off and, it is said, danced reels to help keep warm.

The Jacobite forces were split into two, one group of 2,000 under Murray heading north through Ecclefechan, Lockerbie, Moffat and Douglas to Hamilton. The plan was to give the impression that the returning soldiers were going back to Edinburgh. However, at Hamilton the route north-west was followed and the Jacobites entered Glasgow on Christmas Eve.

Bonnie Prince Charlie took the larger part of the army, around 4,000 men, by a more westerly route, heading for Annan, Dumfries and Drumlanrig Castle, before crossing the Lowther Hills to Douglas, arriving there a day after Lord George Murray.

Charles travelled along to Annan, where he spent the night. On the following day he marched his men to Dumfries and he found lodgings in the Blue Bell Inn. Many of the army were found lodgings in the town, but most camped in the fields south of what became Shakespeare Street.

The Jacobites held ex-Provost Crosbie and Walter Riddell, merchants in the burgh, as hostage against a payment of £2,000, 1,000 shoes and as many arms that could be found within the burgh. This was later paid to free them. The soldiers were also responsible for pillaging some shops and the demand for shoes seems to have been so great that they even pulled shoes off the feet of men walking in the streets! On the Sunday there were no sermons in the churches.

From Dumfries the Jacobites made their way north up Nithsdale to Drumlanrig Castle, seat of the Duke of Queensberry, and arrived there on Monday 23 December. They took with them two hostages, for the folk of Dumfries had only managed to raise £1,195 and 255 pairs of shoes. Ex-Provost Andrew Crosbie and Walter Riddel of Glenriddel were taken as far as Glasgow where they were eventually released on payment of the missing sum.

At Drumlanrig the officers were billeted in the castle. Within were portraits of King William III, Queen Mary and Queen Anne, images that so annoyed the Jacobites that they slashed them with their dirks.

From Drumlanrig the men crossed the Lowther Hills to Douglas, where they spent the night. A third hostage was taken from near Thornhill – Robert Paterson (1716-1801) was a stonemason who is better known in literary circles for being the original of Sir Walter Scott's 'Old Mortality'. He was captured by the soldiers and taken as far north as Glenbuck, on the border between Ayrshire and Lanarkshire, in order to show the Jacobites the route through the Lowther Hills.

From Douglas the route was followed to Hamilton. A contemporary report details their activities in the town:

> Upon Tuesday the 24th December, in the Afternoon, there
> came in here 1900 Horse and Foot, tho' they gave themselves
> out for 2500. They were commanded (if I may call it so) by
> the Lords, George Murray, Nairn, Elcho, Ogilvie and
> Glenbucket and others. Upon the Wednesday Morning, Part
> of them went off for Glasgow; and that Afternoon, their
> Prince, the Duke of Perth, their French Ambassador, Lochyell

and others, with Part of the Clans, came in. Both these
Nights the People of the Town, tho' greatly throng'd, were at
greater Peace, than on the Thursday's Night, when the
Camerons, MacPhersons and MacDonalds of Clan-Ranald's
Party came up, (after having burnt some houses in
Lismahague and rifled one of the minister's Houses; and had
it not been for two of Lochmoidart's Brothers, they would
have laid the whole town in Ashes and plundered the
Country about) and then indeed we felt the Effects of an
undisciplin'd ungovernable Army of Highland Robbers, who
took no more Notice of their nominal Prince, or
Commanders, than a pack of ill-bred Hounds. The
Provisions, Ales and Spirits, beginning to run short in the
Town, they threatened the People with Death, or the
burning of their Houses, unless such Victuals and Drink were
got as they call'd for; which Victuals were not of the coarse
Sort, Herrings, Onions and a Butter and a Cheese, —
which we look'd upon as their best Food, such they would
not taste. The People of England have taught them such a
bad Custom, that they would scarce taste good Salt-beef and
Greens, the meanest of them calling for roast or fried fresh
Victuals; if such were not got, they treated the People very
ill. My Lodgers were so luxurious, that they would not teast
boil'd Pork, a little pickled, unless we would cause dress it in
a Frying-pan, with fresh Butter. Amongst this Set of Ruffians
there were some civil People, some of whom my Aunt and
her two Neighbours had the good Fortune to get for
Lodgers. I had no less than 33 of them, the last Night, of the
worst Kind, besides Horses and naked Whores.

Whilst at Hamilton, Charles spent some time hunting in the Duke's
Park and the same correspondent recorded that he shot two pheasants,
two woodcocks, two hares and a young buck; these were taken back to
Chatelherault where he dined in style.

From Hamilton the Jacobite force made its way on to Glasgow.
The Jacobites took over the city from Boxing Day until 3 January 1746.

In Glasgow, which was a Whig town, the Jacobites took control to some extent, much to the annoyance of the residents. The citizens of the burgh feared the worst, for after Prestonpans they had failed to pay the full amount of the levy demanded by the Prince and on hearing of the initial rising the city had raised two battalions of 600 men in each to fight against him. The Jacobites on entering the city looked tired, hungry and rather dejected.

The soldiers made their way into Glasgow Cross by a variety of routes, a ploy to display themselves to the citizens in order to make them think that there were more of them than there actually were. James was proclaimed king and Charles was proclaimed as Regent of Scotland.

A demand for equipment was sent to the council. This included requests for 6,000 short coats, 12,000 linen shirts, 6,000 shoes, 6,000 pairs of socks, 6,000 waistcoats and 6,000 blue bonnets. The Provost Andrew Buchanan (1670-1759), was fined £500 for having allowed the city residents to raise a subscription on behalf of the Hanoverian soldiers, earlier in the previous year. He was asked to provide a list of those who had subscribed, but he refused, even under threat of hanging. The fine was levied instead.

The Jacobites were quartered on the residents of the city, but contemporary accounts claim that they were well behaved and fairly honest. There were some, however, who were keen to burn the city to the ground, in reprisals for their Hanoverian support. However, Lochiel is said to have prevented this from going ahead and for many years thereafter the bells on the tower of the Trongate Tolbooth were rung out whenever the Chief of Clan Cameron entered the city.

A number of Charles's troops camped around the newly-constructed St Andrew's Church. To help protect their valuable horses, these were stabled within the church itself.

Prince Charles took over the Shawfield Mansion, which was located in the Trongate, the property of Colonel William MacDowall of Castle Semple. He is said to have eaten twice a day there, in full public view. He was described as being very princely in appearance, wearing fine clothing, but that he was rather dejected looking.

It was in Glasgow that the Prince came into contact with Clementina Walkinshaw (1720-1802), youngest of ten daughters of John

Walkinshaw of Camlachie and Barrowfield; the latter had taken part in the rescue of Princess Clementina Sobieski when she was taken prisoner at Innsbruck en route to her wedding. Clementina Walkinshaw was to travel to France at a later date and was to be the Prince's companion for the rest of his life, bearing him a daughter, Charlotte.

Prince Charles held a review of his troops on Glasgow Green. He was delighted to note that he had only lost 40 men since his retreat from Derby. A local later recounted his opinion of Charles:

> He had a princely aspect and its interest was much
> heightened by the dejection which appeared in his pale, fair
> countenance and downcast eye. He evidently wanted
> confidence in his cause and seemed to have a melancholy
> foreboding of that disaster which soon ruined the hopes of
> his family for ever.

On 3 January the Jacobite army packed up in Glasgow and set off for Stirling. The route took them through Kirkintilloch, where a straggling soldier was shot by one of the locals. A number of the Jacobites returned to the town with threats of burning lest the person responsible be given up, but the authorities managed to persuade them that the individual who carried out the murder had done so without the express permission of the council. Instead of burning the town, the Jacobites let it off with a fine instead.

The Jacobites halted at Kilsyth and camped there for the night. The minister, Rev James Robe, was a supporter of the Prince and determined to join his army. Accordingly he purchased a sword and a pair of pistols for himself and acquired a horse. He sent this to an ex-soldier for training. When he received the horse he decided to practise riding around the glebe; at one point in his enthusiasm he decided to fire his pistol, at which the horse reared up, threw him to the ground and bolted. When the minister was later able to pick himself up he challenged the soldier, claiming that the horse had not been 'broken in'.

'Broken in!' the soldier responded. 'It's been broken in fine. It reared up because ye shot it in the lug!'

Charles spent the night in Kilsyth House, the property of

Campbell of Shawfied. The laird's steward was told that he was to provide everything necessary for the Prince, under promise of payment, but the following morning, when the Jacobites left, he was informed that the account should be sent to the laird, to be payable from the rents of Kilsyth, which was at that time a forfeited estate.

On 4 January the way was made northwards to Stirling, stopping a few miles out of the town. The main army camped at Middle Third, near Sauchie, just two miles or so short of the castle.

Joining the Jacobites in Glasgow had been a local packman, Dougal Graham (1724-79). He followed the army to Stirling, all the time recording its exploits in verse. His poems were not particularly good, but as a record of events they make interesting reading:

In the Moor of Touch that night they lay,
And some in villages nearby,
To Stirling then they marched down,
And through that place Cambusbarron town.

Dougal Graham followed the Jacobites all the way to Culloden, after which he disappeared for a time. Graham was to have his poems printed in later years and he returned to Glasgow where he sold his 'History of the Rebellion' in the streets.

The Jacobites built trenches and barricades on the outskirts of Stirling on Saturday 5 January. They knew that they had little chance of taking the castle, but they were intending to take the burgh for Prince Charles. A drummer was sent at eight o'clock in the evening to the burgh gate with a message, but the guards fired a shot at him and he took fright and left, leaving his drum behind. This was quickly lifted by the residents and kept as a trophy.

Prince Charles made his headquarters at this time in Bannockburn House, home of a keen supporter, Sir Hugh Paterson, who had been active in the 1715 Rising and had his estates confiscated. For some unknown reason he was still able to reside there.

On 6 January a second drummer was sent to the burgh gates, this time with a demand for the surrender of the town to the Jacobites. The message read:

CHARLES, Prince of Wales, &c., Regent of Scotland, England, France and Ireland and the Dominions thereto belonging: To the Provost, Magistrates and Council of the Town of Stirling.

Intending to take possession of our town of Stirling, we hereby require and command you to give our forces peaceable entry into and possession of the said town and to receive us as the representative of our Royal Father, James the Eighth, by the grace of God, King of Scotland, England, France and Ireland and the Dominions thereunto belonging; and as we have a list of all the persons now in arms in the said town, you are expressly required to deliver up to us all their arms and likewise all cannon, arms and military stores presently in the said town; assuring you hereby that if you refuse or delay to receive us, or to deliver up the arms or military stores aforesaid and thereby oblige us to use that force which Providence has put into our hands, after our discharging one cannon against the said town no articles or capitulation of protection shall be given to any of the inhabitants for their persons, goods and effects; and as the town is now blockaded on all sides, if any person therein now in arms shall be apprehended without the walls of the town they shall be carried to immediate execution. An answer to this is to be returned to our quarters here by two o'clock afternoon this day. Given at Bannockburn, this sixth day of January 1746.

(Signed) CHARLES, P.R.

The council held a meeting and managed to request an extra day before they finally made their decision. To keep them on their toes and to remind them how serious they were, the Jacobites fired 27 cannons at the burgh from their camp. It was decided to accept the Jacobite terms and the gates were opened. The militia retreated back to the castle, where they remained under the command of General William Blakeney.

The Jacobites entered Stirling and established themselves in the town. They then prepared to take the castle, after General Blakeney refused to surrender it. Guns were positioned on rocky outcrops around the fortress and a French officer, Monsieur Mirabel de Gordon, Marquis de Mirabelle, (known to the Highlanders as Mr Admirable) took charge. He related that as soon as he started firing, the castle would be theirs within 18 hours. How wrong he was. The castle was higher than the Gowan Hill where he was based and shots were fired back from the battlements. Within half an hour Mr Admirable had abandoned his notion and fled to safety.

On 13 January Lord George Murray sent a party of soldiers into Linlithgow, where it was thought that the Hanoverian troops were gathering supplies. The government soldiers were indeed in the vicinity and were making their way along the road from Bridgend. Although Murray headed there as fast as he could, the troops did not engage in battle, instead only hurling insults at each other.

CHAPTER TWENTY-SIX

Most Singular and Extraordinary Combat

General Henry Hawley was by this time in charge of the Hanoverian soldiers in Scotland, having succeeded Cope. He was a veteran of Sheriffmuir and believed that the Highland clans would flee from a disciplined cavalry force. Known as 'Hangman' Hawley by his troops, he had around 8,000 men under his command, of which 1,300 were cavalry. He decided that he would march them to Falkirk, with plans for relieving Stirling, which at that time was held by the Jacobites. He expected to face the Jacobites in battle on Plean Muir, on 18 January and had settled upon this as his plan. Alas for him that the Jacobites were unaware of it!

Lord George Murray advised Charles that it would be better to attack the Whig army, rather than wait for them. Everyone in the War Council agreed and so the Jacobites began their march south from Stirling towards Falkirk, reaching Plean Muir, seven miles to the north west of Falkirk. A rearguard was left here, as was the tall pole flying the Prince's standard, by which the Hanoverian scouts were deluded. The spirits of the Jacobite force had risen once more and there had been an increase in recruitment. The army, at almost 9,000 men, was now the largest it had been during the rising.

General Henry Hawley was not expecting the Jacobites to take the offensive and had accepted an invitation from Lady Kilmarnock to have breakfast at Callendar House. He was enjoying the company so much that he remained there until mid-day, by which time he was partaking of tea. The Hanoverians had discovered that the Jacobites were advancing and sent word to Hawley informing him of this. Still enjoying the company, he responded, stating that the men should start preparing for battle, but he remained where he was.

The Jacobites sent an advance party that crossed the River Carron at the Steps of Dunipace between one and two o'clock in the afternoon. Sir Archibald Primrose of Dunipace showed them the route and later claimed at his trial that he was forced into guiding the army under pain of death. The folk of Falkirk were frightened by their arrival and word was sent as quickly as possible to General Hawley. He came back running, as fast as he could, flustered and embarrassed.

The two sides raced for the higher ground of Falkirk Moor, the MacGregors claiming it for the Jacobites. Some of the Hanoverian army had no real desire to fight and managed to bog down the ten cannon before reaching the battlefield.

The two armies, which had around 8,000 men each, faced each other on the slopes of Falkirk Moor. The Jacobite front line (from south to north) comprised the MacGregors and MacDonald regiments – Keppoch, Clanranald and Glengarry, Appin Stewarts, Camerons, Frasers and MacPhersons. The Second Line comprised the Atholl Brigade, Ogilvie's two battalions, Lewis Gordon's, Farquharsons and the French. The Third Line comprised mainly of cavalry. Prince Charles stood immediately behind the centre of the foot at a spot from where he had a wide view of the field.

Hawley had a larger cavalry, which he was relying on to win the field. He had twelve battalions of regular soldiers, 1,300 horsemen, militia from Argyll and the cities of Glasgow and Edinburgh, a Battalion from the Black Watch and volunteers from Yorkshire; this latter group were known as the 'Yorkshire Blues'. The weather was vile, with the wind raging and rain battering against the soldiers.

The locals who lived on Falkirk Moor were fleeing from their homes, not wishing to get caught in the midst of a battle. They gathered what valuables they could carry and ran with their young families and elderly relations away from the moor. Some of the residents of the burgh climbed the church steeple, which was built like a fortified tower and from there had a wide view of the proceedings.

At four o'clock Hawley sent his cavalry to attack. He expected the horsemen to repel the Highlanders back over the hill, but they were taken aback when the MacGregors and MacDonalds stood firm. When the advancing cavalry was within pistol-shot a volley of bullets reigned across the moor, bringing down waves of horses and their riders. One troop, commanded by Colonel Shugbrough Whitney, was keen to fight and advanced further among the Highlanders, only to have their steeds dirked from beneath them and the riders killed or taken prisoner. Whitney himself was killed.

The strength of the Highlanders' resolve frightened the remainder of the cavalry, which turned around and fled for their lives. The Chevalier de Johnstone, who was with the Jacobites, recorded the events in his journal:

> The most singular and extraordinary combat immediately followed. The Highlanders, stretched on the ground, thrust their dirks into the bellies of the horses. Some seized the riders by their clothes, dragged them down and stabbed them with their dirks; several, again, used their pistols, but few of them had sufficient space to handle their swords ... The resistance of the Highlanders was so incredibly obstinate that the English, after having for some time engaged pell-mell with them in their ranks were at length repulsed and forced to retire.

The infantry were ordered to attack, but after witnessing the retreating cavalry they had little desire to attack such wild men; after wavering for a time, they too turned and fled, heading for the shelter of Falkirk. En route, they set fire to their tents, lest they fall into enemy hands, but they left behind a considerable amount of equipment and arms. In Falkirk, General Hawley is supposed to have struck the market cross with his sword, breaking it into two. The Jacobites were to compose another victory song:

> Up and rin awa', Hawley,
> Up and rin awa',

> Tak' care nor Charlie's guid claymore,
> May gie your legs a claw.

Only three regiments on the far right of the Hanoverian front had any effect in battle. The line had been so long that they outflanked the Jacobites and so were able to wheel round and face the line from the end. As the Highlanders attacked the line in front of them, the Hanoverians were able to fire shots from the side, bringing down a number of victims. These regiments then retired, awaiting developments, before heading back to Falkirk. They had been under the command of Colonel Francis Ligonier, but he was to die within a few days of pleurisy and the exposure suffered on the battlefield.

The battle was basically a victory for Charles; he had lost only 32 men and 120 suffered injury. The Hanoverians lost 12 officers and 280 men at least, with up to 700 men taken prisoner on the battlefield or on the following day. Many of these were held in Falkirk church. One of the prisoners was able to write to his family in Glasgow:

> This is to let you known that I am alive and in pretty good health considering my ill bedding. I'll warrant you there are more than three hundred of us lying upon straw in the kirk, but there are many more in the Tolbooth of the town and in the cellars of Callendar that do not fare so well. The Highlanders are not so cruel as we thought them. When the minister of Fala reads the Bible and we sing psalms, the Guards take off their bonnets. But I am sorry to tell you that the English redcoats go to the other end of the kirk and all the time of our worship are cursing and swearing and damning us as Presbyterian Dissenters.

The left flank of the Jacobites had no real commander in charge of them and they actually pulled back at the attack from the Hanoverians. Some of these men were to retreat back to Plean Muir and took with them a report that stated the Jacobites had suffered a defeat.

The Hanoverians retreated to Linlithgow where they spent the night. General Hawley then returned to Edinburgh, but on the gibbet he had erected there in readiness for Jacobite rebels he strung up 14 of his own usurping dragoons. A further 32 were shot for their cowardice. Other soldiers were whipped in public to add to their shame and five officers were court-martialled. To avoid his humiliation, Captain Archibald Cunningham committed suicide.

Only one Jacobite had been captured; MacDonell of Tirnadris had taken a horse from the government forces and mounted it, only for it to bolt back into the Hanoverian side, where he was easily arrested. He was taken south to Carlisle where he was hanged a few weeks later.

The Jacobites sent Lord Kilmarnock into Falkirk to reconnoitre the area. He returned with the news that the Hanoverians were fleeing towards Linlithgow. The Jacobites therefore determined to take Falkirk and the Jacobite force entered the town from all sides. Lochiel came in through the West Port, Lord George Murray entered by Roberts Wynd and Lord John Drummond by the Cow Wynd.

When Lord John Drummond entered the High Street he came upon a small group of straggling Hanoverian soldiers. A skirmish erupted in which some of the government troops were killed; Lord John was himself injured.

Prince Charles came into Falkirk later in the day. He made his way to Mrs Graham's house, which thereafter became known as the Grand or Great Lodging. Her husband had been a surgeon and a supporter of the Jacobite movement.

On the day after the battle, the Jacobites made their way back onto Falkirk Moor, where they began the sorry task of burying the dead of both sides. However, during the night a number of robbers had been on the field and stripped the dead of anything of value. Some of the men still lying there were suffering from severe wounds and there are tales of the worst of these being buried alive. When one of the wounded being interred complained, he was told, 'Och, jist you go in quietly and please the Prince!'

Chevalier Johnstone was one of those who took part in the burial of the bodies. His journal recounts how he felt:

> The sergeant carried a lantern; but the light was soon extin-
> guished and by that accident we immediately lost our way

and wandered a long time at the foot of the hill, among heaps of dead bodies, which their whiteness rendered visible. To add to the disagreeableness of our situation from the horror of the scene, the wind and the rain were fill in our faces. I even remarked a trembling and strong agitation in my horse, which constantly shook when it was forced to put its feet on the heaps of dead bodies and to climb over them … on my return to Falkirk I felt myself relieved from oppressive burden: but the horrid spectacle I had witnessed was, for a long time, fresh in my mind.

During the Jacobite occupation of Falkirk, Angus MacDonnel of Glengarry the Younger was accidentally killed. A young soldier of the Clanranald regiment had acquired a new musket on the field of battle. He had it in the upper floor of a house he was occupying in the town and was showing the piece off to a friend. A ball that had been put in it for demonstration purposes was removed and the man then fired the powder out into the street to clear out the barrel; unfortunately he was unaware that the gun had been double-loaded and the men he aimed at included Young Glengarry. The musket pierced his body and he fell to the ground, mortally wounded. His friends grabbed him, but it was too late.

The soldier came from the house to help and explained what had happened before Glengarry died. The young chief begged his clansmen to forgive the lad and not to punish him; however, the lad was taken to a park wall and there he faced a firing squad. One of the guns used belonged to his own father, who was keen that the lad should die as instantaneously as possible.

The body of Young Glengarry was taken to Falkirk kirkyard where it was interred next to the grave of Sir John de Graeme, the Scots hero from the 1298 Battle of Falkirk.

Other victims of the battle, but from the government side, were also laid to rest in Falkirk. Colonel Sir Robert Munro and his brother, Dr Duncan Munro, were both killed by the Camerons and, their bodies being recognised, were brought back for interment in the kirkyard. Sir Robert had been a commander of the Black Watch at Fontenoy and was the senior officer in Hawley's force. Another who merited burial there was William Edmonstone of Cambuswallace.

Among the Hanoverian prisoners taken at Falkirk, many were transported north to Doune Castle, where they were held in the vaults by MacGregor of Glengyle on behalf of the Prince. One of those held was the writer, John Home (1722-1808) and Rev John Witherspoon (1723-94). John Home later wrote a *History of the Rebellion*, in which he recounted how he and five other prisoners managed to make their escape from the upper floor of the kitchen tower using bedclothes tied together to form a rope. Witherspoon was later to become the president of Princeton College in New Jersey.

CHAPTER TWENTY-SEVEN
Stirling to Inverness

The Jacobites heard of the advance of the Duke of Cumberland and his soldiers and decided to pull out of Stirling on 1 February. The plan was to leave a rearguard at St Ninians, which lies a mile and a half to the south of Stirling, whilst the main bulk of the troops escaped north over the Forth. The retreat was uncoordinated and the force split into smaller groups so that at no time were there more than 1,000 men in any one party.

Argyll's men captured a detachment of troops in Stirling and these were taken back to the tolbooth where they were imprisoned. Thirty-four men were held there and the council sent Argyll a daily account for £3-8 shillings to cover the cost of their keep. In March the burgh gaoler, Archibald Moir, was given 30 shillings sterling by the town treasurer for his part in 'cleaning the prisoners, serving the prisoners and furnishing ane servant to his assistance for the better doing thereof.'

Whilst at Stirling the Jacobites kept some of their gunpowder in the parish church of St Ninians. On 1 February the powder was set alight, either by accident or by design, and the main part of the church was blown up; a number of local folk were killed by the blast. The clock tower survived the blast and was left to stand alone from then onwards.

On the same day as the Jacobites left Stirling, the Hanoverian troops under Cumberland and Hawley left Linlithgow Palace, leaving large fires burning in the grates and a bonfire in the courtyard. With no one to guard them, a spark seems to have set some straw alight and soon the whole palace was ablaze. Word was sent to Provost Bucknay (a supporter of the Jacobites) to inform him about the blaze, but he replied, 'Weil, weil. Those who kindled the fire had better put it out!'

From Stirling the Jacobites headed north. They crossed the Fords of Frew and entered Dunblane, where most of them spent the night of 1 February. Prince Charles marched a further ten miles to the north and took up residence in Drummond Castle, the seat of the Duke of Perth.

On 2 February Charles and the army made their way further north, into Crieff. The Prince had his residence in Fairnton, or Ferntower, which stood a mile north-east of Crieff. His horse had lost a shoe and it was sent into Crieff to the local smith, John Wright, for a replacement.

The rest of the Jacobites made their way into Crieff. A review of the troops was held on the Market Park, where Prince Charles was angered to discover that the reports of the many deserters had been an exaggeration.

A Council of War was held on 3 February in the Drummond Arms Inn, where Charles and Lord George argued as to what to do next. Eventually they decided to split into two groups and head for Inverness, Murray taking the lower route by the coast via Montrose and Aberdeen. Prince Charles was to follow a more direct route north, over the mountains. The forces were to unite once more at Inverness.

Lord George's men made their way up the east coast of Scotland and arrived at Aberdeen; he left a force here to guard the town. The way to Inverness took them across country, and, after crossing the River Spey, George left a second force behind which was to prevent the Hanoverians from crossing easily. Murray's men reached Inverness and rejoined the rest of the Jacobites on 20 February.

Prince Charles and his followers marched further north, through the Sma' Glen, Amulree and Glen Cochill, before crossing the River Tay at Aberfeldy. They spent two nights camped around Castle Menzies.

General Wade reached Crieff within a few days. As he was making his way along the road to the south of the town he was surprised by a bunch of young lads, banging pots and rattling drums; they even had a few old guns with them and managed to fire some shots into the air. Some of the Hanoverian soldiers were taken aback at the noise and were ready to flee, thinking that the Jacobites were about to attack, when it was discovered that it was in fact just a bunch of lads welcoming the government soldiers into the village. To encourage their support, Wade threw a scramble of coins at the lads.

Prince Charles reached Blair Castle on 6 February and the Jacobites remained there for three days. On 9 February Charles's half of the army pushed on through Glen Garry to Dalnacardoch and Dalwhinnie towards Ruthven. The weather had turned for the worse and the Jacobite forces experienced their worst snows for years. Nevertheless, the advance guard reached Ruthven barracks and, with three Swedish guns and a cannon taken from the field at Falkirk, was able to force the soldiers there into surrender. Three shots were fired at the barracks' walls, creating three holes in the masonry.

From Ruthven the route north went by way of Aviemore and the Slochd to Moy Hall, south east of Inverness and seat of the chief of clan Mackintosh, which the Jacobites reached on Sunday 16 February.

Donald Fraser was the estate blacksmith on Moy estate. The estate was long possessed by the chiefs of the Clan Mackintosh and still remains in their hands today. He was a respected man in the district and accounts of him remark that he was 'a trusty stout fellow', devoted to the Mackintosh family.

On Sunday 16 February 1746 the blacksmith heard that Prince Charles had arrived at Moy House. He was escorted by a band of Camerons and a few MacDonalds and he spent the night in the company of Lady Anne Mackintosh (1723-1787), better known as 'Colonel Anne' and her sister, Margaret, daughters of Farquharson of Invercauld. Lady Mackintosh is one of the heroines of the Jacobite cause, who raised a regiment for the prince with the promise of a kiss to each man willing to serve. Her husband, the chief of the clan, was a soldier in the Hanoverian army, so it must have been an interesting marriage.

Prince Charles arrived at Moy, just ten or eleven miles short of the Hanoverian forces in Inverness. Lady Anne made him most welcome and the Prince was fed a supper that was both 'exceedingly genteel and plentiful.'

The Prince's arrival at Moy was leaked and soon word reached Lord Loudoun at Inverness; Mackintosh was with him at the time and it was decided that an attack on Moy House should be made during the hours of darkness. At midnight Loudoun led 1,500 soldiers southwards towards Moy. An advance party comprising 70 men was under the command of Sir Norman MacLeod, 19th Chief of the MacLeods. However, there were spies on both sides and a servant who had been waiting at the tables in Inverness sent his 12-15 year-old son, Lachlan MacIntosh, to Moy to warn the Prince.

Colonel Anne took command. She sent for Donald Fraser and four others, local men she held in high regard. The Cameron men, who had come with the Prince, were sent out into the fields around Moy, to guard against attack. The Prince was sleeping at the time and he had to be roused from his bed. He seems to have spent some of the time wandering around in the courtyard of the house, before Colonel Anne persuaded him to make an exit along the shores of Loch Moy. The Prince's precious belongings, which had been left behind in the house, were taken up to a turret room and hidden. Likewise the horses and baggage train were removed from the vicinity of Moy House and hidden in a nearby wood.

Donald Fraser and the four others were sent along the Inverness road, to look out for the approaching soldiers. They hid on either side of the road two miles from Moy, at the point where it leaves the narrow Stairsneach nan Gaidheal and enters the wide plain of Moy. As they stood on guard, the rain began to pour heavily and the wind was howling through the trees. They tried to find as much shelter as they could in some peat stacks, fashioning the peat blocks into little sentry boxes for themselves. As they tried to make themselves comfortable, they became aware of advancing soldiers.

Fraser yelled out and fired his musket. In the darkness the impression received by the soldiers was that each peat stack was a bunch of soldiers. The others fired their guns and Fraser yelled out 'Advance Camerons, advance Frasers, advance, advance, my lads!' He was kidding on that he was commanding Jacobite regiments into action. 'I think we have the dogs now!'

The ruse was sufficient to fool Loudoun's men and they about turned and made their way back towards Inverness. In the tumult a few men were trampled underfoot, but survived. Back in Inverness, Lord

Loudoun wrote out a letter to his superior, the Earl of Stair, in which he explained what had happened:

> All faced to where they saw the fire. They were ten
> men deep and all presented and a good many dropping
> shots, one of which killed a Piper at my Foot whilst I
> was forming them. The rest fell all back out of the
> Road to the Right a considerable way, in the utmost
> confusion and it was a great while before I could get
> them brought up and formed and the Panick still so
> great that it was with the greatest difficulty when the
> Party came in, which they did in twos and threes, that I
> could, standing before the Muzzles of their pieces,
> prevent them firing on them and when I came to
> count the corps (if I may call Independent Companies
> by that name) I found I had lost the Five Companys in
> the Rear, of whom, after all the search I could make, I
> could hear nothing. After remaining an Hour on the
> ground and finding that I had lost one third of my Men
> in a Body, besides those who had left the Companys
> that remained with me and finding then the whole
> country was alarmed, I thought it improper, especially
> in the condition the men were, to march on to a
> superior Force.

The Jacobite men managed to kill one of the government soldiers, Donald Ban MacCrimmon, who was the piper to MacLeod. MacCrimmon seems to have been unlucky in life, for the Jacobites had previously captured him. However, being a piper, he was regarded as something of a sacred person and the Jacobites released him so that he could return to MacLeod.

MacCrimmon was also one of the most famous pipers of the time. Before he left Skye to join MacLeod, he is said to have had a premonition of his death and composed *Cha Till Mhic-criomain*, or 'MacCrimmon Will Not Return', better known as 'MacCrimmon's Lament':

MacLeod shall come back,
But MacCrimmon shall never.

Donald Fraser was celebrated for his part in forcing an army of 1,500 men into retreat; indeed, so exaggerated were the accounts of the Jacobite forces waiting at Moy that the Earl of Loudoun made plans for abandoning Inverness and retreating into the wild fastnesses of Ross-shire. Fraser was appointed as an officer in the Mackintosh regiment and earned the soubriquet *Caiptin nan Coig*, or 'Captain of the Five.' He was later to fight at Culloden, which he survived. After the Jacobite Rising had been brought to an end, he moved to live near to the Slochd, but on his death in June 1804 his corpse was returned to Moy, where it was interred in the parish kirkyard. A rather fine marble gravestone was erected over his grave, the stone being sent from Italy by Jacobite sympathizers; later, in 1903, a red granite memorial was added. At Moy Hall the smith's anvil is preserved, along with a sword that belonged to him.

On Tuesday 18 February the Jacobites under Prince Charles marched along the road from Moy into Inverness. The Jacobites expected to come face to face with the government soldiers somewhere on the moor north of the River Nairn, but they were nowhere to be seen. The soldiers had reports of the strength of the Jacobite force and had decided to quit Inverness by boat; any vessel that was available was used to ferry the troops across the firth to Port Kessock. The Jacobites were able to watch the Hanoverians from the shore and fire a few volleys from their cannon towards them.

The Jacobites then entered Inverness where they spent the night. Prince Charles slept in the townhouse of the Mackintoshes. He was later to move to Culloden House, recently vacated by Duncan Forbes, the Lord President, where he remained for a number of days.

A garrison of Hanoverian soldiers held Inverness Castle and on the following morning the Jacobites set about building a battery from where they were to lay siege to the defences; however, someone determined that there was a part of the defences where the walls could be undermined and work started on this. The occupants of the castle decided that it would be better to capitulate and so on Friday 21 February they surrendered. Within the building the Jacobites found a good supply of arms and ammunition, meal, beef, cheese and coal. They removed this from the castle and then set about demolishing it.

There is a tale that relates how one of those responsible for demolishing the castle was a Frenchman. He laid out the fuse train from a pile of gunpowder and set it alight, and, watching the spark make its way towards the castle, thought that it had gone out; as he approached to relight it, he was shocked to discover that the fuse was still burning. Within seconds it blew up, and the blast was sufficiently strong to throw him and his faithful dog into the air and across the River Ness to the green on the west bank, a distance of 300 yards. The Frenchman was killed, but it was reported that the dog survived.

A party of Jacobites were sent south to attack Fort Augustus and that defence capitulated on 1 March. A battalion of 3,000 men were ordered north, to pursue Lord Loudoun and his men; a lack of boats in the Inverness Firth meant that vessels had to be acquired from further along the Moray Firth, the Hanoverian soldiers having taken all local vessels with them on their retreat north. The Royal Navy fleet was in the firth at the time, but a fortunate mist prevented them from seeing what the Jacobites were up to; they were able to sail out of Findhorn and land at Tain. The Jacobites then came upon some of the government soldiers and in a small skirmish were able to capture a number of them. Among the prisoners was Mackintosh of that Ilk, Major MacKenzie and ten other officers, as well as 30-40 soldiers.

Lord George Murray forayed south towards Rannoch, where he captured around 300 government soldiers, most of whom were Campbells. Lord John Drummond guarded the approach to Inverness from the east, where he had a posting at the side of the River Spey. An advance guard of Cumberland's soldiers were making their way towards Keith when Drummond's men spotted them. In the affray a further number of prisoners were taken.

As well as attacking various government garrisons, the Jacobites spent the time at Inverness building up their stock of supplies. Various officers were sent with men out into the surrounding shires to collect meal, corn and forage for their horses, more horses and levy money. One of these parties came into contact with some French soldiers during their foray into the parish of Dallas. The 24 Jacobites were surprised by the French, who had been informed that they were Campbells, and various shots were fired; the Jacobite force suffered a number of wounded men as a result.

During Charles's time in Inverness, he relaxed and enjoyed himself. He spent a few days hunting and in the evenings there were balls and concerts to attend.

On 13 April Prince Charles decided to review his troops. The men were gathered back into Inverness. Information was supplied that the Hanoverian troops under Cumberland were fast approaching, so Prince Charles and a few others rode out to look at them from the distance.

On the evening of 14 April the Jacobite forces met in Inverness where they were all supplied with arms. They then marched eastward to the fir woods of Culloden where they encamped for the night. The following morning they arose and marched a further half mile to Drummossie Muir, where they encamped once more.

CHAPTER TWENTY-EIGHT
Culloden

Cumberland marched his men westward from Aberdeen, leaving the city on 8 April. On 11 April his army arrived at Cullen, on the Banffshire coast, where the Jacobites under the Duke of Perth held the village. Perth decided that it would be better if he and his band of Highlanders should make a retreat before the government soldiers arrived, which he accordingly did. Cumberland then had a straight run along the coast to Nairn, where he arrived on 14 April.

Prince Charles's army had been divided and spread around the Highlands to some extent; many were quite distant from Inverness, either besieging the garrisons at Fort William or else pursuing Loudoun's men in Sutherland. The Prince called together as many of the clans and army as he could and they gathered together on Drummossie Muir.

The Jacobites were outnumbered, which left Charles with a problem. Should he retreat and try and gather more men together, or else stay and face the government soldiers? The redcoats were almost 9,000 strong – around 2,400 cavalry and 6,400 infantry – and all were seasoned soldiers.

It was decided that the best plan for the Jacobites was to make a surprise attack. Cumberland's birthday was 15 April and it was thought that he would not wish to fight that day; indeed, the Jacobites reckoned that many of his troops would be drunk, having taken part in a celebration. The Hanoverian soldiers were all issued with a fairly generous allocation of brandy that was to be drunk as a toast to their leader and other spirits had been acquired.

The Jacobites were determined to make a night-time attack on the Hanoverians. It was their theory that the government soldiers would be rather inebriated and that they would be easy prey in the middle of the night. So that they could kill as many as possible without waking the rest, no firearms were to be used; instead, only dirks and claymores would be used, the Jacobites creeping up on the enemy and killing them in silence.

At eight o'clock in the evening the Jacobites set off, with the Prince in charge of the main army and Lord George Murray in charge of the vanguard. The nine-mile route should have taken them a little less than two hours and it was hoped that the attack would take place around midnight. However, the Jacobite soldiers were exhausted, starving and in no fit state for a forced march in complete darkness.

By two o'clock in the morning the vanguard was still three miles short of its target and the main body of men was further behind. Murray realised that the planned attack was now futile; it would be almost morning before they would be on the opposition and the element of surprise would no longer be theirs. He then decided that the best thing to do was retreat.

The Jacobites made their way back to Culloden moor, where they arrived at seven in the morning. They had nothing to eat with them and were so tired that the men huddled down on the moor and fell asleep. A Jacobite officer recorded this in his journal:

> So back they march'd and arrived at Culloden about sev'n
> o'clock in the morning. The fatigue of this night's march,
> joyn'd to the want of sleep for several nights before and the
> want of food occasion'd a prodigious murmuring among the
> private men, many of them exclaiming bitterly even in the
> Prince's hearing, which affected him very much. Many of
> them fell asleep in the parks of Culloden and other places
> near the road and never wakened till they found the enemy
> cutting their throats.

Four hours later the alarm was raised. The lookout had spotted the redcoats making their way up and across the moor. Two lines of soldiers were spread out across the moor. They spied the clansmen in the distance and came to a halt, one mile short of the foe. The battalions were drawn up in three lines: six battalions in the front line, five in the second and four in the third. The battalions were arranged in an offset way, so that the soldiers formed a brick effect; a regiment of cavalry flanked each infantry regiment and a third was placed to the rear. In total the Hanoverians probably numbered around 7,500, although estimates vary this figure as high as 10,000.

Rising as quickly as possible, the Jacobites formed up in battle order. The front line comprised, from south to north, the Atholl men, Camerons, Appin Stewarts, MacPhersons, Frasers, Mackintoshes, Farquharsons, MacLeods, MacLeans, Clanranald MacDonalds, Keppoch MacDonalds and Glengarry MacDonells. On either flank were placed two guns, with a fifth and sixth in the centre.

The second line of Jacobites was formed of Lord Ogilvie's, Lord Lewis Gordon's, Glenbuchat's and the Duke of Perth's regiments and the Irish and French; the small troops of horsemen were arranged on the flanks. In total the Jacobites probably had only 3,000 to 4,000 men, though again estimates vary this as high as 8,000.

The Hanoverian solders were ordered slowly forward by Cumberland until they were around 500 yards away from the Jacobites. Cumberland took time to arrange his men, moving James Wolfe's regiment forward and placing them at an angle to the front line.

At around one o'clock in the afternoon the first shots were fired. Prince Charles's artillery fired their cannon across the moor towards the redcoats. The balls did little damage.

Cumberland ordered his guns to reply in a similar manner. They were more effective, killing many soldiers who were unlucky enough to be in their line.

As the battle continued the weather got worse. A shower of rain gradually turned to driving sleet and snow, blowing towards the Jacobites' faces. They were itching to fight at close combat and Charles realised this. He sent a messenger to tell Murray that the men should charge, but the man was killed before he could pass this on.

The clansmen, however, had been so impatient that they decided amongst themselves that they needed to attack. The Mackintoshes broke ranks first of all, rushing headlong towards the enemy. When the other clans saw them moving forward, they did likewise, rushing across the moor with their swords and claymores flying.

The Hanoverians continued to fire their guns, and musket balls were shot into the advancing clansmen. But the Highlanders were running on their second wind and no army was going to stop their charge; they battered their way through the front line of Cumberland's men and then through much of the second line. It was only as they reached the third line that their impetus began to wane and their speed faltered. The third line held firm, their bayonets engaging the clansmen, and many were killed here.

The charge spent, the clansmen tried to return to their own side of the battlefield. As they retreated the Hanoverians fired into their backs and many more were killed in this way.

The Jacobite soldiers tried to reform their front line, but there were many missing soldiers. When the line was assembled as best as they were able, a second charge was attempted, but the firepower of the redcoats was too great and most of the clansmen halted their advance and then tried to flee and save themselves.

The redcoats saw the Jacobites failing in their charge, so an attack was launched. As they made their way forward, the second line of the Jacobite force held firm; the Irish men and the Gordons were particularly notable in their resoluteness.

The redcoats turned around and started a second attack. This time they were more successful and the final defence of the Jacobites was broken. The battle was over and the hopes of the Jacobites were broken.

Many of the Jacobite standards were targeted by the Hanoverian soldiers as prizes of war. The Mackintosh standard was saved by Donald Mackintosh who managed to rescue the colours from the hands of the dead standard bearer. He wrapped the material around his body and managed to escape, earning the epithet 'Donald of the Colours' thereafter. A second standard that was saved belonged to the Appin Stewarts; seventeen soldiers in the regiment had lost their lives trying to save the colours, but eventually Donald Livingston, one of the soldiers, cut the flag from its staff and took it away.

A third standard rescued belonged to the Camerons; the hereditary standard bearer to the Lochiel, a MacLachlan of Coruanan, saved it. He wrapped it around his body and made it home to Lochaber. It was handed down through the MacLachlan family for generations until it was handed over to Lochiel in the 20th century and displayed in Achnacarry.

Prince Charles would not accept that the Jacobites were defeated. He was determined to keep on fighting and would not concede that the game was over. It is said that it required some force to persuade him to leave the field and flee for his own safety.

Of those who died on the battlefield, we can only mention a few; numerous deaths occurred on both sides, with the Jacobites probably losing 1,200 men and the Hanoverians 310.

On the battlefield was an old well, which soon came to be known as the Well of the Dead. A stone adjacent to it today records that 'Here the Chief of the MacGillivray's fell'. Colonel Alexander MacGillivray, 8th of Dunmaglass, was in charge of the Clan Chattan regiment in the Jacobite force, which may have numbered around 350; the regiment probably suffered the most losses, including all of their officers except three, one of which was seriously wounded.

On the field of Culloden, MacGillivray was wounded by a musket shot. He was unable to walk and tried to crawl across the battlefield. He was thirsty and suffering from exposure, but he managed to make his way towards a spring, where he hoped to drink the water; however, as he reached out for the cold liquid he breathed his last. He body was disinterred at Culloden a few weeks after the battle and re-interred at Petty churchyard.

MacGillivray had been engaged to a young lady, Elizabeth Campbell of Clunas. Her fiancé did not return to her and she died of a broken heart two years later.

Lachlan MacLachlan of MacLachlan (17th Chief) came out in support of the Prince in 1745. He made his way from Castle Lachlan in Argyll towards Edinburgh, where he joined the Prince at Holyrood on 18 September. MacLachlan almost did not reach Edinburgh, for soon after leaving his home country, with just 20 men, his horse turned around in an anti-clockwise direction three times; the clansmen regarded this as a bad omen and it took much persuading to get them to continue. By the time MacLachlan reached Edinburgh, their support had risen to 150.

Lachlan MacLachlan was in charge of the MacLachlans and the MacLeans at Culloden, fighting on the right wing. He was killed by a cannon ball as he led his men in battle. As a consequence of the clan's support for the Prince, the MacLachlan lands, which were virtually surrounded by the Campbell homelands, were harried and a frigate in Loch Fyne shelled the castle, leaving it uninhabitable.

With the battle over, the Hanoverian soldiers carried out one of the most brutal acts of warfare ever. Though there was no longer any threat of attack, the redcoats roamed over the battlefield and searched for survivors; any injured Jacobite that was found was put to death by bayoneting, no matter how helpless and defenceless they were. A Hanoverian soldier wrote that 'the moor was covered with blood; and our men, what with killing the enemy, dabbling their feet in the blood and splashing it about one another, looking like so many butchers.'

As the Jacobites fled into the distance, scattering in all directions, soldiers pursued them and those that were caught up with were killed where they were. Thus, it was reported that the road from Culloden Moor into Inverness was strewn with bloody bodies.

The orders for this bloodshed were given either by the Duke of Cumberland, or else by General Hawley. They stated that on the morning after the battle, the government soldiers were to return to the field of battle and search among the bodies lying there for any signs of men who were wounded or in the last breaths of life. The soldiers were to gather these men up and drag them into two separate heaps. Once they were all piled up, a six-pound gun was to be fired into the bodies, to make sure that not one remained alive.

One man managed to survive this final act of barbarism. A private in the Jacobite forces, he was surnamed MacIver. He had suffered a number of serious wounds to his body, making it impossible for him to get away from the battlefield. In a weakened state, he lay overnight. After the Hanoverians had attempted to kill all the wounded and left the field, he was later collected by a friendly servant. MacIver survived and lived for another 50 years, dying near Beauly in Inverness-shire in 1796.

John Gordon, 'Old Glenbuchat', survived the field and managed to escape. He was a wanted man, however, with a price of £1,000 on his head and he spent some time in hiding before he was able to escape onboard a Swedish sloop on 25 November 1746; he spent time in Norway before making his way south to France. Living in exile, he was often in the company of the Prince. When the British government passed the Act of Indemnity in June 1747, Glenbuchat was exempt.

John Gordon died in exile at Bolougne on 16 June 1750. The Hanoverian King George is said to have suffered nightmares about Gordon; it is said that he would wake up in a sweat, wondering how to pronounce Glenbuchat and screaming in terror at the thought of him attacking the monarch.

Glenbuchat's regiment had Father John Tyrie as a chaplain, a Roman Catholic priest from Strathavon. He suffered wounds at the battle.

CHAPTER TWENTY-NINE

Aftermath
of Culloden

The Hanoverian soldiers were sent around the countryside to search for Jacobites who had taken part in the Battle of Culloden. They were told to have no mercy and they carried the orders to the full; anyone known to have fought for the Jacobites was harried down and run through with a bayonet, or else shot in cold blood. Even those suspected of assisting the Jacobites, or hindering the Hanoverian troops as they inquired after the hunted, were liable to be killed.

In Inverness, the nearest large town to the battlefield, the government soldiers paraded through the town, searching for men who had taken part in the battle. The Duke of Cumberland was amongst those who searched the town. Provost John Hossack approached the Duke, requesting that he be clement in his treatment of the Jacobites. The Duke was so incensed at his request that he kicked the provost down the stairs of the Town House.

After Culloden, the soldiers under Cumberland spent the next few months searching for those who were known, or suspected of, taking part in the battle. These searches covered much of the Highlands.

A number of Jacobites fled the battlefield and sought shelter at Achindown House, a fairly small laird's house that stands near to the Kirkton of Barevan, a clachan that lies one mile south of Cawdor in Nairnshire. The house dates from around 1700 and was at the time home to Hamish Munroe and his family. The Hanoverian soldiers arrived at the house and forced an entry. No-one was to be found in the main floors of the building, but when they went down to the basement the soldiers found a bunch of Jacobites huddling together. The soldiers dragged them from their hiding place and marched them out into the garden. One by one they were shot dead. Hamish Munroe was also shot for his part in hiding the fugitives. There are still marks on the wall that are said to have been made by bullets ricocheting off the masonry.

A group of soldiers arrived at Balnacraig House, which lies on the south side of the River Dee, near to Kincardine O'Neil. This was the home of the Innes family, who were Roman Catholics and who had their own small chapel adjoining the house. The men had instructions that they were to find Innes, failing which they were to burn down the house. Innes was not present when they arrived, but his wife was. Seeing the soldiers coming, she ran to the yard and killed all the hens that she owned. She then prepared a massive feast, which the soldiers so enjoyed that they spared the house and did not leave a guard at it when they went away.

A similar tale is told of the soldiers who arrived at Bailly, on Eilean Shona in Loch Moidart, Inverness-shire. The only person in the house was the wife of the tenant and she managed to bribe the men to leave their property alone by offering them milk, bread and cheese.

The Hanoverians attacked the home of Donald MacDonald of Kinlochmoidart. The house was set alight, but not before Margaret Cameron, the old bed-ridden mother of the chieftain, had been carried from her room and lay in the shelter of four ancient yew trees in the garden. Other accounts claim that the soldiers camped beneath these trees also. Donald's wife, Isobel, took her children and moved to the lonely Glenforslan cottage, awaiting word of her husband. On 12 November 1745 he was heading for Edinburgh from Carlisle when he was recognised near Lesmahagow in Lanarkshire. He was captured by the soldiers and taken to Edinburgh where he was held for some time. MacDonald was then transferred to Carlisle Castle. He was tried and sentenced to be beheaded; this took place on 18 October 1746, when he and Major MacDonell of Tirnadris were led out to the scaffold. After the execution had taken place, the two men's bodies were cut down, disembowelled and beheaded. The heads were displayed on the battlements of Carlisle Castle for many years thereafter. On hearing of her husband's execution, Isobel Cameron is said to have gone mad with grief.

At Dundreggan in Glen Moriston, the government troops were passing through the glen in 1746 when Major Lockhart spotted three men. The Jacobites had captured Lockhart at one time, but he was able to persuade his guard to allow his release; as a result, he was always keen to capture and kill Jacobites. Lockhart lifted his gun and shot the three men without warning them or checking who they were. The three men were lifted up and their bodies were suspended from a makeshift gallows, to serve as a warning to other Jacobites. Major Lockhart also captured Grant of Dundreggan and ordered that his cattle be rounded up, to be taken as a fine. As the animals were being gathered, Grant was forced to strip and watch as the three men were strung up on a tree. It took some persuasion to prevent Lockhart from hanging Grant also, for he had in fact helped the government soldiers on more than one occasion. Nevertheless, Lockhart stole his cattle, set his home on fire and stole the clothing and rings that his wife was wearing.

A party of Lockhart's men were in the Braes of Glenmoriston when they came upon Isabel MacDonald, wife of Alexander MacDonald of Aonach. He was a fugitive and was hiding nearby. The soldiers tried to get information from Isabel, but on her refusal to tell them where her husband was she was raped; her husband could only watch helplessly from the nearby hillside. Another rape was committed on Flora MacDonell, a neighbour, within a short time. The two women resolved not to lie with their husbands for nine months thereafter in case they were pregnant. Fortunately, neither was.

In April 1746 a group of soldiers made their way to Strathdearn, a valley in the middle reaches of the River Findhorn. They robbed the house of Sir Archibald Grant of Monymusk and relieved him of 36 guns, ten swords, eight bayonets, one pistol, 13 culters from ploughs and 14 socks from ploughs. Another party approached the Dalmagarry Inn, which stood by the side of the Funtack Burn, south east of Loch Moy. The inn was robbed of its remaining goods, a few residents were killed and before the soldiers left with the cattle the inn was set ablaze.

Another group of Hanoverians approached Moy Hall, which had been newly erected around 1700 to replace the old Moy Castle that stood in an islet in the loch. The house was the seat of the Mackintosh of that Ilk, who was a Hanoverian supporter and his lady wife, 'Colonel Anne', a devout Jacobite. The soldiers arrived at the front door of the Georgian house and battered at the door, demanding 'that damd Rebell Lady McIntosh'.

The uproar was witnessed by the local minister, Rev James Leslie, who made his way to the house hoping that the presence of a man of the cloth would prevent any atrocities. At one point he put his hand in his pocket and revealed his pocket watch. A soldier spotted it and within an instant swiped it from him.

Lady Mackintosh witnessed the theft and, feeling sorry for the minister, offered to buy the watch from the soldier for one guinea. 'Dammit, you have got money,' yelled the soldier and took Lady Mackintosh's purse from her. Within it were 50 guineas, which were quickly stolen. A second soldier reckoned that she had more money and withdrawing his bayonet, held it at her face. Lady Mackintosh stated that she had no more money, at which the soldier swiped the bayonet across her breast, ripping the skin. A third soldier saw this action and intervened, telling the second soldier that should he insult the lady any more, then he would have no conscience in stabbing him; it later transpired that Lady Mackintosh had intervened when the third soldier had been due to be flogged at Perth.

A further troop of soldiers arrived at Moy under the command of Sir Everet Falconer. Lady Mackintosh was arrested, but when Sir Everet heard what injury had been inflicted on her, he tried to find out who was responsible. However, he was unable to do so and Lady Mackintosh begged him not to enquire any further. She was taken to Inverness where she was held prisoner in a house for six weeks. She seems to have been given what food she requested and it was worked out that she used 12 loaves each day. These she shared among the poor folk who were held alongside her.

In Inverness a number of Jacobite prisoners were put to death. There is a long-standing tradition that many of them were executed in the kirkyard of the Old High Church. There, in the yard, were two simple headstones, facing each other; one was ideal for sitting on, whereas the other had a suitable notch out of the top on which a soldier could comfortably rest his musket. The church tower was used as a temporary prison and from here the Jacobites were led out into the yard, placed on the smaller headstone and shot at from the other.

One of those held in the tower was a Mr Bradeshaw, who survived and was later able to tell his tale to Bishop Forbes:

> I was put into one of the Scotch kirks together with a great
> number of wounded prisoners who were stript naked and
> then left to die of their wounds without the least assistance
> and though we had a surgeon of our own, a prisoner in the
> same place, yet he was not permitted to dress their wounds,
> but his instruments were taken from him on purpose to
> prevent it; and in consequence of this many expired in the
> utmost agonies.

One of the most notorious of those given the responsibility of tracking down the Jacobites was Captain John Fergusson, or Fergussone, whose ship, HMS *Furnace*, patrolled the waters off the west coast of Scotland. He moved from place to place, sending soldiers ashore at various locations to capture known Jacobites, or in their absence, to destroy much of their property. There are many accounts of his and his men's exploits, recorded in oral tradition in the West Highlands, but the most damning evidence is from his own diaries.

On 12 May 1746 we find him sailing near the island of Raasay, off the west coast of Inverness-shire, where he discovered that the Jacobites were still willing to fight:

> [The] next Morning being the 10th I stood into Loch Alliard
> [Ailort] and Landed my Men at Break of Day and took
> possession of a Little Hill with 60 of them, untill the rest
> Search'd amongst some Caves, where they found 650 Stand
> of Arms, 2000 Weight of Balls and some Flints, but no
> Powder. By this time the Rebells had gather'd into a Body of
> 4 or 500 Men Commanded by Young ClanRonald and made
> several Attempts on my People, who Still kept their ground
> and drove them back with the Assistance of some Grape

Shott, fired in amongst them. Wee got all the Arms etc. off
and took two of the Rebells Prisoners, without any Loss, but
one of the Tenders Men being more intent on Plunder than
getting off, was taken Prisoner by them. My Prisoners assures
me that the Pretender went off in an open Boat three days
before the French Ships arrived ... The French Ships Landed
a great Deal of Arms, Money and Ammunition and gave out
that there were several more Ships on their Passage, Loaded
with the same Cargoes, & has gott 8000 Men on board. The
Cheifs I find still Endeavour to keep as many together of
them as they can; They had a meeting on the 8th Instant of
all the heads of them and afterwards they gave out Orders for
all of them to be ready to joyn in a Days Notice and that
they were to be joyned by some thousands of the French and
gett payed all their Arrears. I am now Cruizing off of the Isle
of Rarza [Raasay] and has my Boats Manned and Armed
ashore, burning and destroying the Lairds Houses with some
others that belong to His Officers. I have very good
Information where all the Arms Brandy etc. is Lodged that
came in the Last two Ships, But not having Strength enough
of my own to attempt carrying it off I have sent an Express
to acquaint His Royal Highness with it, for if he will Order
me a reinforcement of 200 Men, from the Isle of Sky, I shall
forfeit my Life if I do not Bring it all off. I shall Cruize
between this and Loch Mudart untill I receive His Highness's
Answer.

Fergusson's men landed on the island of Raasay, where they ranged from
one end to the other, burning the houses and slaughtering the livestock.
The island was left in a state of waste after their visit and it took many
years before it recovered.

Another series of burnings took place in the Mallaig and Arisaig
area. On 18 May 1746 Fergusson's men landed on the shore at Morar,
south of Mallaig. They made their way to the laird's house and set it
alight. The men also burned every hut or building that they could find
and plundered or destroyed the livestock they could catch. On the same

day they seem to have sailed south towards Borrodale, where John MacDonald of Borrodale's house was burned. Here they also took around 20 barrels of gunpowder and 84 stand of small arms.

Any known Roman Catholic building was a major target for the destructive acts by the Hanoverian soldiers. In the summer of 1746 a number of soldiers made their way from Arisaig in Inverness-shire across the hills towards Loch Morar. On an islet, Eilean Ban, on that freshwater loch, was a small building that was used as a seminary by the Catholics of the district, as well as by more important figures from the Highlands; among those known to have been on the island at times were MacDonald of Morar, Bishop Hugh MacDonald, his brother and Lord Lovat. The navy vessels anchored off Morar Bay and the little ship's boats were brought ashore and carried across the short stretch of land towards Loch Morar. Using these boats the soldiers were able to row the 700 yards towards Eilean Ban where they ransacked the building. All of its valuable contents, including a notable library and manuscripts, were burned and the soldiers used the robes and other items to dress up in fun. The occupants of the islet had managed to escape, landing on the southern shore of Loch Morar at Ceann-Camuis-Ruaidh.

One of the servants on Eilean Ban was left behind by those who escaped and he had to run to the shore of the loch and hide himself in the water, where the long heather stems fell down into the loch. He was able to remain concealed so securely that the soldiers, despite passing within yards of him, did not discover his whereabouts.

It was after this escape from Eilean Ban that Lord Lovat decided that he would have to give himself up. He was now over 80 years of age and, suffering from asthma, gout and other infirmities, he felt that he could not continue living rough, never knowing when or where the soldiers were about to attack him. He spent a few days at Meoble, in Inverness-shire and then sent a messenger to the soldiers who were at that time based in Arisaig, notifying them of his intentions. The soldiers quickly arrived and apprehended him, then sent him off to London for trial. He was found guilty of rebellion on 18 March and was beheaded on Tower Hill on 9 April 1747, the last noble to be executed in Britain.

A more important Roman Catholic centre was located at Scalan, in Glen Livet. Here there existed a seminary for the training of priests, founded around 1714 after the Jacobite Rising at that time had turned the country against Catholics and pushed them into hiding. The seminary had been attacked a number of times in its life, but one of the most serious attacks took place after Culloden; on that occasion the simple building was burned to the ground and all the possessions of the training centre were destroyed. The Catholic Church was undaunted, however, for they re-established themselves in a nearby farmhouse and continued to train priests in this remote spot until 1799.

It was not only chapels and Catholic buildings that came under pressure; parish priests were also subject to severe punishments and cruelty. Many of the priests were no doubt Jacobite in their leanings and some acted as chaplains to the Jacobite forces, but most had little to do with the risings and were being punished for nothing. Father James Grant, priest on the island of Barra in the Western Isles, was one who suffered considerably and his tale is recounted by Bishop John Geddes:

> Early in the spring of 1746, some ships of war came to the coast of the isle of Barra and landed some men, who threatened they would lay desolate the whole island if the priest was not delivered up to them. Father James Grant, who was missionary then and afterwards bishop, being informed of the threats in a safe retreat in which he was in a little island, surrendered himself and was carried prisoner to Mingarry Castle on the western coast, where he was detained for some weeks. He was then conveyed to Inverness and thrown into the common prison, where there were about forty prisoners in the same room with him. Here he was for several weeks chained by the leg to Mr MacMahon, an Irish officer in the service of Spain, who had come over to be of use to the Prince. In this situation they could not in the night time turn from one side to the other without the one passing over the other. The people of the town, out of humanity, furnished them with some little conveniences and among other things gave to each a bottle, which they hung out of the window in the morning and got filled with water. But one morning the sentinels accused the prisoners to the

visiting officer of having entered into a conspiracy to knock them on the head with bottles, which they had procured for that purpose. Father Grant and the others pleaded the improbability of this ridiculous accusation, but they were not heard and the bottles were taken away.

A further five priests were simultaneously incarcerated in the same gaol, before being sent on board a ship to London. On a prison hulk in London, Father Alexander Cameron took ill and died, so the gaolers threw his corpse overboard. The other priests were held in London for a time before being called before the Duke of Newcastle. He informed them that as they were men of the cloth he would be lenient with them; they were to be banished abroad and were to lodge bail of £1000 that they would never return. They were sent to Holland but within a short time most had returned to Scotland. Father Alan MacDonald then wrote an account of Prince Charles's time in Scotland, though this manuscript has been lost.

Similarly, a number of Episcopal churches were burned or destroyed in various places. At Enzie, near Fochabers in Moray, the local Episcopalians had used a barn as a place of worship for a number of years. After Culloden, followers of this church were seen as being Jacobites and their ministers as 'agents' of Jacobinism; at Enzie the barn was pulled down, leaving the congregation with no place to worship; at Banff, a county town and seaport on the Moray Firth, the Episcopal chapel was also destroyed; the chapel at Arradoul, near Buckie was pulled down.

Rev Robert Forbes (1708-75) was an Episcopal clergyman in Leith and an ardent Jacobite. In 1745 he was imprisoned for his part in the rising, but was later released. In 1762 he was appointed as Bishop of Ross and Caithness. After the Act of Indemnity was passed in June 1747 he spent the rest of his life collecting together accounts of the atrocities and other memoirs by those who had fought on the Prince's side, or else suffered in the aftermath of Culloden. These were later published with the title *The Lyon in Mourning*. On 10 July 1749 Forbes wrote to the poet, Alasdair 'MacMhaighstir Alasdair' MacDonald (c.1700-70), informing him, 'how anxious I am to make up as compleat and exact a collection as possible of some certain memorable events, etc. And therefore I hope I need not to use many words to prevail with you to give me all the assistance in your power. You told me you intended to take up your abode in Egg or Canna, which if you do, then it will be in your powers to make up an exact account of the severe pillaging and plunderings that were committed in these islands. You know I like much to have everything minutely and circumstantially narrated. Forget not then to give the names of those who were principally concerned in pillaging Egg and Canna, such as officers or sogers, commanders of ships, sloops or yachts. Be mindful likewise to make as exact a calculation as you can of the damages sustained by the inhabitants of these two islands.'

Alasdair MacDonald contributed many reports to Robert Forbes, among them the following account regarding the island of Canna:

Upon the 3d of April 1746, Lieutennant Thomas Brown, an Irish gentleman with a command of 80 men, did sail with a tender from the *Baltimore* man of war by Captain Fergusons order, which layed then at the harbour of Lochnadaal at Sky, at whose end Lord Loudon had a camp then, came to the haven of Canna and after sending for James M'Donald, bailie of the Island and uncle to Glenaladal, told him he was sent by Captains Ferguson and Dove for some fresh beef and mutton, vizt., 20 fat cows and so many wedders. The gentleman asking his orders was answered he would show him noe commission of that kind, but if he would not present his demands without further controul he would take them *brevi manu*. He had 60 armed men at his heels; the flower of the Islanders was with the Prince; soe that the bailie judged it safer both for himself and inhabitants to grant his request and consequently sent off to the meadows for the above number of cattle and took them up in proportion to the number of the tenements the Isle consisted of.

But being wind-bound for 4 days in Canna harbour, behold! they complained to the said bailie the beef of the cattle slaughter'd stunk and that the country should give them the same number over again. The bailie reckoned this both unjust and cruel and that it was enough for the poor inhabitants to gratify him of what they received already. Upon which the officer was petted and said with a rage he knew where and by whom he woud be served. He meant Laaig's cattle, whom he heard was in the Prince's army. So he hurls away his 60 armed men, gathers all the cattle of the Isle into a particular creek, shot 60 of the best dead, threw the old beef overboard and woud not allow the poor distressed owners to finger a gobbet of it, no, not a single tripe of the first or former. 40 of the last cattle belonged to Laaig, 20 to the tennants.

Captain Duff and Captain Ferguson aboard the *Commodore* came again a little, or about the 15 of April, harrass'd all the Isle and at a certain night when they became fully acquaint through all the country, they (I mean all the young luxurious men among them) combined to make ane attack upon all the girls and young women in all the Isle married or otherwise. But a certain marine who had some grains of Christian principles about him advertised the whole and was obliged to climb to hide themselves in grottos and in the hollow of hideous precipices that were somewhat unaccessable, which rescued them from the unhumanity of those libidinous hounds.

A certain company of them came to execute their sensuality into a certain family, Evan More MacIsaac, his house, from which fled two girls, the landlord's daughters. Their mother who was fifty years old, worn with sickness and within a month of her time, stayed at home as dreading noe danger of that sort. But they missing their aim and geting none of the females within a house roof but that poor creature, they setts a strong guard with drawn swords upon the door of her house, fettered her husband in order to quench their concupiscence on his spouse. Providence favour'd the creature so far that she wonn out through the guard and the darkness of the night concurrd to make her rescue. For they got out in pursuit of her a great hurry and 12 of them was at her heels, when she meeting and sinking down into the very depth of a quaggmire, they leaps over her believing she was still before them. The poor woman contented herself to continue there all the night, till she understood they were all back to their ships. But when she was so much afflicted with the rigour of the cold and she being bigg with child, turned ill, aborted and died next night. The rest continued their sculking in a starving condition till the men of war sail'd off.

After the battle of Culloden was hard fought, Captain Dove and Captain Fergusone went to Canna successively and committed several branches of cruelty upon the poor people, wanting them to inform them of the Prince or any of his officers. After General Campbell turned back from the search of his Royal Highness from the Western Coast, he calls at Canna and hurls away the honest bailie prisoner into his ship without allowing him to speak for himself, or as much time as to shift himself for take leave of his wife. At this stretch he was brought the length of Horseshoe in the shire of Argile, from Horseshoe was brought back to Canna. Then he believed he would be liberate, but instead thereof they caus'd 40 of his cows to be slaughtered, would not permit him as much liberty as goe ashore to take leave of his wife or children, or to bring his cloaths with him, but brought him prisoner to London where he continued upwards of 12 month, notwithstanding of Loudon's protection in his pocket.

The same sort of disturbance, rape and pillaging was repeated day in, day out throughout much of the Highlands. Soon after the ship made its way to the island of Eigg, where they suspected Captain John MacDonald, brother to Kinlochmoidart, was in hiding. Alexander MacDonald, the poet, sent the details to Forbes:

The islanders stifly denied the doctor to be there with their knowledge. With this [the captain] sent about a 100 men,

divided into small corps, in search of him. One Mr Daniel
MacQueen, minister of the gospel at the Isle of Rum,
happen'd to be then at Eigg and was both agent and
interpreter 'twixt the inhabitants and the ennemie. He, Mr
MacQueen, well knew the very place where MacDonald was
hiding himself and understood by reason of the narrow
scrutiny they were resolved to make after him, they would
fish him out. Therefore, he goes himself in person where he
was and, after explaining him the danger he was under,
prevailed upon him to surrender. Accordingly he did. He was
first well us'd. But behold the unluckiness of the poor Eigg
people; for one of the party that was traversing the country
back and forward, found out so many stands of arms that
they reserved for their own use. Captain Ferguson did not
seem to be much disobliged at this; but reflecting that
notwithstanding what they had already delivered, they still
reserved their full compliment. However, he bespeaks
Captain MacDonald, the doctor and earnestly desires him,
for the poor people's own safety and good of the country, he
should call them all and perswad them to come in, with their
whole arms of all kinds and that he would give them full
protections for both their persons and effects that would save
them against future danger: otherwise, if they should not
come heartily . . . he woud immediately cause his men burn
all their houses, destroy all their cattle and carry the whole
men away. Mr MacQueen advises Captain MacDonald to
send for the men for the remainders of the arms in the terms
spoken by Ferguson. He sends dozen of lads for them. They
were seen comeing in a body. Immediately Ferguson ordered
Captain MacDonald to be seiz'd upon and made prisoner of,
brought into a house and confin'd there for ane hour. The
men laid down their arms, such of them as had any. The few
old people that came among them were picked out and
dismissed home. Then, Captain MacDonald was brought out
of the house, was stript of all his cloaths to the skin, even of
his shoe and stockins, brought upon the *Furnace*, barisdall'd in

a dark dungeon. And to the poor people's additional misfortune, there was a devilish paper found about him, containing a list of all the Eigg folks that were in the Prince's service. Then that catalogue was read by their patronimicks in the name of giving the promised protection, which ilk one answered cheerfully and was drawn out into another rank, so that there were noe fewer than 38 snatched aboard the man of war, were brought to London, from thence transported to Jamaica where the few that lives of them continue slaves as yet. Many of them dyed and starved ere they arrove at the Thames. The most of them were marryed men, leaving throng families behind them. They slaughtered all their cattle, pillaged all their houses ore they left the isle and ravished a girl or two.

Of the 18 men who survived the trip to London (the rest died en route), 16 were found guilty of their part in the rebellion and were sent abroad to work as slaves in Jamaica; only two were set free.

CHAPTER THIRTY
The Prisoners

Thousands of prisoners were taken at Culloden and in the following days; in most cases they were treated cruelly and many died as a result of their privations. Thousands of the prisoners were sent south for trial, which in many cases resulted in execution. Others were sent abroad to the Americas, where they were employed as slaves.

A considerable number of prisoners were taken initially from Culloden into Inverness, where they were held within the kirks; many of these men were stripped naked and left in the cold. They had wounds and sores, but no one treated these. As a consequence, many of the prisoners died.

Four hundred Jacobite prisoners were taken south to Carlisle, where they were held in the Castle; perhaps the third time they had been there. The vaulted cells were packed with the men and they had to endure the heat of the summer months there.

Eventually it was decided that 96 of the prisoners should be executed, the remainder to be transported abroad. The executions took place in October 1746 and the deed was carried out in various batches. The group of prisoners were led out into the courtyard where they were restrained. At the command of the sheriff the men were taken through the gateway and across the castle drawbridge, before making their way to the Gallows Hill, located outside the English Gate. On the knoll the prisoners were hanged, after which their bodies were drawn and quartered. A few had their heads severed from their bodies and these were displayed on pikes above the Scotch Gate, the last time such an action took place in Britain.

One of the prisoners who managed to escape before reaching Carlisle was Donald MacLaren of Invernenty. He had escaped from Culloden but was captured in the Braes of Leny, near Callander in Perthshire. The redcoats transported him firstly to Stirling and thence to Edinburgh, where he was held in the Canongate tolbooth. The authorities sent him south to Carlisle, where he was set to be tried. However, as the soldiers escorted him south along the road from Edinburgh towards Moffat, he made an escape by lunging headlong down the steep precipice of the Devil's Beef Tub, a massive natural cauldron by the side of the road. He requested that the soldiers should let him down from his horse, so that he could relieve himself. The weather was rather dreich, so that as soon as he stood by the roadside, he was able to jump off the edge into the mist. The soldiers were not able to follow him, but fired their muskets at random into the thick mist.

MacLaren was able to make an escape and headed north, spending his first night in hiding at the Crook Inn, home of George Black. A party of soldiers were also in residence at the inn, but MacLaren was able to keep his identity hidden and eventually returned to his homelands at Balquhidder.

John MacNaughton was captured and tried at Carlisle. He had joined the Prince early on in the campaign, after being sent by his chief, Menzies of Culdares. 'Old Culdares' as the chief was known, was a devout Jacobite, but he was elderly and unfit to take part in the campaign. As a sign of his support, however, he wished to donate his best horse to the Prince as a gift. Culdares sent his personal servant, MacNaughton, in search of the Prince; MacNaughton enlisted in the Jacobite forces when he caught up with the prince and handed the horse over. At his trial in Carlisle the offer was made to him that his life would be spared if he would reveal who had gifted the horse. MacNaughton refused. Just before he was about to step onto the scaffold the offer was again put before him, but again MacNaughton refused, preferring to die rather than reveal the name of his chief.

Coll MacDonald of Barisdale in Knoydart was out in the '45 rebellion at the head of the Knoydart men. He was captured after

Culloden, but his captors offered him a deal by which he would be allowed to return home if he supplied information as to the whereabouts of Charles. Coll did not wish to betray the Prince, so informed the authorities that he was in hiding in Perthshire whereas he was in fact at that time out in the Hebrides.

It was not too long before the information supplied was proven false, so the authorities sent a party of Ross-shire militia to his home at Inverie, where:

> ... they were presented with a sight of the stocks that lay
> upon a green, opposite to the door and these they kindled
> first, then set fire to the house, which was beautifully covered
> with blue slate and contained eighteen fire-rooms, besides as
> many without chimnies; the flames burnt with great violence
> and in a few hours the building was reduced to ashes.

Captain Fergusson arrived at Inverie in May 1746 and at six o'clock in the evening fired 48 guns at the house. His account of the burning makes interesting reading:

> ... having gott Information that there was a great many
> Arms and Money, in McDonalds of Barrasdales house, in
> Loch Navis, I stood in for it under Spannish Colours and
> came to an Anchor within Gun Shott of it; I landed 120
> Men with Orders to burn and destroy the House (which was
> one of the best in this Country) But before my boats gott on
> Shore I saw a great Number of Men assembling Armed from
> all Quarters, that made me wish I had my Men on board
> again, for they began to fire on the Boats very Briskly. I soon
> gott a Spring on my Cable and began firing amongst the
> Middle of them, which made them retreat with great hast up
> to the Mountains, but they still Lurked about among Rocks
> and fired on my people, but they soon Destroy'd the House
> and two or three Villages about it and not one of them
> received the Least hurt, although there were above 300
> Armed Men against them; they found in the House 150

Stand of Arms, 130 Cutlasses, 30 Anchors of Brandy and
some small plunder. But I had the Misfortune to Loose six of
my Men. No Body could give me an Account what was
become of them; My Lieut is a very Carefull Diligent
Officer and Endeavoured all in his power to keep the Men
together, But how soon they gott at the Brandy, a great many
of them fell to Drinking, which makes me believe that they
either deserted (being all of them Highlanders or Irish Men)
or gott Drunk and Stragled from the rest in quest of Plunder.

Coll made an escape, crossing to France onboard a man-of-war, but
there he was unfortunate enough to be taken prisoner by Prince
Charles, who was there by that time and believed that he had supplied
information against him.

After two years, Coll managed to escape from France and returned
back to Britain, only to find himself taken prisoner for a third time in
1749. He was held in Edinburgh Castle, where he died in gaol in 1750.
Coll's son, Archibald, had taken part in the rising at the age of 22 and
escaped to Knoydart after Culloden.

The tenants on Knoydart estate continued to pay their rents to the
MacDonalds of Barisdale, despite their attainder; however, they had little
choice in the matter, for the Barisdales had a band of armed men who
ranged across the estate, taking the rent from them. This band was
known locally as 'Barisdale's Guard' and was something of an embar-
rassment to the authorities. Eventually, Archibald was captured and taken
to Edinburgh Castle where he was held for some time. He was
sentenced to be hanged, drawn and quartered, but this was never carried
out. Nevertheless, Knoydart was taken over by the Forfeited Estates in
1755 and all rents were payable to the government. Archibald managed
to return to Knoydart in 1764, but by this time he had abandoned his
Jacobite principles and had accepted the incumbent royal family. He
became something of a model tenant on his own estate.

One who survived imprisonment was William Jack from Elgin.
He was captured and held on board one of the prison ships that were
anchored in the Moray Firth. Most of the others held with him died as
a result of the conditions and he later noted that, 'There is none in life

that went from Elgin with me, but William Innes of Fochabers. James Brander Smith in Conloch dyed seven months agoe. Alexander Frigg dyed in Cromarty Road. Jo Kintrea that lived in Longbridge dyed also.'

The Earl of Cromartie and his heir, John MacKenzie, were captured at Dunrobin Castle on the night before Culloden and held prisoner; the two were tried for High Treason and both of them pled guilty. They were placed on board a Royal Navy ship and taken south to London, where the Earl was held in the Tower of London for two years and John was held in a prison ship off Tilbury. The Countess managed to obtain a pass from Cumberland's men that allowed her to travel south to visit her husband. This read:

> Permit by Sir Edward Fawkener in Favour of Isabella
> Countess of Cromartie and the Ladies Isabella, Mary and
> Anne MacKenzie, her daughters, their servants, equipage,
> horses, etc. freely to go from hence to London by sea or by
> land as will best suit their conveniency.
> Given at Inverness by His Royal Highness' command, April
> 24 1746.

Both he and his son pled guilty to the charge of rebellion, but in March 1748 they were pardoned and released, on condition that they stayed in England.

CHAPTER THIRTY-ONE
The Dispersal

With the Battle of Culloden Moor lost, the Jacobites had to fend for themselves. From the moor thousands of soldiers dispersed as quickly as they could, trying to escape the pursuing Hanoverians. Some went towards Inverness, only to be slaughtered if they were caught. Others headed south, into the Grampian hills, where they expected to lose themselves in the mountains.

Many of the Jacobites thought that the Prince would reform the army, ready for a future assault on the government. It was widely regarded that the location where this would take place would be Ruthven in Badenoch, a remote steading that lies near the headwaters of the River Spey, on the south side of the Corrieyairack Pass. Accordingly, those keen to keep the cause alive made for this place.

At Ruthven there must have been thousands of men gathered over the weeks after Culloden, all wondering what the next move would be. They were keen to hear news of the Prince and what his plans were.

According to the Chevalier de Johnstone:

> I arrived on the 18th of April at Ruthven. There I found the
> Duke of Atholl, Lord George Murray, the Duke of Perth,
> Lord John Drummond, Lord Ogilvie and many other chiefs
> of clans with about four or five thousand Highlanders all in
> the best possible disposition for renewing hostilities and for
> taking their revenge …

Lord George Murray immediately despatched people
to guard the passes and at the same time sent off an aide-de-
camp to inform the Prince that a great part of his army was
assembled at Ruthven; that the Highlanders were full of
animation and ardour and eager to be led against the enemy;
that the Grants and other Highland clans, who had till then
remained neuter, were disposed to declare themselves in his
favour, seeing the inevitable destruction of their country
from the proximity of the victorious army of the Duke of
Cumberland; that all the clans who had received leave of
absence would assemble there in a few days; and that instead
of five or six thousand men, the whole of the number
present at the battle of Culloden – from the absence of those
who had returned to their homes and of those who had left
the army on the morning of the 16th to go to sleep – he
might now count upon eight or nine thousand men at least,
a greater number than he had at any time in his army.

Everybody earnestly entreated the Prince to come
immediately and put himself at the head of this force. We
passed the 19th at Ruthven without any answer to our
message and in the interim all the Highlanders were cheerful
and full of spirits to a degree perhaps never before witnessed
in an army so recently beaten, expecting with impatience,
every moment, the arrival of the Prince; but on the 20th, Mr
MacLeod, Lord George's aide-de-camp, who had been sent
to him, returned with the laconic message, 'Let every man
seek his own safety in the best way he can.'

One of those that met at Ruthven was David, Lord Ogilvy (1725-1813),
who had commanded the Forfarshire Regiment. He and his wife, Lady
Margaret Johnstone, had stayed the night at the home of Gordon of
Killihuntly. With no plans to reform, Lord Ogilvy marched with his men
back towards Angus, crossing the Monadh Ruadh to Deeside before
heading over the Capel Mounth to Glen Clova.

Lord Ogilvy hid himself away in Cortachy Castle for a time, but
later caught a ship in the Firth of Tay and escaped to Norway. He was

held in prison there for a time, but managed to escape to Sweden and from there to France. There he commanded 'Le Regiment Ogilvy' on behalf of the French king and earned the sobriquet 'Le bel Ecossais'.

Lady Ogilvy did not travel with her husband, expecting to take a more leisurely route home; unfortunately she was captured and taken to Inverness where she was held prisoner, having joined the Jacobite camp at Glasgow. She was then transported south to Edinburgh Castle, where she was held along with other Jacobite heroines, including the Duchess of Perth, Viscountess Strathallan and Jean Cameron. During her time in prison, Lady Ogilvy had her laundry done by an old crooked woman. In her absence, Lady Ogilvy mimicked her walk and on 21 November 1746 she persuaded her to swap clothes. Lady Ogilvy, dressed in simple clothes and carrying the basket of laundry, was then able to walk freely from the castle. On reaching the top of the High Street she threw away the basket, stood up straight and ran away.

Lady Ogilvy escaped to the Continent, where she met up with her husband. They had a son, also David, who was born back at Auchterhouse in Scotland, where she had been brave enough to return. After the birth she returned to France, but did not survive long, however, for she died in exile in 1757 at the age of 33.

Many Highlanders settled in new homes following the final Jacobite Rising. There are numerous records of whole families moving from one place to another, usually to get away from their past and try to start afresh. Many of them found themselves on estates run by the Commissioners for the Forfeited Estates and, as Jacobites, found their homes uncomfortable to live in.

The search for Jacobites went on for years. Numerous tales exist in the Highlands of soldiers coming to houses in search of known activists, whether or not they still posed a threat to the government. One of these was John MacLean, who lived at Staonaig on the island of Iona. He was responsible for piloting a Spanish ship to the island of Barra in November 1745. On board were arms and money destined for Prince Charles. The soldiers later arrived at Staonaíg, but not before a young lad named MacInnes managed to warn MacLean of their arrival. MacLean and the lad made their way from the farmhouse to a large cave, supposedly big enough to allow the whole population of Iona to hide in it, where they remained undetected.

At a later date, in July 1746, MacLean offered to give himself up to the Duke of Argyll at Inveraray on condition that his home, belongings and family should remain untouched. At the subsequent trial there was insufficient evidence to charge him with high treason, but he did suffer imprisonment in London for three months in 1747.

A Fraser of Foyers had taken part in the Battle of Culloden and had to flee for his life. He found himself in the hands of his friends, the MacKenzies of Gairloch, who hid him for some time within a secret recess at Flowerdale house; a few floorboards in an upper room could be removed to reveal a secret chamber in which he concealed himself. At one time the soldiers on board a man-of-war patrolling in the western islands came into Gairloch bay, where they sent for Sir Alexander MacKenzie to come onboard. MacKenzie, who had not been active at Culloden due to his lameness, although many of his tenants took part, turned the offer down, telling the soldiers that he was due to attend a dinner party and invited the captain. The captain did not attend, however, and when the ship set sail it fired an eighteen-pound cannon ball at the house, the shot lodging in the gable and being visible for many years thereafter.

CHAPTER THIRTY-TWO

West Highland Wanderings

From Culloden, Bonnie Prince Charlie made his way across the River Nairn and travelled by way of Tordarroch, Aberarder and Farraline to Gorthleck, which lies on the west side of the present Loch Mhór, originally Loch Farraline. He was accompanied by a number of close advisers, including Sir Thomas Sheridan, Sir David Murray, Alexander MacLeod, John William O'Sullivan, Captain Felix O'Neil, John Hay of Restalrig, Edward Burke, Allan MacDonald and a servant. At Gorthleck they met Lord Lovat, who was keen that the Prince should keep trying, citing as an example his ancestor, Robert the Bruce, who lost 11 battles before winning the all-important twelfth. Charles did not heed Lovat directly, but left Gorthleck and continued south-westward to Invergarry Castle, seat of John MacDonell, which he reached early in the morning of 17 April.

The owner was absent and the castle had a lack of provisions, but the group made themselves at home, catching two salmon and eating them with wine they found.

At Invergarry it was decided that it would be safer and easier if the Prince travelled with a smaller group. Accordingly, from this point onward only Edward Burke, Allan MacDonald and John O'Sullivan accompanied him. As a further precaution, Charles swapped clothes with Burke.

Shortly after Culloden the redcoats came to Invergarry and burned the houses in Glen Garry, with the exception of the castle. They returned on 29 May under the command of Captain Lofthus. Their first task was to pillage the castle of anything that was of any worth, after which the castle was set alight. Part of the castle was blown up with gunpowder and two large chestnut trees were also subject to the same destruction. 'By the indulgence of the officers who commanded,' MacDonell's wife and nine children were allowed to keep two small Highland cows, a chest of drawers and six pairs of blankets for themselves, with 'not so much as a hatt left to cover them.' The goods pillaged from the castle were taken to Fort Augustus and offered for sale, the money used for prize-money in races run by the soldiers based there.

From Invergarry Prince Charles made his way down the west side of Loch Lochy before heading west, along the northern shores of Loch Arkaig. He travelled up through Glen Pean and arrived at the home of Donald Cameron of Glenpean, where he spent the night; the first decent sleep he had had for days.

On the following morning, Cameron acted as a guide, showing Charles and his men the route through Glen Pean to the head of Loch Morar. He waited for some time for a boat that had been arranged, but it failed to arrive. Eventually the party walked over a rough stretch of countryside to a nearby cottage, occupied by a MacDonald, who fed them with butter, milk and curds. After spending the night there, Charles made his way to the home of Alexander MacDonald of Borrodale, near Arisaig, where he remained for six days.

On his arrival at Borrodale, Charles was able to eat heartily in the MacDonald home. MacDonald's wife supplied him with a new set of clothes, garments more recognisable as Highland daywear and thus less likely to draw attention to him. Nevertheless, the MacDonalds felt that it was still too risky to allow Charles to remain in their house all the time and advised him to hide in various locations in the district; thus we find a few 'Prince Charlie's Caves' appear on the map.

Near to Arisaig House, at Druimindarroch, is one of these caves, located near to the shore and adjacent to the woods; another cave is found on a steep wooded slope at the west end of Loch Beoraid.

Whilst in hiding, Charles had a meeting with Donald MacLeod from Galtrigal in Skye. After some discussions, Charles persuaded him to take him by boat across the Minch.

Having acquired an eight-oared vessel, that had been owned by John MacDonald who had been killed at Culloden, Charles, Donald MacLeod, John O'Sullivan, Felix O'Neil, Allan MacDonald, Edward Burke, Roderick MacCasgill, John MacDonald, Duncan Roy, Alexander MacLeod and the latter's fifteen-year-old son, Murdoch, set out across the water.

Murdoch MacLeod was a schoolboy at Inverness Grammar School. He was keen on warfare and when he heard Prince Charles's men were in the town, he ran away from school to join them. He armed himself with a claymore, pistol and dirk and made his way to Culloden Moor, where he joined the Jacobites. MacLeod fought in the battle and survived, after which he was able to leave the field. He fled to the west coast of Scotland, searching for his father, whom he eventually found.

Donald MacLeod had not been keen to sail that night as he predicted a storm, but Charles was impatient and persuaded him to go. The storm did arrive, one that was fierce and wild, and Charles realised his mistake. He asked Donald to take them back, but he refused, stating that, 'Since we are here we have nothing for it but, under God, to set out to sea directly. Is it not as good for us to be drowned in clear water, as to be dashed in pieces upon a rock and to be drowned too?'

The men rowed on into the night, fearful of returning back, for the boat would likely be forced onto the rocks and wrecked. Instead, they headed westward, passing through the Sound of Rum and across the Minch to the Western Isles.

CHAPTER THIRTY-THREE
Western Isles

Charles and his small party landed on the island of Benbecula on the morning of 26 April 1746. Charles remained in the Western Isles for the next two months, though he had not planned to stay so long. The party landed at Roisinis, or Rossinish, a headland on the north-east edge of Benbecula. The shore was sandy and the men managed to salvage their boat. They immediately fell asleep, the Prince lying on the sail. An old hut was located nearby and they set a fire in it to dry their clothes. A cow was killed and the men sat down to eat.

The party remained at Roisinis for two days whilst the storm raged around them. When it settled one of the party walked to Clanranald's home, which was a few miles away; the chief was absent, but his second son was there and he was able to return to Roisinis with meal, biscuits and fresh butter.

From Benbecula the Prince and his adherents sailed northwards and landed on the little island of Scalpay, which lies at the southern tip of North Harris, at the mouth of East Loch Tarbert. He informed the tacksman, Donald Campbell, that he was an Orcadian who had been shipwrecked further south and that these men were helping him to make his way back home; that he was supposed to be an Orcadian was used to explain his poor grasp of Gaelic. Whilst on Scalpay Charles joined in the family's chores; he went fishing with the tacksman's son and even took part in the rescue of a cow that had sunk into a peat bog. At some point, however, no doubt once it was decided that Campbell could be trusted, he was told who the Orcadian really was.

Whilst on Scalpay, there was an attempt at capturing the Prince by the local minister. Rev Aulay MacAulay was the Presbyterian minister of Harris and like his brother, Rev John MacAulay of Uist, had been trying to find Charles whilst he was known to be hiding in the Western Isles. Rev Aulay arrived at Scalpay with a party of men ready to trap the Prince on what was a little island with few places to hide. He met Donald Campbell as he landed and informed him of his plan; Campbell responded by telling the minister that he would not break the Highland code of hospitality and that he was willing to die to protect the Prince. Rebuffed, Rev MacAulay returned to Harris, no doubt ready to inform the authorities and form a larger party. The Prince, however, made plans to leave as soon as possible.

Donald and Murdoch MacLeod made their way into the town of Stornoway, the capital of Lewis. They headed for the harbour, where they met a number of sailors and dealers and began negotiating with one for the hire of a vessel with which they proposed transporting quantities of meal from Lewis to the Orkney Islands; the sailor was Captain MacAulay, a Stornoway ship-owner, and a deal was struck.

MacLeod then sent word back to the island of Scalpay, where Prince Charles was still in hiding. He was to make his way north to Stornoway as quickly as possible, for the cargo of 'meal' was but a front and the true cargo was the Prince and the true destination was France.

From Scalpay Charles and his men set sail in a small boat across the Sound of Scalpay to the mountainous coast of Harris, from where they sailed up the long and narrow saltwater Loch Seaforth. This loch splits the island of Lewis to some extent and was an ideal way to travel north towards Stornoway. From Airidh a' Bhruaich, or Arivruaich, at the head of the loch, Charles and his party headed north over the wild moors and lochan-covered countryside that drains into the River Laxay; the landscape here is particularly barren and damp, the numerous lochs causing difficulties in finding a route. The men lost their way for a time, taking a most circuitous route before eventually finding the correct direction; the journey was made even worse in that it took place in the darkness of night and the rain and wind were driving into their faces.

Charles then made his way eastward, to the southern side of the natural bay known as Stornoway Harbour, arriving at Arnish, sodden, famished, exhausted and rather downhearted. At the side of Loch Arnish the Prince and his men sank down into the heather to take a rest.

Word reached Donald MacLeod of the Prince's arrival, but by this time the deal had been cancelled. Somehow word had escaped that the ship had been booked for the transportation of the Prince and Captain MacAulay refused to get involved.

Donald MacLeod tried to make arrangements with another ship-owner but no-one was willing to risk transporting the Prince. The Presbyterian ministers of the district were hot on Charles's tail. The rumour in Stornoway had Charles making his way north with an army of 500 men, desperate for provisions and ships and ready to burn the town to the ground. The town drummer was organised and he wandered the streets raising the alarm. A large group of men gathered ready to guard the town and set about holding a council of war to make plans for the expected attack.

Donald MacLeod heard of the meeting and, being particularly brave, decided to address it. He made his way into the centre of the crowd and demanded to speak to the men. The gathering was in an uproar, for they could not believe the audacity of this man. However, they eventually agreed that he could speak to them.

Donald decided that it would be best to tell the simple truth. He explained that the Prince was not ready to attack the town with an army, but that he was actually in hiding with just the services of two friends. MacLeod told them that Charles just wished to escape from Scotland and he requested that the folk of Stornoway should help.

The men gathered together and wondered what to do. They could quite easily capture MacLeod and force him to show them where Charles was in hiding and thus claim the £30,000 reward. A naval ship was just offshore, patrolling the islands in search of the Prince and it would be quite simple to get him onto it. Their chief, MacKenzie of Lewis, had warned them that they should support the government at all costs. However, after due consideration, the men of Stornoway decided that they would do nothing. They would neither capture nor help the Prince and simply asked that he would go away from Lewis.

Donald MacLeod made his way back to Arnish, where Charles was staying at the farmhouse of Mrs MacKenzie, widow of Colin Mackenzie of Kildun, who had fought at Sheriffmuir. On his arrival she slaughtered a cow and butchered it into smaller parts. She gave the Prince meal, sugar and brandy and helped him as he set sail on his boat once more.

From Arnish the small boat sailed down the east coast of the Western Isles and landed on the little island of Eilean Iubhard, at the mouth of Loch Sealg. From the heights of the island the men looked out over the Minch where they observed two men-of-war; it was not known whether they were English and thus the enemy, or else French and probably friendly. Charles tried to persuade some of the men to act as though they were fishermen and pull up alongside. If the ships were friendly, then they were to signal back to the island so that he could make his escape on them. However, the boats sailed off before this idea could be tried.

The men camped for the night on Eilean Iubhard, spending the time in a fishermen's hut, where they feasted on cod, ling and drank a brandy punch. The following morning they set sail again for the island of Scalpay. There they found their host, Donald Campbell, was absent, so they continued sailing south, dodging ships, until they landed at Loch Uisgebhagh on Benbecula.

A storm raged up once more and the men were forced inland to look for shelter; they came upon a shieling and stayed there for the following three nights. One of the party was sent to Clanranald's home once more to see if he was home and this time returned with him, as he wished to visit the Prince. He was laden with fine foodstuffs and the men were glad to feast on trout, biscuits, beer and wine. The following day Clanranald sent them new shirts, stockings, shoes and a silver cup.

On 16 May 1746 a servant of Clanranald came to the Prince and his men and told them that they would be safer living in a hut on a little island in Loch Skiport. He showed them the way there, crossing from Benbecula to South Uist and making their way onto the island. They spent the night in relative comfort, but the following day spotted a government ship offshore. Deciding that the remote location was too open to the sea, they determined to find a new hideout.

From Loch Skiport the men sailed south, around the headland of Rubha Sheallacro to the wild glens that drop down to the sea from the mountains of South Uist; one of the wildest of these glens was Gleann Coradail, which drops quickly down from the heights of Beinn Coradail to a rocky bay. The Prince spent the next three weeks there, in a shieling that was better than he had been accustomed to. Most of this time was spent hunting and fishing and he regarded this as one of the best times he experienced during his time as a fugitive. As well as the sheiling where he stayed, Charles also hid in a cave, known ever since as Uamh a' Phrionnsa, or 'the Prince's cave'.

From Coradail Charles sent letters to various folk, asking to be kept up to date with the state of play elsewhere in Scotland. One of his contacts was Alexander MacDonald of Boisdale, who lived nine miles to the south; they corresponded as 'Johnston' and 'Sinclair', the Prince adopting the latter name. Boisdale would not visit the Prince, more perhaps for his own safety – he had not come out in support before – than to protect Charles, claiming that if he was to head to his place of hiding it would attract the attentions of others.

Charles sent Donald MacLeod across the Minch to the mainland of Scotland, to find out what was happening. MacLeod took with him letters to Lochiel and Murray of Broughton, requesting money and brandy. Despite meeting Murray and Lochiel at the head of Loch Arkaig, they did not give Macleod any cash, even though they had some, and he also had to purchase brandy himself. It was 18 days before he returned to Coradail.

One of those who came to visit the Prince at Coradail was Hugh MacDonald of Baile Sear (Baleshare), who was made most welcome. He was able to tell the Prince what it was that the people of Great Britain objected to over his claim to the crown:

> I told him that Popery and arbitrary government were the two chiefest. He said it was only bad constructions his enemys pat on't. 'Do you know, Mr MacDonald,' he says, 'what religion are all the princes in Europe of?' I told him I imagin'd they were of the same established religion of the nation they liv'd in. He told me then that they had little or no religion at all. Boisdale then told him that his predecessor, Donald Clanranald, had fought seven sett battles for his, yet after the restauration, he was not ound by King Charles at Court. The Prince said,

'Boisdale, don't be rubbing up old sores, for if I cam home the case would be otherwise with me.' I then says to him, that notwithstanding of what freedome wee enjoy'd there with him, wee cou'd've no access to him if he was settled at London; and told us then if he had never so much ado, he'd be one night merry with his Highland friends. Wee continued this drinking for three days and three nights. He still had the better of us and even of Boisdale himself, notwithstanding his being as able a boulman [drinker], I dare say, as any in Scotland.

With word spreading that Charles was in hiding on South Uist, there was little time to spare. The island, though wild, extends to only 140 square miles, which would not be too difficult for the various independent companies of soldiers to search. Government ships were patrolling the coast around the island, so there was little chance of the prince escaping by sea.

When all was quiet, Charles left Coradail and sailed up the east coast of the island of South Uist and arrived on the island of Fuidhaigh, or Wiay, which lies off the south east corner of Benbecula. This island, which is just over 900 acres in extent, was never densely populated; indeed it was described as 'deserted' by O'Sullivan. Charles and his party remained here for four nights.

The group split up for a time, Charles and Felix O'Neil making their way north to Roisinis once more, where they met Lady Clanranald; Donald MacLeod and John O'Sullivan remained on Fuidhaigh. Charles spent two nights at Roisinis, but on the third word was given to him that it would be better for him to return south to a more remote hideout. A return to Fuidhaigh was difficult because of the government ships patrolling the coasts, but MacLeod and O'Sullivan managed to reach Charles during the hours of darkness and take him southwards by boat.

The party did not reach Coradail, as perhaps was planned, but landed two and a half miles short of it, at Uisinis. That day they spent hiding and resting in a narrow cave by the shore, near to where the lighthouse now stands. By now it was 13 June.

At nightfall the party once more set sail and headed further south. They passed the mouth of Loch Aineort and headed for the island of

Stulaigh. They had spotted 15 boats on the journey and realised that the net was closing in on them. The party took their small boat into Caolas Stulaigh where they rested for a time, before making the last dash south into Loch Boisdale, reaching it on 15 June.

The news at Lochboisdale was grim. The redcoats patrolling the area had arrested MacDonald of Lochboisdale, who had never openly come out in favour of the Jacobites. MacDonald had tried to persuade Charles to return to France when he had landed at Eriskay, but in recent weeks had been active in assisting him. Boisdale had been taken on board HMS *Baltimore*, where he was held for questioning.

Despite Boisdale's absence, Charles remained in the vicinity for five days; Lady MacDonald of Boisdale was still at home and she knew of Charles's whereabouts, sending brandy and other goods to his hideout.

Whilst hiding at Boisdale, a ship sailed into the vicinity and landed 700 men. Caroline Scott captained the *Baltimore*, a man noted for his harsh treatment of Jacobite supporters. It was thought that the men knew where Charles was hiding and a messenger was sent in haste from Boisdale's house to the hideout. Arriving there, the messenger told Charles that the men were searching Boisdale's house for arms and Spanish money that was said to be kept there. The party were ready to leave as quickly as possible, at first proposing leaving all their food behind, but Charles would have none of it.

'A Gad, they shall never say that we were so pressed, that we abandoned our meat,' he said. Charles then gathered together some of the food himself, before they all headed for their boat.

The party sailed up Loch Boisdale, heading further inland. On arriving at the head of the loch, it was decided that the party would need to split up in order to avoid being captured. Accordingly, all the men apart from Felix O'Neil and Neil MacEachain were paid off by Charles, who gave the boatmen a shilling per day plus maintenance. As they parted they resolved that they would meet once more at a specific place some time in the future.

From the head of Loch Boisdale, Charles and O'Neil, with MacEachain as guide, made their way over the hills towards Ormacleit, a township on the west coast of South Uist. It was there that Prince Charles came into contact with Flora MacDonald.

CHAPTER THIRTY-FOUR
Battle of
Loch nan Uamh

The last battle of the '45 rebellion took place at sea. Prince Charles was still in hiding in the Western Isles and a variety of French ships came and went, each with the intention of rescuing the Prince. On 3 May 1746 two French privateers from the port of Nantes were sailing in the Sound of Arisaig. The Minch and other waters on the west coast of Scotland were dotted with numerous Royal Navy vessels, each one searching for the fugitive Prince.

The *Mars* and *Bellone* had appeared off the coast of Arisaig early in May. On board was a supply of money, which was intended for the Jacobite cause, as well as arms and brandy; the money totalled 35,000 gold Louis-d'or, which the French king, Louis XV, intended to pay the Jacobite soldiers with. The money was successfully landed and transferred from Arisaig to Lochiel's country, where it was hidden near to Loch Arkaig.

A few days after the two French ships had landed their cargoes, they came into sight of three vessels from the Royal Navy; these were the *Baltimore, Greyhound* and *Terror*. The largest naval vessel was commanded by Captain, later Lord, Howe.

The two French ships were large and difficult to manoeuvre, whereas the navy ships were smaller and armed to the teeth. The three navy vessels came towards the French ships, which failed to respond in a friendly manner to their demands. A number of cannon were fired from both sides, the larger French guns being more successful. The battle continued for around 12 hours and to start with the larger of the two French vessels was crippled so much that its sister ship had to fire twice as hard. The Royal Navy tried to force a boarding of this second French ship a number of times, but on each occasion was forced back. It was only after Howe's ammunition ran out that the British ships withdrew and the French privateers managed to make their way out into the open sea.

A considerable number of men from both sides were killed. The laird of Borrodale, John MacDonald, noted in his diary that after the battle he found 15 dead Frenchmen washed up on the shores of his estate. He noted that there were no English navy men washed ashore, for the ships kept their dead and did not throw them overboard until they had rounded the Point of Ardnamurchan. It is reckoned that around the same number of Englishmen were killed as Frenchmen, although the figure was never released.

The money that was hidden became known in history as the 'Loch Arkaig Treasure'. What happened to the cash is not wholly known and some believe that there is a considerable sum still hidden somewhere along the shores of the loch.

What is certain, however, is that John Murray of Broughton misappropriated some of the money. Cluny MacPherson held most of the capital; he is known to have given much of what he had away, in order that those who had suffered after Culloden, either from having their homes burned to the ground or their cattle stolen, could purchase new belongings.

CHAPTER THIRTY-FIVE
Flora MacDonald

The famous Jacobite heroine, Flora MacDonald (1722-90), was born at a cottage that survives in ruins at Mingearraidh, on South Uist. Her father was Ranald MacDonald of Milton and her mother was Marion MacDonald, daughter of Rev Angus MacDonald, minister on South Uist. Flora's father died in 1723 and her mother had remarried, to another of the same clan, Hugh MacDonald of Armadale in Skye. Hugh was actually a captain in MacDonald of Sleat's company that had been active in South Uist searching for the Prince; this may have been a fortunate link, for word was always sent to the MacDonald household of the captain's movements, which could then be passed on to the Prince.

The first person to meet Flora on 18 June was Felix O'Neil and he inquired of her whether the independent companies were due to pass by that day. Flora replied that they were not and that they were not due until the following day. Finding this out, O'Neil told her that he had brought a friend to meet her.

'Is it the Prince?' she asked, her eyes expectant with excitement. O'Neil told her that it was and the three fugitives went into her cottage.

Trying to come up with a means to get the Prince away from the hotbed that was currently South Uist and the Western Isles was difficult; the group eventually came up with a plan. Flora's mother was living by now on Skye and it was thought that it might be possible for a small party to cross the Minch to visit her. At this time passes from the military were required for travel in the isles, introduced as a means of tracking down the Prince; as Flora's step-father was a Captain, it was thought that she might easily procure one.

At first Flora was unwilling to risk the escapade, but eventually she was persuaded to take part. To start with she headed north, planning to visit Lady Clanranald at her home at Nunton, whom she was to inform of the plan. The journey was also important in that she needed somehow to acquire a pass.

As Flora and Neil MacEachain were crossing a ford a group of soldiers came upon them and asked where they were going. On further inquiry it was discovered that they did not have a pass and so the militia arrested them. Flora asked to which company they belonged and on finding out that it was her stepfather's, she refused to answer any more questions until she could speak with him.

The soldiers held Flora overnight, until her stepfather could come on the following day, Sunday, 29 June. On hearing from his daughter, he issued her with the relevant pass, which covered her, her man-servant (Neil MacEachain) and her maid, Betty Burke. On the pass Betty Burke was described as a good spinner and Captain MacDonald added to the cover by writing a letter to his wife, recommending Miss Burke as being ideal to spin the large amount of lint she had:

> My dear Marion,
>
>   I have sent your daughter from this country, lest she should be any way frightened with the troops lying here. She has got one Betty Burke, an Irish girl, who, as she tells me, is a good spinster. If her spinning pleases you, you may keep her till she spins all her lint; or, if you have any wool to spin, you may employ her. I have sent Neil MacEachain along with your daughter and Betty Burke to take care of them.
>
> I am your dutiful husband,
> Hugh MacDonald.

On being freed, Flora made her way to Lady Clanranald where she was able to inform her of the proposals.

Whilst Flora was away on Benbecula, plans were made to get the Prince into a suitable location for the journey. All the fords on the island were obviously guarded and crossing the landmass was too risky. It was decided to find a boat and make their way by sea. Neil MacEachain found a few friends at Loch Sgiopoirt (Loch Skiport) and persuaded them to ferry the party towards Roisinis; the small party made their way along the east coast of South Uist, crossing the mouth of Bagh nam Faoilean, before landing on Fuidhaigh. From there the boatmen ferried Charles across the water and landed him on a remote corner of Benbecula. Totally exhausted, Charles lay down in the heather and fell asleep.

Flora and Lady Clanranald planned crossing the island of Benbecula from the western side, where Nunton stands, to the peninsula of Roisinis, where they were to meet up with Charles. As the Prince and his two companions neared the bothy where they had stayed before, MacEachain went ahead to check that it was safe to enter. He was surprised to find the building occupied by its tenants and even more shocked to hear their news; the militia had searched the building within the last few days and indeed were still encamped nearby. Keeping calm, he managed to return to Charles with the news.

A second bothy was located nearby and here the small party rested, all the time watching just in case the militia came to search the place. The soldiers were active in the area and word was sent to Charles that it was unsafe to stay there, for the militia were in the habit of visiting that bothy to get milk. Charles therefore had to leave the protection of the building and find a little shelter behind a rock near to the shore. The weather was deplorable and there was little protection from the elements, so it was resolved to move once more.

The Prince and MacEachain headed west, walking the three miles or so towards the highest point on Benbecula, the solitary hill of Ruabhal. There the pair could survey the whole island and were able to watch for any sign of Flora and Felix O'Neil, who had gone to see what was keeping her.

Next morning things began to move. Flora, Lady Clanranald, Flora's brother and sister-in-law and Lady Clanranald's seven-year-old daughter sailed from Nunton along the north side of Benbecula and through the straits to Roisinis. Charles walked back from Ruabhal to the headland and the whole party met up in the bothy. A hearty meal of roast lamb was had, as plans and tales were related.

Suddenly the door banged open and a shepherd lad who worked for Clanranald entered with pressing news. General John Campbell of Mamore (later 4th Duke of Argyll) had landed at Nunton with 1,500 troops. The group lifted all their food and belongings and sailed southwards over Loch Uisgebhagh to the southern side. Landing there, they found a bothy and finished their meal.

Captain Fergusson, of HMS *Furnace*, had entered Nunton where he carried out a search and then spent the night sleeping in Lady Clanranald's bed. A second group under Captain Scott were also on the island and estimates now put their total strength at nearer 2,000 men. There was little time left; the Prince had to move.

Lady Clanranald hurried back to Nunton, where she met the soldiers. They inquired of her where she had been, to which she replied that she had been visiting a sick child. Further questions followed and the Lady managed to supply reasonably convincing answers. The soldiers eventually left, but within a few days returned, arresting her and her husband.

The soldiers similarly captured Felix O'Neil. He had skulked around Benbecula for a couple of days, but was caught by the soldiers and arrested. His answers to the questions put to him were dubious, so he was sent to Edinburgh Castle where he was held. As he was a foreign officer he was treated comparatively well and was allowed visitors.

Flora MacDonald now supplied Charles with a set of women's clothes that she and Lady Clanranald had put together. He wore a dress of calico, white in colour with a blue floral pattern; he had on a quilted petticoat, a mantle of camlet and a cap that covered most of his head and face; his legs were covered with stockings and he wore a pair of women's brogues. Charles wanted to hide a couple of guns on his person, but Flora refused to let him, 'For if you are searched, then they would give the game away.' At length she assented to him hiding a cudgel beneath his dress, just in case someone attacked him.

It was still too early to attempt a crossing of the Minch, so the three found shelter by the Lochside where they built a fire. As they were waiting for nightfall, four boats filled with soldiers sailed past. The three ran away from their fire and hid, but fortunately the soldiers did not land.

When it was dark enough, the Prince and his supporters set sail. The boat was nine cubits in size, complete with a mast, sail and oars. A few boatmen had been hired to row the vessel and Charles was noted for his high spirits as they crossed over the waters in relatively calm conditions.

As the night wore on the wind got up and the rain came in from the west. The boatmen began to argue over which direction to head and basically followed the wind eastwards. At first light they were able to make out the island of Skye.

The point reached on Skye turned out to be the headland of Waternish, at the mouth of Loch Dunvegan. Dunvegan Castle was the seat of the MacLeods, who were supportive of the government, indeed, the chief had previously written to Duncan Forbes of Culloden:

My dearest Lord,

To my no small surprise, it is certain that the pretended Prince of Wales is come into the coast of South Uist and Barra and has since been hovering on parts of the coast of the Mainland; that is, between the point of Ardnamurchan and Glenelg. He has but one ship of which he is aboard; she mounts about 16 or 18 guns. He has about thirty Irish or French officers with him and one Sheridan, who is called his governor. The Duke of Athole's brother is the only man of any sort of note (that once belonged to this country) that I can hear of that is along with him. His view, I need not tell you, was to raise the Highlands to assist him, etc. Sir Alex. Macdonald and I not only gave no sort of countenance to these people but we used all the interest we had with our neighbours to follow the same prudent method; and I am persuaded we have done it with such success that not one man of any consequence north of the Grampians will give any sort of assistance to this mad rebellious attempt. How far you think we acted properly, I shall long to know, but this is certain, we did it as our duty and for the best, for in the present situation of affairs in Europe, I should have been sorry to see anything like disaffection to the Government appear, though ever so trivial; or that there was occasion to march a single company to quell it, which now I hope and dare say there is not.

As it can be of no use to the public to know whence you have this information it is, I fancy needless to mention either of us, but this we leave in your own breast, as you are a much better judge of what is or is not proper to be done. I have written to no one else; and as our friendship and confidence in you is without reserve, so we doubt not of your supplying our defects properly. Sir Alex is here and has seen this scrawl – I ever am, most faithfully yours,

Norman MacLeod
Dunvegan 3rd August 1745

As they neared the shore, soldiers on the land, who fired one or two shots from their guns, spotted them. The Prince and his men did not land there, but sailed along the coast, until they found a narrow inlet where they could come ashore. Eating a meal of bread and butter, they rested for a while before setting out to sea once more.

From Waternish, the boat sailed around Waternish Point and across the mouth of Loch Snizort before landing once more on Trotternish, the northernmost wing of the island of Skye. The boat was pulled up onto the stony shore at Port Kilbride, at a place ever after known as Prince Charles's Point. Just over the hill above, but hidden from the bay, stood Monkstadt, seat of Sir Alexander MacDonald of Sleat.

Sleat was a Hanoverian and was away at the time, searching for the man who was now standing in his home. His wife, Lady Margaret MacDonald, was a devout Jacobite and was an admirer of the Prince. At Monkstadt there were a few soldiers visiting and it was required to send 'Betty Burke' away to another part of the house. Flora MacDonald kept the soldiers busy in conversation, whilst Lady MacDonald spoke with a neighbour and fellow Jacobite, Alexander MacDonald of Kingsburgh about what to do with the Prince.

It was determined that the Prince would be better off hiding on the smaller island of Raasay, which lies to the east of Skye. Its owner, Malcolm MacLeod of Raasay, was a devoted Jacobite and there were plenty of places to conceal the fugitive in the remote island. From Monkstadt MacDonald of Kingsburgh accompanied the Prince south the nine miles or so to Kingsburgh. En route they passed a well, where the Prince slaked his thirst, thereafter known as Prince Charles's Well. As they were making their way south, Flora, who had managed to leave Monkstadt, eventually caught up with them.

It was around half past ten at night, on Sunday 29 June, that Prince Charles, still dressed as Betty, arrived at Kingsburgh with a small party. Mrs MacDonald was not expecting her husband home and was getting ready for bed when they arrived, so she told the maid to see to them. However, MacDonald's daughter was unsure of the strange woman in the company and Mrs MacDonald's nose began to get the better of her.

'Who is this strange carlin?' she asked her husband. He replied that she would find out in good time and that she should make them some supper. She kept on at her husband, who eventually admitted to her that it was 'The Prince – you have the honour to have him in your house.'

'O, Lord. We'll all be ruined now and undone forever! We'll all be hanged next,' she responded.

Kingsburgh replied, 'Hoots, guidwife, we will die but ance and if we are hanged for this, I am sure we die in a guid cause.'

After a simple supper the family went to sleep. The following morning Charles abandoned his disguise and dressed up as a Highlander as he made his way from Kingsburgh. Not long after they had gone, Captain John Fergusson arrived and arrested Kingsburgh and his daughter.

The Prince and a few followers crossed over the hills of Skye to Portree, on the east side of the island. There, in MacNab's Inn (now the Royal Hotel), Flora was left behind and the Prince boarded a small vessel that was to take him to Raasay. On the rocky foreshore at the base of the steep cliffs of Creag Ulatota, four miles north of Portree, the map indicates 'Prince Charles's Cave'; it is doubtful whether he actually spent some time here, but if he did, then it was most likely at this point, prior to sailing for Raasay, or else when he sailed back again.

Flora was never to see Charles again, despite him promising that they would meet again in St James's. As she was returning to her home she was arrested by Fergusson and placed on board his ship, HMS *Furnace*. From there she was transported to the Tower of London, where she remained until 1747, when the Act of Indemnity resulted in her release. She afterwards married and lived in North Carolina for five years, before returning to Skye. She died in 1790 and was buried at Kilmuir, not too far from the spot where Charles landed on the island.

CHAPTER THIRTY-SIX
In a Cold Country

From Portree harbour to the west shore of Raasay was a distance of just under four miles, assuming the party sailed in a direct line. The route would more likely be a circuitous one, for the men set forth in the early hours of Tuesday 1 July; with the Prince were John and Murdoch MacLeod, sons of the laird of Raasay, Captain Malcolm MacLeod, Raasay's second cousin and two boatmen, Donald MacFriar and John MacKenzie. In the boat they had a bottle of whisky, a bottle of brandy and a cold roast chicken to keep them going. The sail was completed the same day and the boat was hauled up on the shore at the foot of the Glam Burn.

On Raasay the Prince discovered a devastated island. Murdoch MacLeod had been at Culloden and survived, though he was badly wounded. The rest of the family were noted Jacobites and the government forces were taking revenge. As Charles wandered around the island he was horrified to discover that the soldiers had burned most of the houses, leaving the residents homeless and trying to build new homes. Charles was appalled at the sight; he could not believe that the soldiers would carry out such atrocities and it made him wonder whether the same story was repeated elsewhere across the Highlands.

Charles spent two days on Raasay, but he soon discovered that although the residents were friendly towards him and would not give him up, the island's geography was not conducive to hiding. Raasay is a long thin island, 12 miles from south to north but only two or three miles or so from east to west and narrowing to the north; should soldiers flood the island, a sweep search would almost certainly uncover the Prince.

It was decided that the Prince should return to Skye; accordingly plans were made to ferry him back across the Sound of Raasay on the evening of 2 July. Soon after they had left the shores of Raasay, however, a very rough sea swelled up, tossing the boat from wave to wave. Most of the sailors wanted to return to Raasay, fearing for their lives as the waves crashed over the sides. Captain MacLeod spent most of his time trying to bail out the vessel and the oarsmen struggled to make any headway in the Sound. To try to divert their attentions from the conditions, Charles sang the sailors some jolly Highland songs.

By nine or ten o'clock in the evening the boat eventually reached the shores of Skye. They landed at a place known as Nicholson's Rock, near to Scorrybreac, just north of Portree; there the party rested in an old byre and ate some bread and cheese.

Charles wished to head south to Strathaird, on the southern side of Skye, land of the MacKinnons. Malcolm MacLeod agreed that he could go there, but tried to persuade the Prince that it would be safer to journey round the island by boat, rather than head across country. Charles would have none of it, probably being fed up of rough sea crossings by this time, and coaxed him round.

On the night of 3 July the party left Torvaig. Charles acted as Captain MacLeod's servant, named Lewie Caw, and walked a few yards behind. MacLeod noted at one point that Charles was troubled by something and on further investigation discovered that he was infested with lice; Charles worried little about it, claiming that he was only one man and the little he had to worry about was nothing compared with the troubles of the many brave lads who had suffered in his cause. Charles also reflected to MacLeod:

> When I was in Italy and dining at the king's table, very often
> the sweat would have been coming through my coat with
> the heat of the climate; and now that I am in a cold country,
> of a more piercing and trying climate and exposed to
> different kinds of fatigues, I really find I agree equally with

both. I have had this philibeg on now for some days and I find I do as well with it as any of the best breeches I ever put on. I hope in God, MacLeod, to walk the streets of London with it yet.

The route taken by the Prince is not known exactly, but there is a cave in the region of Loch Coruisg known as Prince Charles's Cave, which suggests a route up Glen Varragill towards Sligachan and thence through Glen Sligachan towards Loch Scavaig; from there a coastal trackway leads to Elgol, where Charles arrived at the home of Captain John 'Dubh' MacKinnon, chief of his clan.

MacKinnon, who was 71 years of age, was absent, but his wife welcomed them in. Captain MacKinnon arrived home later and Captain MacLeod revealed to them whom Lewie Caw really was. MacKinnon was so overcome by the sight of the Prince and of his poor health that he had to turn away and cry. Charles made himself at home, playing with the young MacKinnon lad, Neil, whom he hoped would grow up to serve in his forces.

MacKinnon had been a supporter of the Jacobite movement for years. He had come out in the '15 Rising, for which he had lost his estate. He had joined the Prince in Edinburgh, shortly after Prestonpans, complete with 120 men. From there he had marched to Derby, returned via Falkirk, but had missed Culloden, having been sent north of Inverness.

It was decided that it would be safer for Charles to return to the mainland. The Highlands was wilder and more extensive than the smaller western islands and it was thought that Charles would have more of a chance evading capture as he awaited a ship from France. MacLeod also reckoned that it would be better if he returned home in order to arouse less suspicion due to his absence, and so passed over the care of the Prince to MacKinnon.

Charles remembered that he had promised to meet Murdoch MacLeod at a certain place and time, to which his brother, Malcolm, responded, 'No matter, I shall make your apologies.' This was not enough for Charles and he wrote a short note to Murdoch:

Sir,

I thank God I am in good health and have got off as
design'd. Remember me to all friends and thank them for
the trouble they have been at.

I am, Sir, Your humble servant,

James Thomson,
Elliguil, July 4th 1746.

Prior to leaving Skye, Charles hid in another cave, located at the
southern end of Strathaird; situated near Port an Luig Mhor, it was from
near here that he set sail on the morning of 4 July. The party headed
south around the Point of Sleat, Skye's southernmost extremity, before
heading east towards Mallaig and the mainland.

CHAPTER THIRTY-SEVEN
Wanderings in Morar

Charles and his men sailed across the Sound of Sleat from Skye and landed on the southern shores of Loch Nevis, at Sron Raineach near to Mallaig Mhor, at around 4 o'clock in the morning. Mallaig at that time was a little crofting community, not the village we have today, and Charles and his followers were able to hide in the vicinity for three days. They then decided to sail further inland, up part of the great sea loch of Nevis. As they were sailing up the loch a party of soldiers on the mainland spotted them and ordered them to come ashore.

Naturally, Charles did not comply with the command. Although pursued by some soldiers in a rowing boat, the Jacobites managed to out-row them. Charles sailed north, crossing Loch Nevis and landed on the remote peninsula of Knoydart. There they ascended a hill near to the coast and gazed across the water to see where the soldiers were. The rowers had given up and were returning back to Morar. Charles and his men then felt it was safe enough to lie down and rest; they slept for three hours in the heather, before rising again.

Back at their boat, Charles and the four boatmen sailed back across Loch Nevis and landed near to Mallaig. From there they climbed over the hills of North Morar, crossed the ford at the west end of Loch Morar itself, before heading to Morar House, seat of Allan MacDonald. The journey was undertaken at nightfall and they arrived early in the morning.

During this journey a light-hearted incident took place at the ford of Morar, near to Rhubana. MacKinnon asked a local guide if he would not mind carrying the poor sick young fellow (referring to Charles) across the water, thereby keeping him dry. The ford was deep and the guide replied, 'The dei'l be on the back he comes, or any fellow of a servant like him. But I'll take you on my back, Sir, if you please and carry you safely through the ford.' MacKinnon turned the offer down, stating, 'If the lad must wade, I'll wade along with him and help him, lest any harm should happen to him.' The guide was never told of his refusal to assist the fugitive Prince.

On their arrival at Morar, Allan MacDonald was a sorry sight; Captain John Fergusson had been there before Charles and had set his building alight. Only the burnt-out shell remained and MacDonald and his wife were living in an outbuilding. MacDonald's wife, who was a daughter of Cameron of Lochiel, recognised Charles and burst into tears. She was later able to compose herself and feed the visitors on reheated salmon. MacDonald then took Charles to a cave where he hid for some time.

From here, Charles moved on to Borrodale, home of Angus MacDonald. Here too he found that Fergusson had burnt the house to the ground and Borrodale was sleeping in a hut. The Prince was directed to another cave, near to the shore at Borrodale, where he hid for three nights.

The two MacKinnons had done their duty and it was decided that they should now return to Skye. As old MacKinnon was making his way home he was captured by the militia on 11 July at Morar and held prisoner. He was taken to Inverness, then to Tilbury and then London, where he was held in the house of a Messenger of the Crown. He was released on 19 January 1749. The Lord Justice asked him, 'If the Prince was in your power, what would you do with him?' The MacKinnon replied, 'I would do as you have done to me this day: send him back to his own country.' His wife, Mary Anne, was also captured and taken south to London with her husband. On 25 May 1747 the Privy Council released her on bail, there being no evidence against her.

John MacKinnon landed near to Elgol, only to be captured by the soldiers and taken prisoner. He was held on board HMS *Furnace*, before being transferred to Tilbury; on board the ship he was examined by

General Campbell, who asked him why he had not given up the Prince for the reward. John MacKinnon replied, 'I would never have done it for the whole world.' At this the officers on board stood up and drank his health. MacKinnon was ordered to be transported abroad, but he was never sent. He became ill later and it was in hospital in Edinburgh in 1761 that he was able to furnish Robert Forbes with information for his *The Lyon in Mourning*, an account of Prince Charlie's wanderings. He died on 11 May 1762.

John MacInnes, who had rowed the Prince from Elgol to Morar, was captured and placed on board HMS *Furnace*. Captain Fergusson came to him to find out where the Prince was hiding, but MacInnes refused to reveal anything to him. Fergusson ordered that he should be stripped to the waist, whereupon he was whipped repeatedly with a cat o' nine tails until the blood poured from his body. Held for some months, MacInnes later turned King's Evidence against the chief of MacKinnon, after which he was released.

Charles moved from Borrodale on 16 July. He was directed to a remote cave on the hillside above the west end of Loch Beoraid, a remote spot in South Morar. Word had now reached him that General John Campbell had arrived in Loch Nevis with six ships and numerous troops, ready to search the countryside. It was too risky to remain in the area and it was resolved to move off. A couple of scouts were sent to Loch Nevis to watch the soldiers' movements, but before they were able to come back word reached Charles's party of Captain Caroline Scott's arrival near to Arisaig, from where he was starting a sweep search.

Charles, Major Alexander MacDonald of Glenaladale, his brother Lieutenant John MacDonald and Lieutenant John MacDonald (Borrodale's son), left the cave at Loch Beoraid as quickly as they could and headed across one of the wildest stretches of the West Highlands. They arranged to meet on the summit of Sgurr nan Coireachan, a major peak in the area that rises to 3127 feet above sea level.

The route taken from South Morar to the peak was not the most direct; instead they travelled east towards Glen Finnan, where they rested on Sgurr Bhuidhe before heading north, probably down Glen Pean and back up Glen Dessarry towards Sgurr nan Coireachan. This was now Lochiel's country. On Fraoch Bheinn, which rises steeply above the northern side of Loch Arkaig, the men were able to witness soldiers in the glen below. The route had to be changed and the party headed north.

Making their way across the mountains to the head of Loch Quoich, Charles discovered that the area was covered with soldiers camped in groups; each of these was no more than half a mile apart, deliberately established to try to prevent the Prince from leaving the Morar area. Soldiers between each camp were arranged within shouting distance of each other and patrols wandered along the line to ensure that the sentries remained awake. With a line extending south from Loch Hourn to Loch Eil and ships patrolling the seas around the promontory, the government reckoned that Charles had no chance of escaping and that it was only a matter of time before he was cornered.

Charles and his men had to hide during the day and as soon as darkness fell made a run for it between the camps, indicated at night by their camp-fires. On the ascent of Druim Chosaidh at the head of Loch Quoich, Charles wandered within hearing distance of one of the camps. He could hear the men talking to each other, but decided to risk a silent passage. However, once he was out of earshot of that camp, he discovered that there was another in Gleann Cosaidh.

They headed west along the ridge for a while, before dropping down into Glen Barrisdale. Walking through the camps was bad enough, but wandering at night was deadly in itself. At one point they were crossing a small burn that plummeted over a precipice; Donald Cameron was first to cross, Charles following; as the Prince straddled the burn he slipped and would have fallen over the cliff had he not been caught by MacDonald of Glenaladale on one side and Cameron on the other.

At Glen Shiel the party met a man who was running from the soldiers; his father had been killed and he, a Glengarry man, was making an escape. It was decided that he should be the new guide and that Donald Cameron could now return home.

Charles was heading north for Poolewe, where they had been told that there were some French ships offshore. Intelligence later reached them that there had in fact been only one ship and it was now sailing home. A new plan was devised and from Glen Shiel the men headed east, towards Loch Cluanie. From the west end of the loch they headed north, up into Coire a' Chait, where they rested in a cave or shelter.

CHAPTER THIRTY-EIGHT

The Seven Men of Glen Moriston

The atrocities inflicted on the Highlands after Culloden goaded seven men into action. They met in secret and decided that they would spend the coming months and years if necessary, in making the lives of the Hanoverian soldiers as difficult as possible; the men were Patrick Grant, tenant in Craskie, who was regarded as their leader, John MacDonald, also in Craskie, Alexander MacDonald, tacksman of Aonach, Alexander, Donald and Hugh Chisholm, sons of Paul Chisholm, in Bhlaraidh or Blairie and Grigor MacGregor, who did not belong to the glen. MacGregor is thought to have deserted Loudoun's regiment and joined the Jacobites in the Corrieyairack Pass.

The Seven Men met together in Coire Dho, a remote part of Glen Moriston where the tributary, River Doe, rises from the Ceannacroc Mountains. Many of the glen folk had fled there to avoid the Hanoverian forces as they plundered their way through the glen, burning homes and stealing cattle. Coire Dho became their headquarters and each man swore an oath that they would 'Never yield to the Hanoverians, but to die on the spot; never to give up their arms for all the days of their lives.'

From Coire Dho the Seven Men made forays down the glen, attacking the soldiers and those informants or guides who sided with them.

In July 1746 Archibald MacPherson, a native of Skye, was guiding a party of seven redcoats through the glens. They were making their way from the garrison at Fort Augustus towards the barracks at Glenelg and had with them two pack horses laden with wine, bread and other foodstuffs. Five of the Seven Men were in the vicinity and fired shots from behind large boulders; two of the soldiers were killed and the rest fled as fast as they were able.

Another killing took place a few days later when the Seven Men came upon Robert Grant, a native of Feith Rob in Strathspey. He was a known supporter of the government and had been suspected of supplying the soldiers with information as to the whereabouts of known Jacobites. The Glen Moriston men shot Grant, the bullet piercing his heart. They then drew their knives and cut off his head, which was affixed to a stick and displayed on a tree near to Bhlaraidh and acted as a warning to others who assisted the soldiers.

The Hanoverians were becoming reluctant to travel through Glen Moriston, but on one occasion had managed to steal some cattle and were in the process of herding them westward, no doubt to act as supplies for the barracks at Glenelg. The cattle had belonged to an uncle of Patrick Grant, so the men were keen to recapture them. The Seven Men made various attempts at finding the soldiers and eventually came across them in Kintail; after a short skirmish they managed to rescue the cattle and bring them back to Coire Dho.

The Seven Men became involved in the protection of Prince Charles, after he had to spend some time in the Highlands when the last ship to France had left. The Prince was in the company of Major MacDonald of Glenaladale, Lieutenant John MacDonald, his brother and Lieutenant John MacDonald of Borrodale and a few scouts. They spent an uncomfortable night on the slopes of Sgurr nan Conbhairean, their clothes soaking and with little more than salted butter and cheese to eat.

Two of the aides were sent down into Coire Dho to try to find the Seven Men. They found three of them and they asked if they would be willing to act as guides to a Jacobite who was being hunted down. The men readily agreed, but they thought that it was MacDonald of Glenaladale, not the Prince himself.

The meeting took place high up in Coire Sgreumh, but when the Glen Moriston men saw the figure, they recognised the Prince, despite his haggard appearance and damp and dirty clothing; in recognition of their leader, they took off their caps and bowed gently. On 29 July 1746 the Prince was taken to a cave or den, known as Uamh Ruaraidh na Seilg or Rory the Hunter's Cave. Food was brought to him and he feasted on mutton, cheese, whisky and bread. Having suffered virtual starvation for almost two days, the Prince was content with his meal and was able to sleep in the warmth of the hideout, the men standing on guard.

Glenaladale administered an oath of allegiance to the Prince, requesting that:

> Their backs should be to God and their faces to the Devil and that all the curses the Scriptures did pronounce might come upon them and all their posterity if they did not stand firm by the Prince in the greatest of dangers and if they did discover to any person – man, woman or child – that the Prince was in their keeping, till once this person should be out of danger.

Prince Charles and Glenaladale were willing to swear an oath themselves, in which they promised to stand by each other should danger come upon them, till the last drop of their blood should flow. The Glenmoriston men refused to accept this, telling the Prince that he should save himself in any way possible, leaving them to their fate.

The following day a live ox and a dead deer were brought up the glen by some of the Seven Men and one even brought bread and gingerbread from Fort Augustus. For three days the Prince was kept hidden in the corrie and he was so well fed and rested that he reckoned that he was now fit to encounter any hardships that he might face.

On 2 August the party moved to Rory's Cave in Coire Mheadhoin, the middle or centre corrie of Coire Dho; since that time this cave has become known as Prince Charlie's Cave. The group stayed here for a further four days and became firm friends. Prince Charles described the Seven Men as his Privy Council and allowed them to call him by the name, Dugald MacCullony, which means 'son of the servant of the Lord'. He also told them not to remove their bonnets in his presence, for he regarded himself as one of them.

Word reached the men that there were Hanoverian soldiers in the vicinity, under the command of Black Campbell of Kintail. These men were within four miles of the cave, so it was decided that they should move further north to Strath Glass, the home country of the Chisholms. For another three weeks the Seven Men and the Prince's close followers moved from place to place, always keeping in front of the soldiers searching the mountains for them. They stayed in a cave in Glen Cannich and in hideouts at Fasnakyle for some time.

On 21 August 1746 the Prince left the Seven Men behind, joining the guiding hands of Lochiel and Doctor Cameron; this took place at Achnasaul, on the north shore of Loch Arkaig. The Prince gave the men a reward, three guineas each. Alexander MacDonald of Aonach was presented with a powder horn, which was passed down in the family thereafter.

The Seven Men survived for some years, but not much is known of what happened to them: Alexander Chisholm died before 1751; Donald Chisholm remained at Bhlaraidh until 1769, when he emigrated to Glengarry in Canada; Hugh Chisholm moved to Edinburgh for a time, where he became acquainted with Sir Walter Scott, who assisted him when he fell on hard times. He later returned to Glen Moriston, before moving to Balnabruaich in Strath Glass, where he died; Alexander MacDonald seems to have died by 1751, whereas Grigor MacGregor was still alive; Patrick Grant joined the British Army in 1753 and served in North America. He retired in 1763 and became an Out-Pensioner of Chelsea Hospital; John MacDonald emigrated in 1775, when he was around 75 years old.

Roderick MacKenzie was one of the heroes of the '45. He had an uncanny likeness to the Prince, which was made good use of in sending the government troops on a wild goose chase, leaving the Prince to escape in an opposite direction. MacKenzie is thought to have been born at Fisherrow in Edinburgh, perhaps the son of Colin MacKenzie, a jeweller in the city; Colin is known to have had Jacobite sympathies. At any rate, Roderick joined the Prince's army and took part in many of his exploits, serving in the Royal Lifeguards.

In July 1746 Roderick was in Glen Moriston when a party of

troops were in the area. They had been very active in the glen and one writer noted, 'few districts, if any, in Scotland suffered more cruelly from the atrocities and the rapacities of the English Butcher and his demon gang than Glenmoriston.' MacKenzie was in a hiding place with Charles and some others when they became aware of the soldiers approaching. They were trapped.

Prince Charles was sleeping at the back of the hideout when the men awoke him. Once they had finished explaining their predicament, the Prince said, 'Then we must die like brave men, with our swords in our hands.' MacKenzie answered, 'No! We still have a few resources to hand. I will take your place and face up to some of the soldiers. I know what fate falls before me, but for as long as I can keep it up, you will have to make good your escape.' With that MacKenzie ran out of the hideout, brandishing his sword. He attacked the soldiers, striking his sword in all directions like a man possessed, making the most of his final minutes. As he did so, the Prince and the others slipped away into the hills.

The soldiers overcame MacKenzie and immediately mistook him for the Prince. MacKenzie was aware of their mistake, but he was willing to die for the Prince; he did not let on that the soldiers had been in error and refused to be taken alive. A shot was fired, the bullet hitting his body. Before he breathed his last, MacKenzie was able to shout out, 'You know not what you have done! Alas, you have slain your Prince!'

The soldiers were delighted at this and felt extremely pleased with themselves. They cut off MacKenzie's head and marched as fast as they were able to Fort Augustus, where it was presented to the captain of the garrison, perhaps even to Cumberland himself. Imprisoned at Fort Augustus at that time was MacDonald of Kingsburgh, to whom the soldiers took the head to have it identified. MacDonald was probably well aware that the head did not belong to the Prince, but he let the soldiers believe that it was and replied in the affirmative when they questioned him. The head was then placed in a box.

From Fort Augustus the head was taken south to London, where it was regarded as a great trophy; however, a formal identification was needed. Richard Morison, who had been a barber and valet to the Prince, was awaiting execution at Carlisle Castle and was considered the only man able to identify the head; however, by the time he had recovered from illness and was fit to travel to London to identify it, the head had shrivelled up and become unidentifiable. Morison had been promised his freedom if he would swear on oath that the head had belonged to Prince Charles.

However, word soon reached the authorities that the Prince was not dead and that the soldiers had killed MacKenzie by mistake. Nevertheless, MacKenzie's act had given the Prince a few extra days in which to make his escape and no doubt had saved his life.

The remaining part of MacKenzie's body was buried where it fell, by the side of the River Moriston, downstream from Ceanacroc Lodge. The nearby stream was renamed the Caochan a' Cheannaich, which translates as the 'merchant's burn'. A wooden cross was raised over the grave in 1873 and a cairn with a plaque was erected nearby. During digging work in the late 19th century a sword was found in the vicinity that was thought to have belonged to MacKenzie.

CHAPTER THIRTY-NINE
Cluny's Cage

When Charles arrived at Achnasaul there was no sign of the Camerons, who had fought with the Prince at Culloden. The rain was heavy and the weather was getting the spirits of Charles and his men down; finding the best shelter they could, they hung around soaked to the skin. They had nothing to eat and by the afternoon were beginning to despair of their condition. Eventually a messenger reached them with the news that the Camerons could not meet with them at that time and that they should move to a wood two miles away and hide for the night; this they had no option but to do. Nevertheless, they managed to kill a deer and feasted grandly.

On the following day the Prince met with the Cameron party. The news was not what Charles had been expecting; the Cameron seat, Achnacarry House, had been burned to the ground and the chief of the clan was hiding 20 miles away, a wanted man. Soldiers were searching for the Prince where Cameron of Lochiel was hiding, so Charles decided it was best to remain near to Achnacarry. He remained there for ten days, from 17 to 27 August, moving from hideout to hideout.

After some time, word reached Charles that he would be safe in the vicinity of Lochiel's hideout, which was over 20 miles to the south east. On 27 August they set off, the party comprising Charles, Doctor Archibald Cameron, Donald MacDonell of Lochgarry, John Cameron of Clunes, his son, Alexander, and three servants. The route, followed at night, went by way of the east side of Loch Lochy, over the Pass of Corrieyairack and then south to the west end of Loch Laggan. From there they made their way south to Ben Alder, where the Prince was to hide.

The following day Charles left from Ben Alder and travelled a few miles to a mountain known as Meall Mor, where Lochiel was hiding. The chief was still suffering from injuries received at Culloden, but he was overjoyed to meet Charles. Lochiel was about to kneel down before the Prince, but Charles stopped him in time, warning, 'Oh no! My dear Lochiel. You don't know who may be looking from the tops of yonder hills and if they see any such motions then they'll immediately conclude that I am here, which may prove of bad consequence.'

Although Lochiel's hideout was rough, Charles enjoyed the company and they feasted on mutton, ham, whisky, cheese and butter. Charles wolfed at the food, eating minced collops from a frying pan, and exclaiming, 'Now gentlemen, I live like a Prince,' even though the only hint that he was anything other than a shepherd on the hill was the fact that he ate with a silver spoon.

Prince Charles was in particularly good spirits. According to Donald MacPherson, younger brother of Cluny MacPherson:

> Upon his entry he took a hearty dram, which he pretty
> often called for thereafter to drink his friends' healths; and
> when there were some minch'd collops dress'd with butter
> for him in a large sawce pan that Locheil and Cluny carried
> always about with 'em, which was all the fire vessels they
> had, he eat heartily and said with a very cheerful and lively
> countenance, 'Now gentlemen, I leive like a Prince', tho' at
> the same time he was no otherwise served than by eating his
> collops out of the sawce pan, only that he had a silver spoon.

For two days the Prince stayed with Lochiel at his shieling, before Cluny MacPherson joined them. He took them further up the Allt a' Chaoil-reidhe to a remote bothy, located in the vicinity of Culra, where they spent a further two nights; this bothy was noted as being particularly smoky and rough and after a short while the party moved on again.

The next hideout was located on the southern slopes of a mountain named Sron Coire na h-Iolaire, overlooking Alder Bay where the Alder Burn runs into Loch Ericht; it was a man-made shelter, built within a wooded part of the steep mountain. This hideout was known as Cluny's Cage; it was quite a unique structure, having two floors and being big enough to conceal seven people. An account of the cage written around 1756 gives a precise description of it:

> [Cluny] observed a thicket of Hollywood; he went, viewed and found it fit for his purpose; he caused immediately wave the thicket round with boughs, made a first and second floor in it and covered it with moss to defend the rain. The upper room served for salle a manger and bed-chamber, while the lower served for a cave to contain liquors and other necessaries. At the back part was a proper hearth for cook and baiker and the face of the mountain had so much the colour and resemblance of smoke, no person cou'd ever discover that there was either fire or habitation in the place. Round this lodge were placed their sentinels at proper stations, some nearer and some at greater distances, who dayly brought them notice of what happened in the country and even in the enemie's camps, bringing them likewise the necessary provisions, while a neighbouring fountain supplied the society with the rural refreshment of pure rock water.

The Prince stayed in this hideout for six days, from 6 to 12 September; he was well looked after, with fresh supplies of meat and vegetables brought up to his fastness from Strathspey. During his time there, he sent MacPherson of Cluny and Doctor Cameron westward to Loch Arkaig, to find out what was happening. As the two men were heading thence, they came upon John MacPherson, known also as John MacCoilvain. He had been sent eastward by Cameron of Clunes to try to find the Prince, for he had important information for him.

MacCoilvain told Cluny and the Doctor that two French warships, *L'Heureux* and *Le Conti*, had arrived off the west coast and were at present anchored in Loch nan Uamh, a sea-loch south of Arisaig in Morar; the ships were ready to rescue Prince Charles and take him back to France. The two emissaries sent by the Prince were delighted at this news and returned to the cage as quickly as they were able. The time saved by MacCoilvain's message meant that the Prince was able to make his way towards the ships and finally escape from Scotland.

On the morning of 13 September Prince Charles, Lochiel, Allan Cameron and MacPherson of Breakachie left the cage behind and began their secret trek westward to Loch nan Uamh. They travelled north to the west end of Loch Laggan and then along the Braes of Roy towards the southern end of Loch Lochy. The weather had been bad and the party was held up at the Fords of Lochy, where the River Spean meets the River Lochy. The river was too high to cross and the men had to camp out for a time. Cameron of Clunes discovered their whereabouts and arrived with an old boat, as well as a bottle of brandy; fortified with the spirits, the party managed to cross the swollen waters and make their way towards Achnacarry.

The home of the Camerons stood as a gutted shell, but the Prince and his men kept their distance, hiding in the woods to the south. At nightfall, after a short rest, the party set off westward once more; the route taken was one of the roughest in the district, but the men were so close to the ships in Loch nan Uamh that they dared not lose the chance of escape. From the slopes above Achnacarry, the route taken went west, skirting around the low lying ground at Invermallie. The route then followed the quieter southern shores of Loch Arkaig, where only the lonely crofts of Giubhais and Geur-oirean existed. In Gleann Camgharaidh, at the croft of Dirlagich, Cluny and Doctor Cameron rejoined the Prince, the two having made a diversion to inspect the Loch Arkaig treasure.

Beyond Kinlocharkaig the route followed was up the lonely Gleann a' Chaorainn to the high pass between the mountains known as Streap and Sgurr Thuilm. From Corryhully the way was made westward over the pass to Gleann Donn and Loch Beoraid; at the west end of the Loch is Prince Charlie's Cave, where he had spent some nights in hiding previously. The route taken then went by way of Gleann Mama towards the sea, thus avoiding the more populated and consequently dangerous, route by the way of Loch Eilt and Lochailort.

On 19 September 1746 Prince Charles Edward Stewart embarked on *L'Heureux*, sailing to France the following day. He was never to set foot on Scottish soil again. He had been in hiding for a little more than five months since Culloden and it was a year and a month to the day that the standard had been raised in Glenfinnan.

CHAPTER FORTY
Cluny MacPherson

After Charles had gone, Cluny MacPherson remained in hiding. Ewen MacPherson of Cluny (c. 1698-1756), was the twelfth chief of a Highland clan that was centred on Cluny Castle in Badenoch. Originally a Hanoverian supporter, he had reported to General Cope at Ruthven on hearing of Charles's arrival. However, he was captured by the Jacobites in August 1745 and was set free on agreeing to swap allegiances. After that he was a notable Jacobite and led his men with distinction in the various battles. At Falkirk he fought with his men against the English dragoons, whose leather helmets contained steel reinforcement plates – MacPherson is said to have remarked, 'Devil take them, these dragoons are the hardest-headed men I've ever met. I've struck at their skulls till my arm's tired and I haven't been able to break more than a few of them.' The MacPhersons had missed Culloden due to Charles leaving them to guard the various passes in Badenoch. After Culloden Cluny went into hiding, for there was a price of £1,000 on his head.

The Hanoverian soldiers searched Badenoch for him, burning his house in June 1746. This had been a new building, erected only two or three years earlier. Not only did the soldiers burn Cluny's home, they also set fire to all buildings in the area that they reckoned belonged to him. Lady MacPherson, who was heavy with child at the time, had to flee the castle on the arrival of the soldiers. She found some shelter in a building that housed a corn kiln and there was to give birth to her son and heir, later nick-named 'Duncan of the Kiln'.

Cluny had to remain in hiding for the rest of his life. One of his favourite hideouts was a cavern on the cliff of Creag Dhubh, known as Uamh Chluanaidh, or Cluny's Cave; this subterranean vault is 26 feet deep and the low and narrow entrance is reached from a thin rock ledge that affords wide views of the lower reaches of Glen Truim and upper Strathspey. A second hideout was at Dalchully House, located three miles west of Cluny Castle; beneath the floor was a wood-lined chamber where the chief hid on many occasions. One day Hector Munro, with some of the 34th Regiment, arrived there and began a search of the house. Cluny was not in the hideout at the time, but disguised as a ghillie. He offered to hold Munro's horse whilst the search was undertaken and later told him, 'Even if I knew where the chief was, I would not betray him, not even for the 1000-guinea reward.' Munro replied, 'I believe you would not. You are a great man. Here is a shilling for you.'

Another hideout was a subterranean chamber, excavated near to Cluny. According to General Stewart, in his *Sketches of the Highlanders*:

> This cave was in the front of a woody precipice, the trees and shelving rocks completely sealing the entrance. It was dug out by his own people, who worked by night and conveyed the stones and rubbish into the lake in the neighbourhood, that no vestige of their labour might betray the retreat of their master. In this sanctuary he lived secure, occasionally visiting his friends by night, or when time slackened the rigour of the search. Upwards of a hundred persons knew where he was concealed and a reward of £1,000 was offered to any one who should give information against him; and as it was known that he was concealed on his own estate, eighty men were constantly stationed there, besides the parties continually marching into the country, to intimidate his tenantry and induce them to disclose the place of his concealment.

Cluny MacPherson was never caught. He received a letter from Prince

Charles in September 1754 requesting him to come to France. In it Charles desires him 'to come as soon as you can conveniently to Paris, bringing over with you all the effects whatsoever that I left in your hand when I was in Scotland, as also whatever money you can come at, for I happen to be at present in great straits, which makes me wish that you should delay as little as possible to meet me for that effect. You are to address yourself when arrived at Paris, to Mr John Waters, Banker, etc. He will direct you to where to find your sincere friend, C. P.'

MacPherson managed to make an escape there in 1755, his wife and children joining him in 1757. He died at Dunkirk in 1758 where he was interred.

CHAPTER FORTY-ONE
Lord Pitsligo

Prince Charles was not the only one who spent time in hiding after Culloden; many others disappeared from their homes and remained hidden for many months and even years. One of the more celebrated was the 4th Lord Forbes of Pitsligo, better known as Lord Pitsligo.

Alexander Forbes was born on 22 May 1678, the son of the 3rd Lord Forbes of Pitsligo and his wife, Sophia Erskine, daughter of the 9th Earl of Mar. The 3rd Lord died in December 1690 whereupon Alexander succeeded to the estate and title. After he came of age, he swore the oaths and took his seat in the Scottish Parliament on 21 May 1700. He was an opponent of the Act of Union and as such refused to take part in the Parliament of 1706-7.

Pitsligo married Rebecca Norton in 1703, but she predeceased him, dying in 1731. He married a second time, to Elizabeth Allen, who died in 1759. Pitsligo was a literary man and published a series of essays in 1734 entitled, *Thoughts concerning Man's condition and duties in this life and his hopes in the world to come.*

Being a cousin of the Earl of Mar, Pitsligo decided to support the Jacobites in 1715. After the failure of the rising, he fled to the Continent. For some unknown reason he was not named on any list of attainder issued at that time and thus escaped any form of persecution or imprisonment. When he became aware of this, he returned home and lived quietly for a number of years.

When the standard was raised in Glenfinnan, Lord Pitsligo came out in support. Despite his advancing years (he was now 67) he threw his wholehearted support behind the movement and it is said that he was instrumental in persuading many other Aberdeenshire landowners to join him. He gathered together a troop comprising between 100 and 200 men, made up of lairds and their servants. On 5 October 1745 he rode into Aberdeen and prepared the men for the ride south. Prior to leaving the city he lifted his hat and said, 'Oh Lord, Thou knowest our cause is just. Gentlemen, march!'

Making his way south, Pitsligo joined the Prince in Edinburgh on 9 October, just after the Battle of Prestonpans. Charles appointed him as commander of a troop of horse and a member of his war council; the cavalry regiment was known as Pitsligo's Horse. He took part in all the activities of the Jacobite army from then on, until finally fleeing from the Battle of Culloden. He was one of the most popular men in the Jacobite movement.

Pitsligo went into hiding and remained so for the rest of his life. His trials were tough and many times he found himself living in squalor. On one occasion it is noted that he was busily eating his simple meal of water-brose, or oatmeal soaked in hot water, when he remarked that it could do with a little salt. The man who had taken him in replied, 'Aye, man, but sa't's touchy', implying that it was too expensive for him.

Sometimes the hideouts were more salubrious and it is known that at one time he lodged with William King at New Miln house, near Elgin, along with other Jacobite fugitives, including Alexander Irvine of Drum (1711-61), Cummine of Pitullie and Mercer of Aberdeen.

Alexander Irvine escaped after Culloden and spent most of his time in hiding; much of this was in a secret room at Drum Castle in Aberdeenshire. On one occasion the soldiers arrived to search for him and it was only the quick-witted actions of his sister in mis-directing the soldiers that saved him. He later moved to Paris but was eventually allowed to return to Scotland, where he lived out his final years. The gardener at Drum Castle had also fought for the Jacobites. He too survived, but being an unknown was not persecuted the same. It is reputed that he made a fortune from selling 'horse nails' and other goods gathered up on the field of Culloden.

In April 1746 Lord Pitsligo was in hiding along the Buchan coast.

The soldiers were searching the area for him, thinking that he was hoping to catch a boat that would take him to France. At this time he concealed himself in a tiny hideout that was located under the arch of the bridge at Craigmaud; this tiny hole was just large enough to let him in and when he thought it was safe to do so he lay out on the moors at Craigmaud. However, the latter hideout could be troublesome as the lapwings were wont to circle overhead, indicating that there was someone there.

On the shore at Aberdour Bay is Lord Pitsligo's Cave, a large cavern in the sandstone rocks where the noble Jacobite often hid. It is said that the soldiers searched this cavern at one time and Pitsligo, disguised as a tramp, assisted by holding a lantern for them.

Pitsligo's wife remained at Pitsligo Castle all the time her husband was in hiding. On a few occasions he dared to venture there, disguised as a beggar; Lady Pitsligo would instruct her maid to give the beggar food and clothing.

The close escapes experienced by Pitsligo were legion. One day he was in the company of a cobbler when the soldiers arrived. The shoemaker had dressed Pitsligo with an apron and had given him some tools, but he was frightened that the soldiers would notice that he was useless with them. Thinking quickly, he ordered him to go out of the house and hold the soldiers' horses whilst they searched the house.

One of Lord Pitsligo's narrowest escapes took place when he visited a local farmhouse. Staying there at that time was a simpleton named Sandy Annand, a well-known character in Buchan. Annand immediately recognised Pitsligo and ran forward to him, greeting him and commenting on his troubles when a party of soldiers entered the house to search for him. They asked Annand whom he was lamenting. The rest of the household waited in terror to hear what Annand would say, for he was bound to give the game away. Sandy Annand was more shrewd than he was given credit for and said, 'I kent him aince, a muckle farmer, but his sheep a' dee'd in the 40.'

For his part in the '45, Lord Pitsligo was listed in an act of attainder, in which his title was removed. The attainder was erroneous in that it listed him as 'Lord Pitsligo', as opposed to 'Lord Forbes of Pitsligo'; using this as a means of appeal, he was successful in having the attainder reversed by the Court of Session on 16 November 1749. However, the government took the case to the House of Lords who reversed the decision again on 1 February 1750.

Pitsligo died at the House of Auchiries, in Aberdeenshire, on 21 December 1762, aged 85, and was buried in the family vault at Pitsligo Church. Auchiries was the home of his only son, John, Master of Pitsligo, who had married Rebecca Ogilvy, daughter of Ogilvy of Auchiries; the Master of Pitsligo died in 1781, but had never been able to reclaim the title.

It is claimed that Sir Walter Scott based his 'Baron of Bradwardine' on Lord Pitsligo.

CHAPTER FORTY-TWO
The Jacobites Captured

The hunt for Jacobites continued long after Prince Charles was safely across the water in France. One of those captured was Donald MacLeod of Galtrigal in Skye, who had been instrumental in looking after the Prince in the western islands and on Skye. He was captured by the Hanoverian troops and had to endure eight months imprisonment on one of the government's prison ships. He was kept below decks in total darkness, without the use of a candle or lamp and had to sleep on the ship's ballast. For his exercise he was allowed to walk around a pen in which were kept a number of sheep – the fresh mutton for eating.

At one point General Campbell asked MacLeod why he had not betrayed the Prince, for if he had he could have been £30,000 richer. To this he replied, 'Thirty thousand pounds! Though I had got it, I could not have enjoyed it eight and forty hours. This conscience of mine would have got up upon me and that money would not have kept it down. Though I had got all England and Scotland for my pains, I would not allow a hair of his body to be touched, if I could help it.'

Donald MacLeod was eventually released on 10 July 1747 and he lived on Skye until his death on 8 September 1749.

Lord George Murray went into hiding and spent some of this time concealed in the attic of a farmhouse near Glendoick in Kinfauns parish, Perthshire; his presence was unknown to even the nearest neighbours. However, one night he heard the sound of footsteps coming up the stairs and the words spoken by an unknown voice, 'Is Lord

George Murray here?' He dared not wait to see if the visitor was a friend or foe and so jumped up, grabbed his sword and barged down the stairway, shouting, 'I'll let you see Lord George Murray!' He rushed out of the house and disappeared into the night. No sign of him was made in the locality thereafter and it was believed that he had been drowned in the Qua Loch. However, Lord George had been successful in making his escape across the water to France.

The Murrays of Stanhope in Peeblesshire were ardent Jacobites throughout history. Sir David, 2nd Baronet, was active in the '15 Rebellion. His grandson, also Sir David, was a captain of horse in Charles's army in 1745. He was taken prisoner and held at York, where he was sentenced to death. This sentence was later commuted to banishment and he was sent abroad. His estates were forfeited and the title eventually passed to his uncle, John Murray of Broughton, in 1770.

Another John Murray, born in 1715, was one of the most important figures in the final Jacobite Rising. He had been active on the Stuart side since 1738, being the Scottish correspondent with the Jacobite court in Rome. When Prince Charles landed on these shores, John Murray soon joined him. Murray's wife, Margaret, was in Edinburgh in September 1745, sitting on her horse with a white cockade in her hat, recruiting men for the cause. Murray was to become Prince Charles's secretary and was by his side most of the time up to Culloden.

After the battle had been lost, Murray had to flee and look after himself. He set off back south, towards his home country in the Southern Uplands. He disguised himself as a drover and dodged the Hanoverian soldiers the long distance home.

Murray arrived at his Aunt Margaret's home at Kilbucho in Peeblesshire, where the elderly lady recognised him straight away. He was taken into the house and treated as an honoured guest, much to the surprise of the servants. They could not understand why she allowed the 'drover' to sit at her table and indulge in her best claret.

The strangeness of the situation probably led the servants to gossip and word reached the authorities that someone strange was in the vicinity. As Murray was a wanted man, it was no doubt suspected that he was there. He left his aunt's home the following day and made his way further up Tweeddale to Polmood, home of his sister Veronica and her husband, Robert Hunter. The soldiers caught up with him there and he was arrested.

To Murray's eternal shame, he turned King's evidence and it was he who was responsible for sending many Jacobites to the scaffold; one of the most important of these was Lord Lovat, who had given himself up at the age of 80 plus.

One of those who were tried was Sir James Douglas of Kelhead. In the dock he was asked if he knew the witness, referring to Murray. 'Not I,' he responded. 'I once knew a person who bore the designation of Murray of Broughton – but he was a gentleman and a man of honour and one that could hold up his head.'

Murray was treated with disgust for the rest of his life. He had sold his soul to gain his own life and it is said that his wife never forgave him for it. She left him and settled in Holland, where she died.

Murray later wrote the *Memorials of John Murray of Broughton*, detailing his activities between 1740 and 1747, trying to vindicate himself. He went mad and died in 1777.

A lady named Jenny Cameron, who had a milliner's business in Edinburgh, was arrested in error early in 1746, it being thought that she was the Jenny Cameron who rode with the Cameron's at the raising of the standard in Glen Finnan. She was held prisoner in Edinburgh Castle until November, but was eventually released. Thereafter, she used the error that associated her with the Prince for advertising purposes, promoting her shop and neither denying nor confirming any connection she had with Charles.

CHAPTER FORTY-THREE
The Appin Murder

The estates belonging to most of the clan chiefs who had taken part in the rising were taken from their possession and in numerous cases sold off. In other situations the Commission for Forfeited Estates took the lands in hand, running them on behalf of the government. In many places the tenants were against this, for they were supportive of their chiefs and saw the introduction of English landlords as an imposition on their traditional way of life.

One of the areas where the Commission was appointed to run three estates was in Argyllshire; Ardsheal in Appin, Callart and Mamore estates were taken from their owners and put under the control of a new factor, Colin Campbell of Glenure in 1749. Campbell was, like the Duke of Argyll, chief of his clan, a devoted Hanoverian, and was regarded as ideal for the job. The locals thought otherwise, for the Stewarts of Appin had been suspicious of the Campbells for years, thinking that they were trying to take over their lands.

Colin Campbell was given a difficult task at his appointment. He was expected to gather in the rents for the previous three years, ever since the estates had been forfeited. The tenants, however, had in fact paid their dues to the original owners, even although they were in exile. On some occasions his attempts at gathering rents were met with resistance and he often had to send reports of verbal assault and threats to his superior.

Although hated locally, Campbell managed to carry out his duties for three years. However, in 1752, he was responsible for forcing a tenant off of his lands for non-payment of his rent; the farm was then offered for let at a roup and the highest bid came from John Cameron of Fassfern, brother of Lochiel. This was the final straw, for Cameron was none other than Campbell's cousin, his mother being a Cameron. This had resulted in much of Ardsheal estate falling into Campbell hands – his cousins were given Glenduror and Auchindarroch, his nephew Ardsheal and he himself held Lagnaha.

The tenants who were being thrown out appealed to the courts to have the evictions overturned, but Campbell's defence was that he was only carrying out the government's orders, for 'these persons had been all Engaged in the Rebellion, one of them being Ardsheall's own Brother.'

The evictions were scheduled to take place on 15 May 1752. James Stewart, acting on behalf of the tenants, had appealed incessantly to have the plans quashed, but with no success. He advised the tenants to stay put as long as possible, hoping that the local Barons of the Exchequer would decide in their favour. Some, however, wished a more direct form of action to take place.

As Colin Campbell was riding through the woods of Lettermore, south of Ballachulish, returning from Fort William with his nephew, two gunshots echoed through the trees. The nephew, Mungo Campbell, turned round and saw his uncle tumble from his horse, two bullet holes in his back. Diving down to protect himself, he made his way to the body lying on the ground. Still alive, Campbell told his nephew, 'Oh! I am dead. Mungo take care of yourself. The villain's going to shoot you.' After a few more breaths Campbell died.

No more shots were fired however, for the murderer made his way deeper into the wood.

The murder caused a sensation in the district and its effect was felt throughout the rest of the country. The authorities were incensed at the death of one of their own and regarded the attack as a possible indication that the Jacobites were willing to rise once more. A reward of £100 was offered for the capture of the murderer.

The principal suspect was a local man, Allan Breac Stewart, a foster son of James Stewart. He was a known Jacobite who had taken part in

Culloden and had escaped to France after the defeat; it was he who had returned to Appin on a regular basis to collect the rents and return with them to France where the chief was in exile. He had argued with Campbell in recent weeks and seems to have disappeared after the murder. A search of the district was carried out and despite its thoroughness, Allan managed to escape to France.

Instead the authorities arrested James Stewart. He was taken to court in Inveraray in September 1752 where he was tried before the Lord Justice General, the Duke of Argyll, as well as the Lord Advocate; these men had been suspected of being soft on Jacobites in recent months, so they wanted to use Stewart as an example of their adherence to the government. Stewart was brought before the court and accused of conspiring with Allan Breac to murder Campbell.

The trial lasted fifty hours, in a single sitting, from five o'clock on the Saturday morning until seven o'clock on the Monday morning. At one point a juror shouted at an advocate for the defence, 'Pray, Sir, cut it short, we have had enough.' Sixty witnesses were brought into the courtroom to give evidence. The jury, which comprised of eleven Campbells out of fifteen men, took five hours to find James Stewart guilty of the murder. He was sentenced to be hanged and, in order to use his execution as a warning to other Jacobites who may rise up against authority, it was decreed that he should hang on a notable eminence at Ballachulish. After he was dead his corpse was to remain hanging from the gibbet for all to see.

Accordingly, on 8 November 1752 James was led up the steep slopes of the little hill above the ferry slip at Ballachulish. Between the hours of noon and two o' clock he was suspended from the rope and the trestle removed, leaving him dangling from the noose; a second hangman was sent up from Glasgow to make sure that no accidents took place, for they did not want anything to go wrong. Stewart claimed that he was innocent and did so right up to the last moment. He recited from Psalm 35, 'False witness did rise up. They laid to my charge things that I knew not,' a Psalm known in the Highlands as James of the Glen's Psalm ever since.

After the body hung still from its rope, it was left on the gibbet for a number of years; the authorities had made the gibbet stronger than normal, with iron plates affixed to it to prevent it from being cut down. For the first few months soldiers guarded the site to prevent anyone from taking the corpse away. In January 1755 the corpse was blown from the gibbet in a gale, but the authorities ordered that it should be restrung. No locals were willing to assist, so soldiers had to be brought from Fort William to carry out the task and even they had to be plied with drink beforehand. Eventually the laird of Ballachulish was able to have the bones gathered up as they fell from the gibbet and buried in the old kirkyard of Keil.

James Stewart of the Glen always claimed that he had nothing to do with the murder and the locals believed him. There are families in the district, or their descendants, who claim to know who the real murderer was and this has been handed down orally to this day, each generation being sworn to secrecy; possible names have included Allan Breac Stewart, though some claim that he was only a front for he was safely away in France; Donald Stewart, a nephew of the laird of Ballachulish, was another suspect, as was James Stewart of Fasnacloich; two sons of Rob Roy MacGregor, James Mor Drummond and Robin Og MacGregor, have also been suggested, as has Allan Stewart, son of James of the Glen.

In recent years one of the descendants has come forward with a name, but many others who claim to know the identity have stated that this was not the killer. It is a mystery that will remain for years to come. The tale has also been used by Robert Louis Stevenson in his novel, *Kidnapped*.

CHAPTER FORTY-FOUR
The Last Execution

On 7 June 1753 the scaffold at Tyburn was made ready for the last execution of a Jacobite prisoner.

Archibald Cameron was born in 1707, the fourth son of John Cameron of Lochiel. His father was keen that he should study law and accordingly he was sent to Glasgow, where he studied for some years. Cameron had a personal liking for medicine, so he transferred to the University of Edinburgh where he studied under doctors Monro and Sinclair; he then moved to Paris, before completing his studies at Leyden in Holland.

On qualifying, Dr Cameron returned to his home country of Lochaber and set up practice there. He had been regarded as fit to practise anywhere in the country, but preferred to work among his kin. He seems to have held ground in Glenkingie, but moved around the West Highlands, treating the sick in various places.

Archibald Cameron married his cousin, Jean Cameron, daughter of Archibald Cameron of Dungallon, and together they had seven children during his life; his eighth child was born after his death.

At the landing of Prince Charles at Boisdale on South Uist, Lochiel sent his brother, Dr Archibald, to meet him at Alexander MacDonald's house; Archibald was to warn the Prince that this was not the right time for the rising and that he should escape whilst he could. However, the Prince sent a summons to Lochiel asking him to attend him and subsequently persuaded him to join the Prince, having previously promised to raise his clan in the Prince's name; he was able to raise almost 1200 men to join the Jacobite cause.

Locheil requested Archibald to join him, but he argued against supporting the rebellion; he even fell on his knees and begged his elder brother not to join the Prince. However, Locheil was resolute, so Archibald decided to join him as his physician, refusing to accept a commission in the Jacobite army. He was appointed the Prince's aide-de-camp, but spent most of his time with Locheil.

The Doctor took part in the main events of the '45. He was at the Battle of Falkirk where, whilst tending the wounded, he was hit by a musket ball; this was to remain in his body for the remainder of his life, causing him a considerable amount of discomfort.

After Culloden, Dr Archibald travelled with the Prince throughout the West Highlands; he advised him where to go and, knowing the countryside, selected the best places for concealment.

In May 1746, two ships landed at Borrodale and 40,000 gold coins were taken from them, bound to pay for the soldiers and support the rising. Archibald was one of those appointed to look after it and he was instrumental in arranging for it to be moved from Borrodale to Loch Arkaig, where a meeting of the chiefs was taking place. The treasure was buried at a secret location, known only to a select few. After Culloden, it was to remain hidden and has since become lost. It is celebrated as the 'Loch Arkaig Treasure'.

When the Prince escaped to France, the Doctor and Lochiel went with him.

In 1747 Prince Charles told Doctor Archibald to return to Scotland, where it was hoped that he could 'keep alight the flame of Jacobitism.' He was also to make contact with Cluny MacPherson regarding the Loch Arkaig treasure. The letter instructed:

> You are to make your way to the Highlands as soon and as
> privately as possible. You are to inform the people that
> H.R.H. has nothing more at heart than to relieve their
> misery, that he has now taken all the care in his power of
> them by the succour granted by the Court of Spain and will
> constantly do the same until he can compleat their

happiness. You are to concert with Cluny the proper
measures about the affair which he and you only know,
which I entirely refer to your prudence and discretion and
desire that no other person, if it can be possibly contrived,
should known anything of it ...

In France Archibald was given a commission in the Spanish Service; he
later had a commission in the French service. Following the death of
Donald Cameron, the 'Gentle Lochiel', at Borgue in France in 1748,
Archibald was appointed guardian of his nephew, John, the young chief
of sixteen years.

In 1750 a public subscription raised money that was intended to
support those Jacobites who had been attainted and had to flee abroad.
Doctor Archibald came to Britain to collect some of this fund in order
that he could treat sufferers in France; his arrival and departure was kept
a closely guarded secret. In 1752 a second subscription was raised,
prompting Archibald to return to Britain; by this time he was in
financial trouble, his pay being insufficient to keep himself and his large
family. Whilst in England, the Doctor wrote a number of letters to his
friends. These may have resulted in word spreading that he was in the
country and a detachment from Lord George Beauclark's regiment was
sent to find him.

Captain Graves was sent with 30 soldiers to the Loch Katrine area,
where it was rumoured that Cameron was hidden. Near the garrison at
Inversnaid he spotted a young girl, who fled as soon as she saw them;
thinking that this was suspicious, two soldiers and a servant were sent to
follow her. She ran to a nearby clachan where she was seen talking to
another boy; she then left. The soldiers caught up with the young lad
and aimed their guns at him. Witnessing this sight, he fell to his knees
and begged for his life. The soldiers asked him where Doctor Cameron
was hiding and promised that his life would be spared if he would lead
them to their quarry.

The boy gave in to the threat of the guns and pointed in the
direction of Benachyle house, home of David Stewart of Glenbuckie.
The soldiers sent for the rest of the party, which surrounded the
building. Whilst the soldiers forced an entry, Cameron managed to

escape; however, he was caught in a nearby wood, taken prisoner and dragged off to Edinburgh. He was then sent south to the Tower of London.

During Cameron's imprisonment, he was denied paper and pens; he was not even allowed to speak with visiting friends unless a warder was present. The Lords of the Privy Council questioned him, but he denied that he was the same Doctor Cameron that was named in the act of attainder. As a result, evidence was required to prove that he was indeed the same person.

Cameron managed to find a small blunt pencil and on a few scraps of paper wrote out his dying testimony; the first recounts his association with the church; the second and third pieces note how he was responsible for preventing the Jacobites from attacking Glasgow and Kirkintilloch, which had been suggested following the murder of two Cameron men who had been servants to Lady Lochiel; the fourth scrap of paper rebukes the 'inhuman son of the Elector of Hanover'; the final piece of paper prays to God to 'hasten the restoration of the Royal Family, without which these miserably divided nations can never enjoy peace and happiness.'

On 17 May 1753 Cameron was taken to the bar of the court of the king's bench; by now he acknowledged that he was indeed the same Doctor Cameron that had been attainted. The Lord Chief Justice Sir William Lee pronounced sentence:

> You, Archibald Cameron, of Lochiel, in that part of Great Britain called Scotland, must be removed from hence to his majesty's prison of the Tower of London, from whence you came and on Thursday, the 7th of June next, your body to be drawn on a sledge to the place of execution; there to be hanged, but not till you are dead; your bowels, to be taken out, your body quartered, your head cut off and affixed at the king's disposal; and the Lord have mercy on your soul!

Cameron was sent back to the Tower to await his fait. He begged permission to see his wife, who was at this time still at Lisle in Flanders; she came to the Tower and spent most of her time there weeping and sobbing. She was able to return to the Tower on the morning of Cameron's execution, but she was so overcome by grief that she suffered many fits. She sent petitions to George II, the Princess of Wales and others, but none was willing to stay the execution. Within a few days she became mentally retarded, but survived for some time after.

On 7 June Cameron was taken from the Tower by the sheriffs. He was placed on a sledge and drawn to the gallows at Tyburn. Cameron asked to see his wife, but he was informed that she had left. As Cameron was being dragged through the streets of London, a large crowd witnessed him making his way; he seems to have been well-dressed and sported a new 'bag-wig'. As he lay on the sledge he looked at those gathered to witness the spectacle and he acknowledged the presence of those he knew.

Cameron reached Tyburn at quarter past twelve. He was untied from the sledge, whereupon he bounded up, making his way onto the cart. He spotted the minister that had attended him making his way forward and Cameron called out to him, 'So, you are come – this is a glorious day to me! 'Tis my new birthday! There are more witnesses at this birth than my first.' The minister asked how he was, whereupon Cameron replied, 'Thank God, I am very well – but a little fatigued with my journey. But, blessed be God, I am now come to the end of it.'

The sheriff was impatient and asked the minister how much longer he would be, only for Cameron to respond on his behalf, 'He requires very little time, for it is disagreeable to be here and I am as impatient to be gone as you are.' Cameron then sang some verses of the psalms, said a few prayers and then hugged the minister. The minister stumbled as he made his way down from the cart, to which Cameron warned him to watch how he went, 'for I think you don't know this way as well as I do.'

Once Cameron was left alone on the cart, the horse drew it away, leaving him hanging from the gibbet. Within minutes his body was left a lifeless corpse. After twenty minutes had passed, the body was taken from the noose and the chest was cut open to allow the heart to be removed; this was then burned. The body was not quartered as had been proposed. On the following Sunday the body was taken to a vault in the Savoy Chapel where he was laid to rest.

CHAPTER FORTY-FIVE
The Last of
the Rebels

In 1824 Peter Grant died at the advanced age of 110. He had become something of a hero and his funeral was one of the largest ever seen in the village of Braemar. His body was carried through the village behind a party of pipers and followed by around 300 Highlanders. He was laid to rest in the old churchyard, to the left of the Invercauld mausoleum. At the funeral there were copious amounts of drink consumed, one account noting that four gallons of whisky had been taken before the coffin was lifted. An old friend, Charles Lamont, who was ninety years old himself, had promised to play a lament at Grant's funeral, should he live longer than he. Accordingly, the piper played the old Jacobite tune, 'Wha wadna fecht for Charlie', as the body was laid in the ground.

A fine tablestone was raised over his grave, which records:

Erected to the memory of Peter Grant, sometime farmer in Dubrach,
who died at Auchendryne, the 11th of Febr. 1824, aged 110 years.
His wife Mary Cumming died at Westside, parish of Lethnot in
Forfarshire on the 4th Febry. 1811 aged 65 years and lies interred in
churchyard of Lethnot.

Peter Grant was born in 1714, the son of Patrick Grant, tenant of Dubrach farm, which lay on the south side of the River Dee, west of the Linn of Dee. On old maps the name is rendered in the Gaelic version – *An Dubh-bhruach* – which means the black slope. Grant was taught by the priest of Inverey before being apprenticed to a weaver and tailor at Auchindryne, or Braemar; Grant was eventually to take over the business.

When 'Colonel' Anne Mackintosh was recruiting for the Jacobite cause, Grant signed up, joining the Clan Mackintosh. He followed the Jacobites south to Prestonpans, where he so distinguished himself that he was promoted to the rank of Sergeant Major. It is not known whether he marched to Derby, but it is known that he was at the siege of Carlisle Castle and probably remained there whilst the Jacobites held it.

When Bonnie Prince Charlie held a review of his men on Glasgow Green, Grant was there. He later took part in the Battle of Falkirk. He then made his way north with the Mackintoshes and fought on the moor at Culloden.

Grant seems to have given advice to the leaders on the best method of fighting. He recommended that fire-arms should not be used, reckoning that they would have greater success with broadswords; however, his advice was not taken on this occasion. On being prevented from taking an early engagement with the enemy, he shouted, 'O, lat's throw away these fashionless things o' guns, ere we get doon upon the smatchets wi' oor swords!'

Grant was captured at Culloden and taken to Inverness where he was imprisoned in the castle. It was decided by the authorities that he should be sent back south and once again he found himself in Carlisle Castle. His knowledge of the building was to be useful, for he managed to make an astonishing escape from the great sandstone fortress.

Peter Grant took to the back roads and managed to make his way northwards to Glen Dee once more. He arrived in the latter half of the summer of 1746 and he was able to attend the Christening of the baby girl of a neighbour, Mary Cumming. Sixteen years later, Grant and Mary were to be married.

Grant's former home at Dubrach in Glen Dee was now being used as an outpost by the soldiers based at Braemar Castle. He kept a low profile for a while, but eventually was able to show his face without fear of being taken prisoner; he returned to his trade in Braemar.

In his old age, Peter Grant retired to the parish of Lethnot, in Angus, where his eldest son, John, had leased the farm of Westside from the Panmure Estate. Peter and his wife lived in a small cottage on the son's farm, but she died on 4 February 1811 and was interred in Lethnot kirkyard.

During Grant's time at Lethnot, a new minister arrived, Rev Alexander Symers. His wife was Clementine, a daughter of James Carnegy of Balmachie, Panbride. The Carnegys had been notable Jacobites and James had been Grant's commanding officer.

By 1814, when Grant celebrated his 100th birthday, he was now the only surviving Jacobite who had taken part at Culloden. In 1822 two walkers met Grant at his home at Westside; they were fascinated by his tales of the rising and were appalled at the poor condition of his home. They started a petition that was presented to George IV when he visited Edinburgh later in the same year. The king found his story most interesting and arranged that he should receive a pension of £52 per annum for the remainder of his life. He instructed that no time was to be lost in making sure the first of the weekly pounds should be paid.

Grant was celebrated for his longevity and story. In 1822 he sat to have his portrait painted by Colvin Smith, R.S.A; the Hon. William Maule commissioned this. Grant posed in full Highland dress.

In May 1823 Peter Grant became very desirous of seeing his birthplace and homelands once more. He made his way north to Braemar where he stayed with his third son, William, who ran a cattle-dealing business. He spent the winter there, but died in February 1824.

Bibliography

Allardyce, Col. James (ed.), *Historical Papers 1699-1750 Relating to the Jacobite Period*, New Spalding Club, Aberdeen, 1895-6.

Barty, Alexander B., *The History of Dunblane*, Eneas Mackay, Stirling, 1944.

Bates, Cadwallader, J., *History of Northumberland*, Elliot Stock, London, 1895.

Baynes, John C. M., *The Jacobite Rising of 1715*, Cassell, London, 1970.

Beveridge, David, *Between the Ochils and the Forth*, William Blackwood, Edinburgh, 1888.

Black, Jeremy, *Culloden and the '45*, Alan Sutton, Stroud, 1990.

Blaikie, Walter Biggar, *Itinerary of Prince Charles Edward Stewart,* Scottish History Society, Edinburgh, 1897.

The Origins of the Forty-Five, Scottish History Society, Edinburgh, 1916.

Chambers, Robert, *Jacobite Memoirs*, Edinburgh, 1834.

History of the Rebellion, Constable, Edinburgh, 1827.

Craig, Maggie, *Damn' Rebel Bitches: The Women of the '45*, Mainstream, Edinburgh, 1997.

Cunningham, Audrey, *The Loyal Clans*, Cambridge University Press, Cambridge, 1932.

Daiches, David, *Charles Edward Stewart*, Thames & Hudson, London, 1973.

Douglas, Hugh, *Charles Edward Stuart, the Man, the King, the Legend*, Robert Hale, London, 1975.

Flora MacDonald: The Most Loyal Rebel, Alan Sutton, Stroud, 1993.

Bonnie Prince Charlie in Love, Alan Sutton, Stroud, 1995.

Jacobite Spy Wars, Alan Sutton, Stroud, 2000.

Duke, Winifred, *Lord George Murray and the Forty-Five*, Aberdeen, 1927.

Prince Charles Edward and the 'Forty-Five, London, 1938.

Erickson, Carolly, *Bonnie Prince Charlie*, Morrow, New York, 1989.

Ewald, A. C., *The Life and Times of Prince Charles Stewart*, London, 1875.

Fforde, Catriona, *A Summer in Lochaber: The Jacobite Rising of 1689*, House of Lochar, Colonsay, 2002.

Forbes, Rev Robert, *The Lyon in Mourning*, Scottish History Society, Edinburgh, 1895-6.

Forbes Leith, William, *Memoirs of Scottish Catholics During the XVIIth and XVIIIth Centuries*, London, 1901.

Gibson, John S., *Lochiel of the '45*, Edinburgh University Press, Edinburgh, 1994.

Edinburgh in the '45, Saltire Society, Edinburgh, 1995.

Gibson, John S. (ed.), *The Diary of John Campbell, a Scottish banker and the 'Forty-Five*, Royal Bank of Scotland, Edinburgh, 1995.

Hewison, J. King, *The Covenanters*, John Smith, Glasgow, 1913.

Home, John, *The History of the Rebellion in Scotland*, London, 1802.

Hook, Michael, & Ross, Walter, *The 'Forty-Five: the Last Jacobite Rebellion*, Her Majesty's Stationary Office, Edinburgh, 1995.

Hunter, James, *Glencoe and the Last Clansman*, Mainstream, Edinburgh, 2001.

Johnstone, Chevalier de, *Memoirs of the Rebellion*, Folio Society, London, 1958.

Keltie, John S., *A History of the Scottish Highlands, Highland Clans and Regiments*, Fullarton, Edinburgh, 1875.

Kybett, Susan Maclean, *Bonnie Prince Charlie*, London, 1988.

Lang, Andrew, *Prince Charles Edward*, Longman, London, 1900.

Lenman, Bruce, *The Jacobite Risings in Britain, 1689-1746*, Eyre Methuen, London, 1980.

The Jacobite Clans of the Great Glen, 1650-1784, Methuen, London, 1984.

Linklater, Magnus & Hesketh, Christian, *For King and Conscience – John Graham of Claverhouse, Viscount Dundee*, Weidenfeld & Nicholson, London, 1989.

Livingstone of Bachuil, Alastair; Aikman, Christian W. H. and Hart, Betty Stuart, *No Quarter Given*, Neil Wilson Publishing, Glasgow, 2001.

Love, Dane, *Scottish Covenanter Stories*, Neil Wilson Publishing, Glasgow, 2000.

MacDonald, Charles, *Moidart, or Among the Clanranalds*, Oban, 1889.

MacDonald, Norman H., *The Clan Ranald of Knoydart and Glengarry*, MacDonald, Edinburgh, 1979.

MacDonald, Stuart, *Back to Lochaber*, Pentland Press, Durham, 1994.

MacKenzie, W. C., *Lovat of the Forty-Five*, Edinburgh, 1934.

MacLean, Alasdair, *A MacDonald for the Prince*, Acair, Stornoway, 1982.

MacLean, Sir Fitzroy, *Bonnie Prince Charlie*, Weidenfeld & Nicolson, London, 1988.

MacLynn, Frank J., *The Jacobites*, London, 1985.

    The Jacobite Army in England, 1745, John Donald, Edinburgh, 1998.

Murray, William Hutchison, *Rob Roy MacGregor- His Life and Times*, Richard Drew, Glasgow, 1982.

Paul, Sir James Balfour, *The Scots Peerage*, (9 volumes), David Douglas, Edinburgh, 1904-14.

Petrie, Sir Charles, *The Jacobite Movement*, Eyre & Spottiswoode, London, 1958.

Pittock, Murray G. H., *The Myth of the Jacobite Clans*, Edinburgh University Press, Edinburgh, 1995.

Prebble, John, *Culloden*, Martin Secker & Warburg, London, 1961.

Price, John Vladimir (ed.), *Selected Poems of Alexander Robertson of Struan*, Tragara Press, 1971.

Reid, A. G., *Annals of Auchterarder and Memorials of Strathearn*, Perth & Kinross District Libraries, Perth, 1989.

Reid, Stuart, *1745: A Military History of the Last Jacobite Rising*, Spellmount, Staplehurst, 2001.

Roberts, John L., *The Jacobite Wars*, Polygon, Edinburgh, 2002.

Sinclair, John, Master of, *Memoirs of the Insurrection in Scotland in 1715*, Roxburghe Club, Edinburgh, 1858.

Sinclair-Stevenson, C., *Inglorious Rebellion: The Jacobite Risings of 1708, 1715 and 1719*, Hamish Hamilton, London, 1971.

Speck, W. A., *The Butcher*, Basil Blackwell, London, 1981.

Stewart of Ardvorlich, John, *The Camerons*, Clan Cameron, 1974.

Tayler, Alistair & Henrietta, *Jacobites of Aberdeenshire and Banffshire in the '45*, Milne & Hutcheon, Aberdeen, 1928.

    Jacobites of Aberdeenshire and Banffshire in the Rising of 1715, Oliver & Boyd, Edinburgh, 1934.

1745 and After, Nelson, London, 1938.

Terry, C. Sanford, *The Rising of 1745*, Cambridge University Press, Cambridge, 1890.

Tomasson, Katherine, *The Jacobite General*, Blackwood, Edinburgh, 1958.

Tomasson, Katherine, & Buist, Francis, *Battles of the '45*, Batsford, London, 1962.

Youngson, A. J., *The Prince and the Pretender*, Croom Helm, London, 1985.

Index